MYTH AMERICA:
Democracy vs. Capitalism

By
William H. Boyer

MYTH AMERICA:
DEMOCRACY VS. CAPITALISM

By William H. Boyer

THE APEX PRESS, NEW YORK

Cover Design: William Boyer and Maverick Publishers
Interior Design: Mary Ellen McCourt

Published by The Apex Press, an imprint of the Council on International and Public Affairs, located at 777 United Nations Plaza, Suite 3C, New York, NY 10017. Its publications office may be reached at (800) 316-2739 or (914) 271-6500, P.O. Box 337, Croton-on-Hudson, NY 10520. Web site: www.cipa-apex.org

Library of Congress Cataloging-in-Publication Data

Boyer, William H. (William Harrison), 1924-
    Myth America : democracy vs. capitalism / William H. Boyer
    p. cm.
    Includes bibliographical references and index.
    ISBN 1-891843-22-2 -- ISBN 1-891843-19-2 (pbk.)
    1. Business and politics--United States. 2. Corporations--United States--Political activity. 3. Capitalism--United States. 4. Democracy--United States. 5. Social justice--United States. 6. Sustainable development--United States. I. Title.

JK467.B69 2003
306.3'0973--dc21

                                                                    2003052224

Printed in the United States of America.

To Ann, David, and Jeff

CONTENTS

PREFACE

The terrorist tragedy of September 11, 2001, produced three shocks to American society—the horror of the attack, the vulnerability that permitted the attack, and the discovery that so much of the world dislikes or even hates the United States. I was surprised only by the attack, for I had been writing for years on the expanding gulf between the world and the American perception of the world. After World War II, the power of the United States increased worldwide as a result of the arms race with the Soviet Union and the global expansion of corporations. European colonialism declined, replaced by American colonialism in Central and South America, Asia, and the Near East, while we claimed self-righteously to bring freedom and democracy wherever we went.

The attack of September 11 combined with economic decline to help Americans face public problems as a community for the first time since World War II. It may also have provided an opportunity to break through the myths that have obscured our real role in the world. The stock market bubble, the collapse of Enron, and CEOs heading to jail helped provide a traumatic, painful lesson about American capitalism. The shock of the disintegration of expected wealth may help people look at the pathology of the institutional games played by corporations that substitute for a just and viable economy.

We cannot afford to move into the twenty-first century using national military power and global corporate capitalism to justify our continued dominance. If instead, we reconsider where we have been heading and act to separate myth from reality, this period of history can be a new beginning, reducing polarization and dominance while laying the groundwork for democracy, human rights, and the rule of law. Our schools, our economic system, and our government are all in need of basic reform, for they are the main institutions that bolster the illusions shielding us from reality.

The myths that dominate a society are likely to serve those who have the most power over the institutions. When such beliefs are treated as truths they become myths that influence political policy. Here are some examples of erroneous assumptions found in mass media and even in some text books.

Isn't self-interest basic to human nature and therefore the necessary basis for an economic system?

No. Many kinds of economic systems can be formed. When greed is rewarded, people will become greedy. Then people will say it is human nature.

If farmers produced more food with biotechnology, wouldn't there be fewer people starving in the world?

No. In the present world system there is plenty of food, but it is only distributed to those who have money.

Didn't dropping the atom bomb on Japan save many lives?

No. Negotiations to end the war were well underway and only required an American decision to retain the emperor. We retained the emperor even after dropping the bombs. The reality has been ignored because it conflicts with our national self image.

If people learned to have more tolerance and love, wouldn't war come to an end?

No. War has nothing to do with interpersonal relations. It has to do with the sovereign power of nations. If there is no law above nations, military power is the ultimate authority and when it is used we call it war.

Isn't the high income of CEOs necessary to provide incentives?

No. CEOs in other countries with much lower pay are at least as motivated.

Television costs are major reasons for the costs of elections, yet isn't this a necessary cost if candidates are to communicate with the public?

No. The airways are owned by the public. Changes in TV licensing could permit free access for political candidates.

If we have more economic growth couldn't we eliminate unemployment?

No. Not under current law where the Federal Reserve is required to have some unemployment. When too many people are employed, the Fed will increase interest rates and depress the economy.

ACKNOWLEDGMENTS

I am deeply grateful for the thoughtful comments and suggestions I have received on preliminary drafts from Gordon Bigelow, David Saari, Lois Tyler, Richard Clinton, Warren Olson, Michael Parenti, Dennis Oshea, and Sidney Peck. Shirley Suttles and Gary Houser not only provided substantial editorial assistance but helped create order from a manuscript that developed over a period of four years. My wife, Ann, has been as usual an indispensable assistant in the writing and the repeated editing.

But the final result is my responsibility. Hopefully it will provide some basis for ideas and theory needed to help produce democratic changes in this promising and precarious period of history.

William H. Boyer

We can have democracy in this country or we can have great concentrated wealth in the hands of a few, but we cannot have both.

—Supreme Court Justice Louis Brandeis

INTRODUCTION

The worldwide protests against globalization that began in 1999 were driven largely by awareness of the bankruptcy of current global capitalism and reaction against the ways in which giant corporations are involved in secret arrangements through the World Trade Organization. The protests recognized that we are not moving toward global democracy but rather toward global oligarchy—control by the rich and the powerful—and the United States has been the leader in this globalization movement.

Enron provided useful unintentional education of the American public in 2001 when its bankruptcy revealed that the corporate managers had lied about their profitability and people throughout the United States lost their retirements, tied to 401 K accounts. At the same time the corporate CEOs skimmed billions for themselves.

As an educator, I am interested in the kind of citizen education where people in and out of schools have information that will help them regain control over government and the laws affecting the economy. Changes are needed in nearly all our institutions in order for them to become more democratic. Unfortunately many people have become accustomed to an anti-democratic culture.

Anthropologists have often used the analogy that if a fish were a scientist the last thing it would discover would be water. Fish do not see water; they only see through it. It explains why people have a problem understanding their own culture: They seldom know how their thoughts are being shaped by the ideas and beliefs imbedded like lenses in the culture that surrounds them.

Extrication from this trap is not easy, but it is essential. People cannot control their future if they are driven by blind beliefs. Harvey Cox, professor of religion at Harvard, says in "The Market as God," (*Atlantic Monthly*, March 99, 18-23) that capitalism has become the new religion. Most Americans are true believers in capitalism as if it were a religion, and most American institutions are driven by faith based capitalistic rules. Even our schools are institutions that prepare us to be efficient contributors to a capitalist economic order, though they tell students that they live in a democracy. The new "age of communication" mainly adds technology to make the current system more efficient, without questioning its goals or values.

Americans lose control over the meaning of capitalism when they equate "capitalism" with "democracy." American foreign policy uses this deception when the United States is said to be dedicated to furthering democracy in the world; but the truth is that the objective is mainly to further capitalism. The most favored term is freedom. When the terms "capitalism," "democracy," and "freedom" are intertwined in domestic or foreign policy, there is no chance of conceptual clarity. They mesh together. That is the point of meshing them—public *misunderstanding is essential to the perpetuation of the power structures of the twentieth and twenty-first centuries.*

The word "freedom" has a positive halo effect in most parts of the world. It is often used to paralyze thought, so that capitalism and corporate power are "free" to carry on. If we distinguish between "capitalism" and "democracy," we engage in radical political philosophy for they are not the same. I want to make such distinctions in this book to help people clarify thinking, gain more control over ideology and social philosophy, and thus have a better chance to control their institutions instead of being controlled by them.

I remember people saying in the 1930s, "The reason the unemployed have no jobs is that they are lazy." At that time I first saw how people were exploited by public ignorance and how politics and beliefs about human nature came together. When shipyards opened and the war economy made work available for everyone, these "lazy" people changed amazingly almost overnight. The problem was not human nature but an obsolete government that denied work to people.

After World War II, the GI Bill was a massive government program provided to veterans to gain higher education. It is now considered to have produced one of the highest national economic returns on investment. The return to the veterans and to the public was equally high. This planned economic stimulation through government produced jobs and housing and provided a basis for optimism, replacing the pessimism of the 1930s.

My life-long interest in democracy began in my three years in the Army Air Force during World War II, for the military was a vivid example of what democracy is not. I was surprised at the ease with which people raised in a "democratic" society could be manipulated and rapidly transformed to obey orders. I saw that the military psychology of "obedience" underlay the psychology of the very fascist countries with which we were at war, and in my first book, *Education for Annihilation* (1972) I raised the question of whether such deep involvement in war would transform most Americans psychologically. It was clearly transforming the United States economically, as Eisenhower correctly warned us in the 1950s regarding our creation of a "military-industrial" economy. The use of Keynesian economics, where government was used to prime the pump of the economy, increasingly became "Keynesian militarism,"as government stimulated the economy through war production. Even Thomas L. Friedman, writing in the *New York Times Magazine* (March 28, 1999), makes this admission: "The hidden hand of the market will never work without a hidden fist—McDonalds cannot flourish without McDonnell Douglas, the designer of the F-15." War production and business continue to be highly intertwined. American capitalism has never been economically successful without the stimulus of military production. America continues to be the world's leading producer of war machines, available for export as a profitable commodity.

The anti-democratic, anti-intellectual character of the military culture encouraged my search in the opposite direction—toward the philosophers of western civilization. I had studied engineering before the war, but after my military experience I returned to the university to study philosophy. My central concern was with the question: *If a social system such as the military could dehumanize, why couldn't a different kind of system **humanize**?*

After graduation, I worked in the democratization phase of the American occupation in Germany. It was a time in history when Americans overseas were actually doing some good deeds, especially with the Marshall plan, which funded European recovery. Later in graduate work and then high school and university teaching, I focused on how people could learn to gain control of their institutions. The right kind of education seemed crucial, and this idea has propelled me ever since. We stand at the end of what is often called a century of progress, yet the chainsaw bulldozer society continues full speed ahead, depriving future generations of a healthy planet and a sustainable society.

In the 1960s I helped develop community organizations to try to save special places—the giant redwoods of California and some undeveloped shorelines in Hawaii. There were some successes but the forces of destruction dominated, so I shifted to the idea of large-scale long range planning of the future as the alternative to our standard piece-meal mitigation and market-oriented non-planning. I proposed a national park to save the old growth redwoods, lobbied for its creation, and contributed to a movement that established the Redwood National Park. A later plan for classifying the Smith River in California was developed on the floor of my cabin with local people and eventually led to protecting this exceptional river under the Wild and Scenic Rivers Act. It remains the only coastal California River without any dam.

But over all, the world is moving entirely in the wrong direction. United States leaders continue to promote world domination by multinational corporations. Instead of schools educating democratic citizens they primarily prepare them to be consumers and producers—grist for the corporate mill. Instead of teaching them how to be involved in democratic planning, we try only to **mitigate** the social and environmental effects of capitalist "growth economics." We avoid real planning altogether.

Oregon and Hawaii (where I taught for 20 years) were pioneers in centralized land use planning, a bold step that limited the old belief in absolute rights of land ownership. During the 1990s I focused on land use planning in Oregon, which had become a national model through reforms started in the early 1970s under Governor McCall.

Public involvement in planning the future has increased in many states, but most government is fragmented by separate interest groups vying for power, while candidates are usually marketed for their personalities. There are no elections of political goals. Think of it: we vote for the candidates we hope will do the things we want done, but there is no way we can vote for the actual things we want done.

The **election of goals** became my central interest. I focused on environmental rights as an extension of human rights, and I initiated a bill and then an initiative that could create environmental rights in the Oregon State Constitution. One objective was to grant legal standing and rights to future generations so that natural ecological systems could be protected in courts of law. The other objective was to shift the burden of proof to polluters, requiring them to show that they were not producing a threat to human health. These steps would extend principles in *The Universal Declaration of Human Rights*, which does not at present include environmental rights.

Such rights would provide more power to the public and permit greater participation in the creation of enforceable human rights. Expansion of enforceable human rights moves us in the direction of a global, legally enforceable system of world law. Naturally, such a future comes squarely in conflict with the current control of the world by multinational corporations and nations.

Since such a future bucks most trends, I am asked: Am I optimistic or pessimistic? Well, pessimistic about most trends, yet optimistic about the largely untapped **potential** of people to recreate their own culture and institutions. But the United States is a major obstacle. Parading worldwide as the leader of democracy, the U.S. in reality is using its power to impose corporate capitalism throughout the world. This requires a system of propaganda through the schools, the media, and advertising—propaganda which puts blinders on the public. However, the great ideas of freedom and democracy still contain the possibilities of a better world and the development of real global community.

What should we do? **We desperately need national and global priorities that are ecologically sustainable and economic systems that are driven by human rights policies.** Then we can and must create institutions where technology is controlled for human use rather than for war and for corporate profit.

How to move from here to there? It will require educational and political movements. It requires understanding where we are going and analyzing alternatives. As the civil rights movement of the 1960s demonstrated, peaceful forms of change can come from democratic means, but if democracy is ineffective, change may require non-violent resistance. Democracy is civilization's great non-violent instrument of social change but when conditions are highly unjust, the failure of non-violent means to produce change can then lead to change through violence.

The central American myth is that democracy is the American way of life. Democracy, however, requires an educated public. The sad reality we face is that the prospect of a public educated to issues and alternatives is perceived as threatening to the privileges of the minority that hold most of our wealth and power, so virtually all of our institutions work to disarm this threat. Operating with an effective confusion of "information" with propaganda, our media, our schools, our corporations, and our government support information technology and produce an increasing flood of its product. Through what I call "the strategic use of trivia," members of the public are under the illusion that the "information" they receive is educating them on subjects that matter. In fact they are by and large being fed what the institutions that perpetuate the power of corporate America wish to feed them.

I am writing this book at age 78 when the temptation is to coast, have fun, and spend one's savings. But after a half century of involvement in education and politics, I believe I can contribute some ideas to help redirect political change. Because I look at alternatives that can create a better twenty-first century, I have been called a "futurist," and this book is my way of developing theory and practical steps for the reform of politics, economics, and education, hoping to lead to that better future. As a professor, an activist, and a llama rancher, I have seen in my lifetime changes which are encouraging and also changes which are so discouraging that they could lead to the termination of the human race. In fact, in the last few years I have personally experienced some of the deadly legacy created in the nuclear age.

In 1945, when I was in the Air Force and stationed down wind from the Hanford nuclear plant, there were high releases of radioactive iodine. I found recently that I had acquired thyroid cancer from the releases and I am now trying to control the progress of the disease. Others were also affected by those radioactive releases; and we are in a class action suit against the Department of Energy. The major corporations involved in Hanford are actual objects of the suit and, unbelievably, the Department of Energy has provided the corporations with over $55 million of public money to pay their attorneys to fight us. This is one of many lessons about connections between government, the military, and nuclear power.

I hope that many others believe, as I do, that we have a fundamental responsibility to future generations. I want to show in this book ways in which future generations are in jeopardy through our present institutions and the ways in which we can make changes that protect them. Creation of the future has usually been limited to the powerful, but it now can be an opportunity for all of us. What we must do is to take the myth of American democracy and turn it into reality. This requires analysis of our institutions to see if they are viable or obsolete. Each chapter involves ways to assess American institutions and how to take steps toward necessary change.

The central theme is how dominance and oligarchy through corporate capitalism is tied to increasing concentration of wealth and power. This must be changed if democracy and human rights are to prevail in the twenty-first century. The belief that a bad society is caused mainly by bad people is a major myth that hinders structural and institutional change. To claim that greedy people are the main problem ignores the way in which an institution such as corporate capitalism makes people greedy. We had better learn to change our institutions if we are to have better people.

A long habit of not thinking a thing wrong, gives superficial appearance of being right.

—Thomas Paine

THE UPSIDE DOWN SOCIETY

If we appear to be headed for a future of societal and environmental disaster we need to recognize that we have the knowledge to design a desirable and workable future. A better future for the human race is now possible but it requires that we conduct an honest assessment of where we are, how we got here, where we are heading, and what needs to be done.

WHY WE NEED TO CHANGE
OUR TWENTIETH CENTURY INSTITUTIONS

We Have An Upside Down Society: Instead of promoting democracy and human rights our government:

- Promotes global free trade without ecological or economic justice standards.
- Blocks empowerment of the poor in order to enrich the wealthy.
- Expands national military power instead of creating world law.
- Advocates human rights but supports national sovereignty.
- Blames unemployment on schools instead of public policy.
- Uses schools to reinforce the trends that create the upside down society.
- Supports petroleum-based transportation while global warming is increasing.
- Accelerates the concentration of wealth and power in the hands of a few.
- Relies on technology rather than public policy to solve environmental problems.
- Subsidizes growth in areas where growth is already destructively out of control.
- Subsidizes products that threaten human health while medical costs expand.
- Creates more and more nuclear waste without having any means of safe disposal.

- Encourages the use of wealth to control elections instead of campaign finance reform.
- Gives more power to contrived corporate "persons" than to natural persons.
- Allows the release of large amounts of chemicals into the environment without knowing the effects on health and the biosphere.
- Avoids policies and discussions of equitable wealth and income distribution.
- Permits people who make money from money and their investments to pay lower taxes (capital gains) than those who work.
- Supports growth by consuming the natural heritage of future generations.
- Permits cities to expand into farmland, diminishing future capacity to grow food.
- Allows over fishing without meaningful controls to sustain the resources.
- Avoids long range planning, reacts only to crises.
- Subsidizes mining operations which destroy public land.
- Provides subsidy to tobacco farmers while their product is killing 420,000 people each year.

(And this list is just a start).

THE EXAMPLE OF GLOBAL WARMING

Leading scientists have been trying desperately to awaken the world to the threat of global warming. In 1995, a team of 1,500 scientists worldwide produced a report called the UN Intergovernmental Panel on Climate Change which concluded that there is "a discernible human influence" on the earth's climate because of the greenhouse effect caused by the buildup of heat-trapping chemicals in the atmosphere. President Clinton admitted that the "overwhelming balance of evidence and scientific opinion is that it is no longer a theory but now a fact that global warming is real." In 1999 even Texas Governor George W. Bush admitted that there is global warming. With only 4 percent of the world's population, the United States contributes 22 percent of the carbon dioxide. This makes the U.S. the largest emitter of greenhouse gases in the world. By being tied highly to a fossil fuel economy, the economic pressures to avoid leadership in controlling global warming emissions are very strong.

The multinational corporations responded to the greenhouse effect in a way that reveals how corporate power has become a threat to the human future. In the past the response to scientific evidence by the Fortune 500 and other major corporations when policies might threaten their profit has often been to find a way to deceive the public by denying the validity of the evidence or to have a public relations misinformation campaign. The Global Climate Coalition was created by some of the most powerful corporations involved with fossil fuel to propagandize the public against taking action.

The group's action was so extreme that some members withdrew, and in 1997 British Petroleum began the break away from corporate orthodoxy by stating that "the policy dimensions of climate change is not when the link between greenhouse gasses and climate change is conclusively proven but when the possibility cannot be discounted." (*State of the World 2002*, 41).

The evidence on the relationship between global release of carbon dioxide and warming of the world's atmosphere became so well documented that it was undeniable and became the evidence for an attempt in 1997 to create the Kyoto treaty to reduce greenhouse-gas emissions by 2012 to 7 percent below 1990 levels. The UN Intergovernmental Panel on Climate Change said emissions must decline by 50 to 70 percent if humanity is to avoid drastic changes. Such changes could include a one-meter rise in global sea levels by 2100, leaving parts of New York, Amsterdam, Bombay, and Shanghai underwater.

Here is how corporations responded. They met after the Kyoto summit. Previous strategy had been to use the corporate sponsored Global Climate Coalition to provide a propaganda campaign for convincing the public that global warming was a "mere theory" for which nothing needed to be done. But when evidence was irrefutable, the next best strategy thought to preserve profits connected to a worldwide petroleum-based economy was to *get the United States to be the nation that would slow the transition instead of leading it*. They launched a national campaign alleging threats to the U.S. economy and with their campaign financing influence they persuaded the U.S. Senate to pass a Senate Resolution which kept the Senate from ratifying the Kyoto protocol. "The fossil fuel lobby spent $13 million on TV adds to reinforce the opposition in the months before Kyoto (Gelbspan, 102)."

The Global Climate Coalition promoted a voluntary, market-based approach advantageous to U.S. business. Heavily supported by Enron and Exxon Mobil they sponsored ads and lobbied congress. Gelbspan said "with their relentless attacks on the world's scientific establishments and with their ceaseless interference in intergovernmental negotiations, the fossil fuel lobbies have been extraordinarily successful in blocking meaningful efforts to address the climate crisis (102)."

This use of the political power of global corporations should be a major lesson to every citizen that corporations will serve their own economic objectives even to the detriment of the rest of the human race. It also reveals that they have the economic power to distort or control governments that are supposed to represent the public.

Any plan for twenty-first century education must include ways to control the power of corporations. They now violate their original authorization to serve the public interest (see chapter 2) and have become controllers of the press and the government. They exploit human labor and consume irreplaceable natural resources. We do not need to totally eliminate corporations but rather to control their size, regulate their impact on environment and people, and restrict their political power. Education should help people understand where we are going so people are able to help provide a political counterforce to support the public interest. Corporations can be expected to provide strong resistance to such "citizenship" education.

Global warming may be the evidence we need to galvanize world wide political action, for the entire human race is in danger. In October 2000 the United Nations Intergovernmental Panel on Climate Change, the most authoritative voice on the issue, concluded that new evidence shows man-made pollution has already contributed substantially to global warming, and the earth is likely to get *even hotter than previously predicted*. From these revised estimates, the scientists concluded that if greenhouse emissions are not curtailed, *the earth's average surface temperatures could increase by as much as 11 degrees by the end of the twenty-first century*. In 2002, the U.S. National Academy of Sciences, the nation's most august scientific body, said that climate change from global warming does not need to be gradual but could dramatically accelerate and that on the basis of inference from the record, it is possible that projected changes will occur not through gradual evolution proportional to greenhouse concentrations, but through abrupt and persistent shifts. The Arctic and Antarctic ice is already melting. If an ecological holocaust equal to the changes of the period that produced dinosaur extinction is possible, should continued profits of corporations be the deciding factor for the human future?

Understanding this clear and present danger could be an effective means of global cooperation to change policies and create new plans for common human survival. If an enemy is needed to unify us, our life threatening obsolete institutions based on fossil fuels might be an appropriate enemy.

The human race is now:
- Altering between one-third and one-half of the earth's land surface.

- Depleting two-thirds of the world's marine fisheries.
- Raising the level of carbon dioxide in the atmosphere by nearly 30 percent since the beginning of the Industrial Revolution.
- Using more than half of all accessible fresh water, with large rivers such as the Colorado, Nile, and Ganges almost drained before they reach the sea.
- Driving about a quarter of the bird species to extinction.

Worse yet, the forces driving us toward disaster are not slowing, but rather are accelerating. In most industrial countries of the world, people think that "progress" requires economic expansion. Competitive capitalism is used as the main driving force. It is based on expansion without ecological sustainability—no limits—the more the better. Global free trade policies drive the system ever faster. With population expansion and with Third World nations just beginning to accelerate their economies by using the pre-ecological western model, forecasts of the future are dismal.

Economists such as Kenneth Boulding in his many speeches throughout the United States in the 1950s and 1960s called this model of expansion through exploitation of nature the cowboy economy—an extension of the eighteenth and nineteenth century view that there really are no environmental limits and that everything—people and nature—is for sale. Herman Daly, who helped pioneer ecological economics, says it is a way of producing massive involuntary subsidy for those who dominate by shifting pollution and resource costs onto others—especially future generations.

Most technology now serves this old order, which is concentrating wealth and power into a worldwide corporate oligarchy in which a small minority have most of the wealth and the power. The first goal of real education is to tell the truth about the world and help people see what is happening, instead of permitting themselves to be used as instruments to accelerate an obsolete world system structure over which people have little or no control. The longer we wait, the more difficult the task; earth's living systems are being run down and may soon prove to be irreversible.

Reverse Priorities

The United States is not only an upside down society but is the world leader of *reverse* priorities. When I ask my students, "What are our country's current priorities in relation to *economics, social needs, and ecological systems?*" they know the obvious answer which is: economics is first. They also know what the correct ordering of priorities should be. Yet this common sense eludes national and state policy.

NOW: WRONG PRIORITIES	**FUTURE: RIGHT PRIORITIES**
FROM	**TO**
1. Economics first	1. Ecology first
2. Human needs second	2. Human needs second
3. Ecology third	3. Economics third

The biological life support system, another name for "biosphere," is the necessary prerequisite for everything—survival and a sustainable future. Therefore, ecological sustainability needs to be given first priority.

With a protected planet, the basic needs of people should be next. This commitment to human life would mean that economics had ethical priorities. Maximizing growth and profit—the current economic objectives—could then be accommodated only by making the environment and human needs the first priorities.

This is how it should work, but not how it currently works—quite the opposite. Economics overrides and is first. Then come some considerations of public needs. Ecological considerations are last, if included at all.

This is the upside-down society. This model is exported worldwide, particularly by the United States. Whether in the name of economic freedom, global markets, free trade, or whatever, the game being sold is really the upside down society.

The rationale is that if an economy expands, it will provide more to everyone, even though those at the top get most of it. This assumes that people's needs are automatically served by the "trickling down" of the wealth spent by the upper classes. Maybe a little safety net is needed here or there, but priorities should be based on economic benefits. If it is profitable, it is justified.

As for ecology, when natural systems have been polluted or degraded (aquifers, watersheds, soils, riparian areas, etc.), the presumption is that effects can be mitigated. This could be called *mopping up*. On the other hand, *correcting these upside-down priorities* would avoid the ecological degradation in the first place.

Mopping up is also used with respect to social needs, for the American model of expansion and trickle down economics always means that many at the bottom don't get much trickle. In that case, social agencies and churches are used as mop up squads to mitigate the effects on people who are left without economic benefits.

Upside down advocates consider the indicator of success to be GNP, the gross national product. Growth begets growth, and the more the better, with a dash of mitigation. The future will take care of itself if everyone works hard, invests, and contributes to increased productive efficiency. The meaning of life is to produce and consume. This ideology has even been introduced to over a billion Chinese and most of the developing world. *Gross production and consumption are increasingly considered the key to the future, not ethical policies or sustainable economics.*

THE OPIATE OF THE MASSES

Mass media—newspapers, television, radio, and magazines—are businesses that need to make sure that the belief systems underlying corporate capitalism are accepted by the public. The dialogue and debate on politics and economics is therefore narrow, shallow, and largely irrelevant to most crucial issues. If the corporate ownership of the media is not enough to ensure ideological orthodoxy, the corporate advertising which is the main source of profit will guarantee that content is carefully selected.

One of the most effective forms of political control is to make life a matter of entertainment to distract the public's attention from issues which could cause discontentment. Fun and entertainment becomes "the opiate of the masses," when it becomes central to the entire way of life. It constitutes an effective form of distraction from politics when golf, beer, television, and spectator sports are the centerpieces of popular culture. It is as if there is a corporate mantra that says:

LET THEM EAT TRIVIA.

SANITIZE.

DO NOT OFFEND.

KEEP THEM LAUGHING.

THEY WILL NOT KNOW WHAT IS HAPPENING TO THEM.

The Constitutional guarantees of freedom of the press and speech have helped to keep enough openness so that it is possible to obtain books and magazines that do not promote corporate capitalism or American nationalism. In a totalitarian society, government would shut these intellectual doors. In the United States the closing of doors is mainly through media that affect the mass public. Corporate television has usually tried to minimize public understanding, while public television has opened some intellectual doors. But these doors have been increasingly shut from the 1980s on by Congressional budget cuts that drive public television programs into corporate sponsorship. Even the Jim Lehrer public television news show was increasingly put under corporate sponsorship. We can now experience reports on energy and the environment sponsored by petroleum corporations with predictable content. Also public radio, which trickles in a few valuable non-mainstream ideas, has increasingly been subject to the same budget restrictions as public television. Programs have become more politically safe. However, some local public radio stations have aired tapes on talks given by some top intellectuals, people ordinarily never heard by the public. The programs that are broadcast by Alternative Radio are a small opening to critical ideas, and people such as Ralph Nader and Noam Chomsky—usually heard only on university campuses—provide analysis of issues that far exceeds what is usually heard in the business controlled media.

CONCEALING ALTERNATIVES TO THE WAR SYSTEM

Our dangerous and obsolete world order is held to its present course by the extent to which people are unaware of the alternatives. For instance we take for granted that "nations" are a normal part of the world, yet they were invented quite recently. The nation-state system developed after the Thirty Years War in Europe with agreements made under the Peace of Westphalia in 1648.

National sovereignty was created in place of the sovereignty of kings. *This "modern" world of sovereign nations in which there is no binding law above individual nations means that the ultimate authority in international conflict is the military violence of nations.*

The violence that nations can produce is connected with the state of technology—from spears, to bows and arrows, to rifles, to cannons, to bombs, etc. This has "advanced" to the level of intercontinental nuclear missiles. Though national military power was as often used for aggression as for defense, the concept of "defense" through military violence turned into "mutual assured destruction," known as MAD. Nuclear violence employed for either aggression or defense leads to human genocide where there is actually no more national defense. All nations become vulnerable but can retain what has they continue to call a "national defense" system, even though it became a mutual annihilation system. With the help of word magic, this is institutional obsolescence at its highest level.

Because of this structural anarchy in the nation-state system, military
is still the ultimate authority. Enforceable representative law replaces vi
within most modern nations, so states such as Oregon and Califorr
never go to war for the reason that enforceable federal law will take
any irresolvable conflict between states. The domestic system was p
that way.

A parallel model is applicable to the world system—a federated st
with enforceable law would serve as the instrument to substitute law fc
Given the current dominance of the United States and the lack of pι
knowledge of world alternatives, the current model, the war system, is lik
to continue. The United States has been a major obstacle in structuι
change, often using its veto power in the Security Council of the UN to prevent change which might reduce American dominance. If the American public follows the media and the old "realist" national-interest view of international politics, the American government will continue to be the keeper of
the old order. What is called "education," therefore, can be either the keeper
of ignorance that could lead to annihilation or the major instrument for
twenty-first century survival.

Designing the future requires consideration of alternative systems, yet modern education is largely devoid of systems education, with the exception of
technical systems—those which fit into engineering concepts and administrative efficiency. For example, it is well known that population increases
tend to be exponential based on doubling time and cannot continue without
disaster. The dominant response is to rely on birth control devices even
though there is now good evidence that the most effective basis for population stability is the education of women. The combination of these two elements is quite effective for stabilizing population in developed countries, but
in most of the world poverty is still increasing, which undermines education
and family planning by women. This increase in poverty results in large part
from capitalist systems that profit from exploiting poverty through cheap
labor—also from autocratic governments that maintain the two-class system
of very rich and very poor.

Few Americans know that the United States conducts a foreign policy that
contributes to population increase in poor sectors of the world, that have the
majority of the world's population. American foreign policy is tied to support
of the multinational corporate economic system and to arrangements with
juntas and dictators that make resources and cheap labor available to these
corporations. Governments that are uncooperative such as Chile, Cuba, or

Nicaragua, receive the full force of American coercion ranging from eco-nomic pressures to direct military intervention. All this is well known to peo-ple who have access to the non-popular media, but for those who have not, books such as Michael Parenti's *Dirty Truths* points out that "U.S. adminis-trations have worked hard to subvert constitutional and popularly accepted governments that pursued policies of social reform favorable to the down-trodden and working poor. . . the United States has supported some of the worst butchers in the world: Batista in Cuba, Somoza in Nicaragua, the Shah in Iran, Salazar in Portugal, Evren in Turkey, and even Pol Pot in Cambodia (59-60)." In the same book Parenti provides a more detailed analysis of U.S. foreign policy in the chapter "Making the World Safe for Hypocrisy."

THE "PROGRESS" MYTH

Economic and political systems tend to be "locked-in" when they are sup-ported by the belief that growth will inevitably provide progress. We have become tied mainly to quantitative economic indicators in which an expand-ing "gross national product" (GNP) is the standard for "progress." The pre-sumption is that quality of life will improve with expansion in the size of the economy as measured in dollar amounts.

Some of these GNP assumptions lead to absurd results. Cigarette sales become "plus" indicators, in which more sales produce more money for doc-tors, hospitals, and drug companies treating cancer, and then more business for morticians. Without any *qualitative* indicators, *all profit* becomes a sign of progress, which of course is moral and intellectual chaos. Even disasters such as tornadoes help the GNP, for if houses are destroyed, the construction industry will benefit. Crime also is an economic contributor, according to GNP, providing jobs for police and construction jobs for new jails.

So when we don't know where we are going, we concentrate on quantitative ways of getting there. Change, expansion, construction, and development are paraded and compared with last year's GNP to show if things are better or worse. Presidential elections can then be based on showing the public whether the nation is going upward or downward. The United States leads the world in selling this conception of "progress" and most other nations have fallen into the trap.

Growth mythology is essential to drive the current economic system. People are encouraged to accept unemployment, environmental degradation (air and water pollution and congestion), and crime, based on the assurance that these are minor aberrations which are the price of progress. The promise is that tomorrow will be better, even if today is somewhat miserable. Drugs are available if there is a bit too much pain. If one's community has more problems than ever, if taxes keep draining us, if fear of job loss is pervasive, the upward movement of the indicated gross national product will tell us that everything is actually OK. So there is no reason to organize with others to take control, for to apply democracy to the economic system is the supreme heresy. Have faith in technology and economic expansion. Tomorrow will be better. The best government is the least government. Let the magic of the market determine the future, here and abroad.

Such a belief system protects itself from verification. If depression occurs, faith tells us that cycles of business will correct themselves. Short-run rewards of income reinforce the belief that society's future is heading in the right direction. Take-home pay is more tangible than loss of air quality or water quality, top-soil, old growth forests, fisheries and other non-renewables that will affect future generations.

The solution is both simple and drastic. The economic process needs to be tied to *sustainable common quality of life indicators. A "better" future needs to be defined by a specific set of indicators that affect the health, security, and well being of the community.* The "market" does not need to be eliminated, but it must be required to operate within the constraints of sustainability, and human needs should be given the first priority over human wants. It is only when the priorities of the economy are under the guidance and control of such public policy that the future has the prospect of improving.

This twenty-first century model requires a change from a deterministic belief system such as the presumed natural forces of "supply and demand" to a system that involves people in cooperative planning—from a future beyond public control to a future under public control. Democracy and human rights, including rights for future generations, will need to supersede the dominant institutions of the twentieth century that treated people as commodities and consumed the life-support system of the entire planet. This can be done if ethical principles guide future institutions, if a new public education helps reconstruct obsolete institutions, and if public movements toward structural change take place.

How Means Become Ends

My first book, published in 1972, was titled *Education for Annihilation*. It extended the Eisenhower concept of the "military-industrial complex" which helped explain that the military-economic system was not merely a means but had become an end. The public began to understand more clearly that corporations were political influences with vested interest in the expansion of Pentagon budgets. The naïve view that the "defense" industries were simply instruments to serve "national security" was given the necessary reinterpretation. This is only one of many examples of how "means" often become "ends." Military expenditure had become a self-perpetuating "end."

In that book I showed how the military cultural complex was also an outcome of World War II. In the 1930s, if a President had proposed compulsory military training, he would not have survived the next election, but by the end of WW II, President Truman was able to institute a military draft on the basis of the argument that it was inherently good for Americans to be in the military—it represented good education. *After four years of war the military had moved beyond being a necessary evil to being a positive good* (Truman 1955, 51). A new meaning of citizenship was being born. This made it easy in the 1950s and 1960s to emphasize that schools should make students into contributors to the military-industrial complex by learning math and science so that the United States could make bigger and more powerful atomic missiles than the Soviet Union. (The objective had nothing to do with actual national security, since nuclear overkill had been achieved by the end of the 1950s.)

John Hersey wrote a novel in the 1950s called *The Child Buyer* that illustrated how the emphasis on science in schools was being used to capture school children for use in the military-industrial complex. About that time, GI Joe dolls became popular and war toys were in vogue, even for celebrating Christmas. Junior ROTC programs were expanding in public high schools to indoctrinate American students in what the Pentagon calls "leadership" and "discipline." The meanings of these terms actually change according to the ideology of which they are a part, thus the "leadership" and intellectual (self) "discipline" in a democracy are poles apart from their meaning in a totalitarian society.

The upside down society involves reversals of means and ends. Few institutions serve the goals they claim to serve, and in the field of law, medicine, religion, social services, or urban planning, the reversal is so ingrained that most people working in such areas do so without understanding the real objectives they serve. The institutions assign members to roles and usually convert them into agents to produce self-perpetuation of the organizations, complete with rationalizations for what people are required to do, with rewards and punishments to sustain the viability of the institution. The research on social psychology has consistently shown how the change in the rules in an institutional "game" changes the behavior of people. The self-interest rules of capitalism produce greed. The public then rationalizes the institution by saying it merely reflects the natural "greed" of people.

The game of Monopoly provides simulation of the immediate conversion to self-interest and the enjoyment of winning and the acceptance of the loss of others. The reality of losing was played out in real life during the high unemployment of the 1930s, and there was no recognition of the irony of the Monopoly parlor game even when it was played by the unemployed.

In the latter part of the twentieth century, public concern for crime increased and became useful both politically and economically. In 1996 Steven R. Donziger as President of the non-profit National Criminal Justice Commission, published a two-year study called *The Real War on Crime*. It describes how crime has become good business, for if growth rates continue apace for the next few years, by the year 2020, our prison population will top 10 million and more than six out of ten African-American men will be in prisons. (In comparison, Canada has roughly the same crime rate but one-fifth the prison population.)

Why are both private and public prisons expanding so rapidly in a time of declining crime rates? Based on this study it has to do with the economic imperatives of the prison industry. The economic well being of a large number of people is tied to the growth of the prison industry and to the existence of crime itself. In addition to the stockholders of CCA and Wackenhut corporations, one need only look at the many depressed areas competing for new prisons and the jobs they bring to understand this phenomenon.

Because there are not enough violent criminals to fill all the new prison cells, we are flooding the criminal justice system with low-level offenders such as marijuana dealers who are savored by private prison companies as ideal for-profit prisoners. They tend to be better behaved, so staffing can be kept to a minimum. They can help run the facility by cooking and cleaning. And, they can be "leased" as in-prison laborers to outside companies for less than the minimum wage.

Like the military-industrial complex, the prison-industry complex has an implacable internal logic that allows it to expand regardless of whether its stated objectives succeed or fail. If crime rates rise, we need more prisons; if crime is down, we need to continue to build more prisons so it stays down. And money is then siphoned away from education, the best crime-prevention measure.

THE LEGAL SYSTEM

So crime pays—not for the criminal but for the prison industry. The legal system has similar characteristics—encouraging the enactment of as many complex laws as possible and using arcane language and courtroom procedures that usually force people to hire expensive attorneys. The "fair" level of attorney fees is authorized by judges who are themselves attorneys, an established conflict-of-interest process. The noble ideal of "the rule of law" and "government under law" has been transformed into an expensive morass which prevents the average citizen from making use of the law without incurring huge costs. But the large wealthy corporations not only can afford such attorneys, they can dominate the less affluent and turn the "rule of law" into the rule of the oligarchy. Through campaign contributions, they can get the best government money can buy and create the laws that will rule.

THE MEDICAL SYSTEM

Even medicine has some of these "means become ends" characteristics. Instead of putting as much emphasis on the prevention of disease as on the lucrative area of treatment, the institution of medicine has itself become a cause of many illnesses. Doctors waited a very long while to challenge cigarette smoking and unhealthy food. The emphasis on "treatment" of cancer is to obtain more and more money for new research for a cure even though at least 80 percent of cancer is from known environmental causes and little of the existing research is being used for prevention (Eckholm 1977, 90).

Doctors are trained in medical school to emphasize drugs and surgery rather than prevention. One example of the unnecessary (but profitable) surgery is the high number of bypass heart surgeries, often conducted to the detriment of the patient's health (Ornish 1996).

Physicians have had control over their own fees, which seem astronomical to the average person. The rising cost of medicine far exceeds the rise in the GNP, and projections of current increases point toward an impossible time when, at current exponential levels, the medical costs could equal the entire GNP! So the system is unsustainable even in capitalistic economic terms. In the meantime, national medical organizations have led the effort to prevent the development of a national health care system. The current one is just too lucrative. And doctors have become major drug pushers. Though many medicines are very valuable and needed, Thomas Moore claims in *Prescription for Disaster* (1998) that by prescribing excessive medicines (drugs) far more deaths result from legal drugs than from all the illegal hard drugs combined.

CHURCHES

Some fundamentalist churches turn morality upside down by working close-ly in elections with the political forces that promote militarism and by con-vincing the poor and uneducated to support an ideology which promotes the concentration of wealth and power in a small minority. Encouraging anti-government politics and hostility toward intellectual dissenters, these funda-mentalists encourage bigotry and racism and do so in the name of "God." American institutional change is discouraged while personal afterlife salva-tion is advocated. Neither compassion nor enlightenment is stressed, but instead these right wing churches promote anti-democratic, ethnocentric, nationalistic, authoritarianism, which concentrates wealth and power in the hands of a clergy that claims to have a direct connection to God and prom-ises personal salvation for the impoverished faithful who often cannot afford such donations. Typically such groups find little inconsistency in supporting anti-abortion politics while also supporting capital punishment, and when they support war-oriented policies it is often in the name of the "Prince of Peace" (Harding 2001).

PLANNERS

The newly developing field of "planning" has produced many people who think of themselves as professional planners dedicated to guiding and imple-menting laws in the public interest. However when they do so, they find that the forces of development—builders and real estate organizations—have usu-ally taken over the politics of local elected officials. Therefore, planners who work for such officials often learn to tilt their reports and recommendations toward the developer's interests. Planners learn that it is through this game that they will be retained. Job security through selling out the public interest then too often becomes the unintended reality of planning. Professional ethics is usually so narrowly defined that it applies only to client relationships and not to the larger public interest. It then becomes easy to conform to political demands and aid the dominant controllers of local politics.

GOING BEYOND OUR UPSIDE DOWN SOCIETY

As formidable as the obstacles appear, people have the capacity not only to change themselves but also to change their institutions. Democracy is the major instrument for civilized and nonviolent change but it requires an informed public. There are many forces that have a stake in an uninformed public, yet the task before all of us is to avoid pessimism and cynicism and to examine the problems and the alternatives.

Democracy has in the past been defined as a set of *procedures and processes.* We now need to stipulate the necessary *ethical outcomes* of democracy, for the procedures must now help achieve ways to enhance human rights. It makes no sense to create a political process called "democracy" which in fact permits exploitation of people and the environment through economic power. Mere voting in conventional elections is not enough, for constitutional guarantees of universal human rights must now be the inherent and prescribed outcome of the political process, in which democratic participation is the method to implement such rights. The alternative is for established inequality to replicate and enhance itself in the name of democracy.

How many institutions in the United States or worldwide can stand up against these "radical" standards of democracy and human rights? These should be the basis for testing current institutions and for prescribing necessary change.

Which road will future generations wish we had taken—upside down or right side up? How will we be able to evaluate our relentless human experiment with the human race? Are some experiments irreversible in their effects? Are they unchangeable in their formulation?

Neither the Republicans nor the Democrats ask serious questions about macro-priorities. While Republicans leave the future to the market, Democrats are usually more willing to throw a lifeline—to fish, birds, and people, providing the system is allowed to continue full speed ahead. In the meantime we are driven by what William Greider calls "the manic logic of global capitalism," where "there are skillful hands on board, but no one is at the wheel. In fact, this machine has no wheel nor any internal governor to control the speed and direction. It is sustained by its own forward motion, guided mainly by its own appetites. And it is accelerating" (1997, 11).

Are we willing to ask where we are going? Or are we, to borrow from Santayana's definition of fanaticism, "redoubling our effort when we have forgotten our aim"?

HOW CORPORATIONS CAME TO HAVE SO MUCH POWER

Why have economic profits become the top priority over social needs and ecological sustainability? A brief look at the history of the corporate rise to power provides some answers.

Many of the original 13 colonies were actually corporations created (chartered) by the King of England to extract timber, animal pelts, and precious metals to benefit England. The charters of these colonies were not written to create democracy or to promote the welfare of the colonial communities, and abuses of power were widespread. The power of non-colony corporations was also a problem for the colonists: the "Boston Tea Party" was a protest over how the British East India Tea Company had pressured the King to raise the tea tax. The tea tax forced colonial merchants to raise their prices so they could not compete with this tea corporation and it was not hard for the colonists to see how a corporation could control their economy.

After the Revolutionary War, citizens of each state (via their legislatures) issued not-for-profit charters to establish such community ventures as firehouses, libraries, and colleges. Legislatures also chartered profit-making corporations to work on such infrastructure projects as the construction of bridges and canals. In exchange for the charter, a corporation was obligated to obey all laws, serve the common good, and cause no harm. Chartering by the legislatures was a privilege—not a right—and charters automatically expired after five to 30 years unless renewed. In the first few decades after the War, very few charters were granted and the citizens of this new country made sure that the abuses they had suffered as colonies were not repeated (Grossman and Adams 2001, 62).

In those days, people were very cautious about creating institutions which could overpower them. There were many limitations written into corporate charters and state constitutions. Corporations had limits on capitalization, debts, land holdings, and sometimes profits. They could not own stock in other corporations nor could they keep their financial books closed to public representatives. They were prohibited from making political contributions. In dramatic contrast to the situation today, corporate stockholders and directors were held personally responsible for crimes and harms committed and debts incurred by the corporation (Grossman and Adams 2001, 61-2).

As David Korten points out, the Civil War changed all this. Public scrutiny of corporations was difficult to keep up during the Civil War when the states were warring among themselves. State legislators took bribes from corporate executives to loosen legal restrictions, grant lucrative business contracts, and to have the government subsidize their businesses (Korten 1995, 58).

President Abraham Lincoln was moved to use these stunningly strong words to describe the situation in1864:

> I see in the near future a crisis approaching that un-nerves me and causes me to tremble for the safety of my country. As the result of the War, corporations have been enthroned.... An era of corruption in high places will follow, and the money power of the country will endeavor to prolong its reign by working upon the prejudices of the people.... until wealth is aggregated in a few hands... and the Republic is destroyed (Wasserman 1983, 89-90).

Following the Civil War, a battle of a different nature emerged as states competed against each other with weakened chartering requirements designed to attract corporations and their money. This bidding war reached such a magnitude that President Rutherford Hayes issued the following striking statement in 1876:

> This is a government of the people, by the people, and for the people no longer. It is a government of corporations, by corporations, and for corporations (Wasserman 1984, 291).

THE SANTA CLARA CASE

This slackening of legal restraints on corporations culminated in a U.S. Supreme Court decision in 1886 known as Santa Clara County vs. Southern Pacific Railroad. It opened the floodgates for the accumulation and consolidation of corporate power. Without even any allowance for discussion or debate, the Supreme Court accepted the Santa Clara decision that corporations are "persons." Even though they are artificial entities, they were granted the same legal status as real human beings and were entitled to all the same Bill of Rights protections including freedom of speech. In one fell swoop, essentially all pretense of meaningful control over corporations was abandoned for the corporations since they can use the First Amendment provision for "freedom of speech" as the basis for making contributions to political candidates. The result, as we know too well, has been to transfer the economic power of the corporation into control of the political system.

From 1886 onward, corporations have used their court-conferred wealth to overwhelm the democratic process. Having now the same rights as real people, they were allowed to participate in the political process. Their unlimited spending in elections permitted them to gain majorities in legislatures and eliminate all remaining troublesome language in state constitutions. Any attempts at control were defeated as "unconstitutional" infringements on their right to "free speech."

The Supreme Court used the Fourteenth Amendment to rationalize its decision by saying that it "forbids a State to deny to any person within its jurisdiction the equal protection of laws." (Santa Clara County v. Southern Pacific Railroad Company, 118 U.S. 394 (1886), available at www.touro-law.edu/patch/santa.) The logic was inescapable once the corporation was deemed a "person."

Corporations increasingly use their economic power to influence government and consider this a normal part of the costs of doing business. Campaign money for political candidates, lobbying in the halls of Congress, soft money to political action committees and political parties often helps provide the kinds of legislation which serves the corporations. This rapidly expanding private power of corporations is often at such variance with the public interest, that the phrase that we now "have the best government money can buy" is understood by the general public. People know that money now buys government.

Back in the 1930s, when Thurman Arnold, an astute political philosopher, wrote *The Folklore of Capitalism*, he saw the effect of "personhood" and stated: "The idea that a corporation is endowed with the rights and prerogatives of a free individual is as essential to the acceptance of corporate rule in temporal affairs as was the ideal of the divine right of kings in an earlier day (1937, 185)." And he also pointed out that "Institutions once formed have the persistency of all living things. They tend to grow and expand. Even when their utility both to the public and their own members has disappeared, they still survive (395)."

His prediction is accurate for our present day. As soon as a "legal" right was established to use corporate money to control the political system the contest between capitalism and democracy had a pre-determined outcome. Corporate power was greatly increased when television became crucial in elections for it is so expensive that the preponderant wealth of corporations over individuals made the personhood fiction exactly what was needed to use money as speech. Once political candidates got most of their campaign money from corporations the tax benefits and access to public resources soon followed. Those same legislators could also make sure that the right people were put in the Federal Communication Commission to keep television under private control and out of reach of the public. When the major nation in the world is under de-facto control of the major corporations, their power will reach everywhere on this planet (Nader 2002, 156,161-162, 239).

So as corporations have grown into multinationals they have gained massive power on a global scale. Corporations are taking the further step of establishing international agreements (such as the North American Free Trade Agreement (NAFTA), the General Agreements on Tariffs and Trade (GATT), and the Multilateral Agreement on Investment (MAI)) through which they are attempting to gain even more power by insulating themselves from all meaningful legislative oversight. Although states still technically retain the legal authority to revoke corporate charters, the exercise of this right has languished virtually to zero as corporations gained more wealth and power to corrupt government officials.

As William Greider points out, NAFTA was adopted in 1993, and under Chapter 11, "has enabled multinational corporations to usurp the sovereign powers of government, not to mention the rights of citizens" (2001, 5).

Mexico, Canada, and the United States forfeited sovereign immunity when they signed NAFTA, which means countries cannot control their own resources. Corporations and "free trade" override nations. Corporate investors from other countries even override the laws created through national elections.

Few people, even among college graduates, know that corporation power was initially usurped in 1886 when the corporation became a "person" and could use the first Amendment of the Constitution as the basis for "money is speech." The lives of ordinary Americans are controlled substantially by the power that resulted from personhood.

Understanding how we lost control and what to do about it is of the utmost importance for the American future and, because of American corporate dominance, for the rest of the world as well. There are steps that can be undertaken to reverse this usurpation of American democracy and various groups have been developing and testing strategies. Since corporations are chartered in States, the responsibilities of corporations can be defined at that level. Changes usually involve a Catch 22, for corporations will use their economic power to protect their privileges. Yet the contest between democracy and oligarchy involves potential power that has not yet been mobilized.

The last chapters of this book will present some proposed strategies and solutions.

No matter how rich you may be, and how well satisfied with your world, you will be better off . . .in a cooperative commonwealth.

—Upton Sinclair

The danger of the past was that men became slaves. The danger of the future is that people may become robots.

—Eric Fromm

INVENTING ETHICAL INSTITUTIONS

People everywhere are forced to adjust to existing institutions even if they are obsolete or immoral. We need to learn to design ethical social goals and create institutions which will serve those goals.

The most likely future will be one shaped by dominant trends driven by our institutions. So where are we going and what are the institutions which are taking us into the future? The first thing we need to know about all institutions—schools, government, churches, economic systems, etc.—is that they were invented. So they can be reinvented. However, the biological life support system of our planet was not invented. It evolved over millions of years during which local ecological systems became part of the global ecological system. This is our natural environmental heritage—given, not invented, essential for the sustenance of life, yet easy to degrade or destroy.

Once people invent an institution they usually forget its human-created origin. Because of this amnesia, an aura tends to become established about a particular institution, suggesting that it has always been and will always continue to be with us. The opposite has occurred with the ecological life-support system. Rather than hold it in high esteem, we freely exploit it and change it—as though it can be perpetually reinvented. Not only that—we undermine and degrade it. As a result, the planetary capacity to support life is progressively diminished. Air, water, topsoil, forest, and species of plants and animals are either reduced or degraded. The life-support system increasingly supports less life while human populations grow larger and larger. We behave as though we were living on an infinite instead of a finite planet.

Only those who are ignorant of these trends can be optimistic about the current human trajectory. On the other hand, only those who do not understand that institutions can be reinvented have any basis for being pessimistic about human potentialities. Institutions are self-perpetuating. They create the future because the public, as yet, is not in charge of the future.

Institutional Obsolescence: Band-Aid Short-Range Planning

Most of our traditional institutions cannot take us into a more desirable twenty-first century, for they developed under different historical conditions. These institutional structures establish the framework and set the rules by which choices can be made. In this way, obsolete institutions limit the possibilities that are actually available to use for solving many of the core problems facing human civilization. Therefore, basic systems change is often necessary.

Modern, industrial civilization has an inertia that requires long-range planning and lead-time for it to change direction, but current political and economic systems involve no long-range planning. As a result, decisions based on short range, piece-meal, ad hoc, reactive, Band-Aid non-planning are foreclosing future options.

Politics as currently practiced is based largely on selecting a person to make decisions in a government that lacks ecological or social priorities. This is a paternalistic model, driven by politicians serving their own goals and those of their campaign contributors. "Public interest" goals are not part of the process, and the public is never involved in voting for priorities or long-range goals. The biosphere and its resources are pre-determined to be degraded in the pursuit of short-range profits. Progress is calculated in economic cost-benefit terms because the rules of the game determine that economic profits have first consideration, while social needs and ecological sustainability are second.

The United States has become an oligarchy of the rich and the powerful cloaked in the costume and trappings of democracy. Most of our twentieth century institutions are not able to respond adequately to emerging human needs and the development of sustainable economics. The solution to institutional obsolescence requires the creation of appropriate institutions as a basis for both a new politics and a new education. Creating a better future that would be more effective in responding to pressing human needs requires understanding the alternative rules of the institutional games.

Some of the principles are clear. The capitalist approach, which gives first priority to self-interest, has prevented economics from establishing ethical goals. Instead, relying on the principles of supply and demand means that there has been virtually no planning for a sustainable future, and movement has been continually toward liquidation of non-renewable resources and toward distribution inequality. Politics that have no goals of ecological sustainability or principles of social justice reinforce existing short-term exploitation of the air, water, land, and biota. And economic "justice" is replaced by "trickle down" economics and the vagaries of market fluctuation.

People who are heavily invested in the current institutional framework, both financially and emotionally, feel threatened by any prospect of institutional redirection. They therefore dismiss as heretics those who are attempting to bring about institutional redesign. The economists who preside over the "religion" of capitalism typically presume that the world is driven by sacred economic laws that people have no control over. These "true believers" are likely to be self-righteous in their persecution of the heretics, because the struggle is seen as between absolute "truth" and "falsehood." So political campaigns often use the strategy of demonizing opponents as "threats to the American way." The "extreme" heretics have been the socialists and the communists. During a period of national neurosis, we were afflicted with McCarthyism that capitalized on such simplistic devil theory.

But the real issue is "Who has the power?" When ideas are a threat to the arbitrary power of a minority, its strategy is to manipulate the belief systems of the majority to get them to support undemocratic power. People are encouraged to go to the poll and shoot themselves in the foot for they are offered choices already controlled by the minority. So the illusion of democracy is maintained though its substance has actually been taken away.

Words such as "freedom, local control, home rule, and free enterprise" are keys to the ideology that becomes part of the secular religion, appealing to ingrained beliefs and reinforced by a ubiquitous culture. An educated person may see through this, but most people are incredulous true believers—not because they lack intelligence, but due to the absence of the kind of education which would help to decode the political system and the effects of widespread ideological indoctrination.

The future is usually locked in through a combination of selectively filtered information and belief, which is transmitted from one generation to the next. This system operates through selective omission and therefore sustains sufficient ignorance in the general public so that the average person is unaware of what has been omitted. Those who have primary institutional control often do not even realize that they are acting as information "screeners," especially if they have come to treat the institutions they direct as "given" by some forces higher than mere mortals.

Typically the schools and other educational institutions (such as mass media, civic clubs, and churches) do not provide people with an understanding of the alternatives. Quite the opposite—nearly all ideas and influences that are presented are aimed at getting people to fit into and accept current institutions. The not-so-golden rule is "adjust." The propaganda process is so subtle and pervasive that only a few escape. Those who are true believers in existing institutions are often rewarded for their loyalty with money and power. They are likely to feel assured that they are doing the right thing and likely to develop hostility toward those who threaten their beliefs and institutions.

This process is revealed continuously. Those who question the basic values of these institutions and seek the "truth" continue to receive some of the same negative treatment as Socrates 2000 years ago. But there has been some social progress. Death as punishment is not as likely now, except in some totalitarian nations. Instead, there may be loss of a job, failure to pass a government "security" check based on being "controversial," or exclusion from access to coverage by mass media.

Noam Chomsky is a case in point. A brilliant contemporary critic of violations of human rights, he is seldom invited to American TV and mass media. His analysis of the actions of the rich and powerful is too accurate and direct to be in "good taste." He is pushed to the side of public perception but is not executed, as he would have been as a dangerous heretic in the middle ages. His ideas are available, and he is enthusiastically greeted on university campuses, especially outside of the United States. As more people learn that his ideas are feared by the establishment, his books and lectures are increasingly popular. This is an important indication of the basis for hope—the door is not entirely shut. We have oligarchy, but not totalitarianism.

Instead of police-state repression, we have two major obstacles to a better future.

1. Most people live in a windowless cocoon of perception and belief as a result of normal social enculturation.

2. The economic power of corporations dominates mass media and the political process at both the national and local level.

Anyone attempting to provide leadership in guiding us toward a better future must understand these two obstacles and the need to assist in the deprogramming of the public, which means helping people understand where we are headed and being able to see political, economic, and social alternatives. People need help to understand the nature of corporate and state power and how to change it.

There are many people in the United States and throughout the world who have emerged from that windowless cocoon and are ready to help others do so. The combination of being well-informed and possessing both moral courage and a social conscience makes them committed to opposing human exploitation and violations of human rights. They have a humanistic mission. Working at all levels—locally, nationally, and globally—they are the leaders of a movement towards a better twenty-first century.

People are easily "bought" when they are adrift and have no direction to their life. Modern life under capitalism consists of pressures to sell oneself into the service of a corporate consumer economy. For many, the choice is between being a "pimp," selling economic exploitation or a "prostitute" selling oneself to serve questionable social values.

The forces of twentieth century institutions are so strong that it is easy to earn a living in earth destroying, people-exploiting activities. CEOs willing to play this exploitative role are rewarded with huge salaries. Doing the right thing is seldom rewarded, so those who protect the earth and treat people fairly have a hard time making a living. Yet many of them, the modern heroes, manage to do so whether it be in human rights struggles or in protecting the environment.

They produce some of the best books, magazines, pamphlets, and newspapers (called "underground" and "little" newspapers), weaning people away from the corporate-controlled mass media in order to move toward social justice and environmental sustainability.

INVENTED MAJOR SYSTEMS THAT INSTITUTIONALIZE VIOLENCE

Each institution has rules and values. When people are exploited or killed as a result of the *characteristics of the institutions*, this exemplifies structural violence. Slavery in the pre-Civil War days is a clear example of structural violence. People were both exploited and killed. There are other examples of current structural violence.

The War System

The world system of nation-states is a war system: it predetermines that military violence will be the ultimate authority in the resolution of conflict between states.. This means that **war is inherent in a fragmented world in which separate nations answer to no overriding authority**. Instead, authority arises from the power of each "sovereign" nation. Between nations there are treaties, trade, and military power. When a nation wants to get what it cannot achieve by other means, military power is available. Military power is a system of organized violence that is used to kill and destroy in order to serve the purposes of the nation. Although much of the time military systems are used for national aggression, they are almost always retained in the **name** of defense.

No institution in its current form is absolutely necessary. If it does not produce the desired results, the rules can be changed for the rules determine the outcomes. The rules of the present international order were largely established in 1648 after the end of the Thirty Year War in Europe. The modern nation was given "sovereignty" and its own military system. International law through treaties and diplomacy was established, but there were no enforceable systems of law higher than the nation-state (Falk 1971, 229-30).

Since military systems increase their level of violence according to the state of the art of technology, power to kill and destroy has gone up exponentially to the point where all out war would now be nothing less than mutual annihilation, dubbed MAD (for "mutual assured destruction") at the height of the Cold War. At this point, the "war system" becomes dysfunctional in addition to becoming immoral. Such an obsolete dysfunctional institution can, if it continues, terminate the human race. The war system, which may have made sense at an earlier period, is now high on the list of obsolete institutions. The main task of keepers of obsolete institutions is to find ways to continue their survival by convincing the public that they are needed. Desperate measures such as a "war on drugs" focusing on South American cocoa plants and "star wars" (missile defense) programs have been contrived to prevent the demise of military budgets.

The George Bush administration used the New York terrorist attack on September 11, 2001 to advance a "war on terrorism" that could be the focus of American policy for many years. Terrorism is not necessarily a war between nations and therefore the word "war" is mainly useful for mobilizing the

Pentagon and providing long-range profits for war industries. Claims of "national defense" in times of international conflict permits presidents to command public support, often by curtailing civil liberties, increasing nationalistic conformity, and enhancing their power.

Solutions to terrorism and criminal acts of violence and killing require a cooperative plan between nations and the United Nations to work within international law. Dominance and exploitation world wide that increases poverty are the driving forces behind most terrorism. Bombing in Afghanistan and Iraq by the Bush administration will have no effect on curbing terrorism and may well exacerbate it by reinforcing an image in the Muslim world of a country that uses bombs to protect oil interests.

Both terrorism and war are largely the result of basic structural conditions such as economic and political exploitation that result from failure, as yet, to have representative world government. National dominance shifts power to those with the capacity to produce the most violence and perpetuates inequality. When there are no non-violent means of redressing grievances and when the world system creates inequality, terrorism becomes politics by other means.

THE ECOCIDE SYSTEM

Much of what is now called "economics," especially capitalist economics, is earth destroying. In using non-renewable resources to produce wealth, the ecological balance of the planet is ignored for the purpose of obtaining short-term benefits from the finite materials of the earth. Forests, fisheries, topsoil, minerals, animal and plant species, and watersheds are used for producing goods and services. If the system is driven mainly by institutional profit instead of ecological sustainability the life support system will be destroyed—I call that an "ecocide system." The dollar pay-off can be high in the short term before resource depletion occurs. It is a "fly now pay later" system in which payment is tragic in the long term. Global warming is giving us a picture of such a future.

There is nothing in economics per se that requires it to be ecologically unsustainable, but the particular kind of economics we have created involves structural violence. When we define current productivity in monetary units without social and political constraints on the ecological and moral outcomes, the economic process exploits both people and the life support system of the planet.

Obsolete political divisions are a part of the ecocide system. The well-known "tragedy of the commons," which Garrett Hardin defined, reveals how **com-**

petition for scarce resources leads to destruction of the common life support system. His illustration showed English villagers who competed with each other to produce more milk by increasing the number of cows they put on the "commons." The escalation moved inexorably to exceed the carrying capacity, leading to the destruction of the commons and the death of the villagers (1968, 1243-48).

This parable is applicable worldwide—with corporate shipping fleets competing for fish and minerals, with nations in competition for water supplies, and with multinationals competing for the lumber from rain forests all over the world. Even states within national boundaries vie for maximum use of water and hydropower. The western states of the United States are becoming a growing battleground over limited water resources. As populations increase and industry demands grow, water, once considered virtually "free" and unlimited, may take the place of gold in the future as the most coveted resource, tied not only to direct human uses but also to the health of forests and fisheries.

THE POVERTY SYSTEM

The World Health Organization reports that 19,000 people, most infants and children, die each day from hunger and malnutrition. WorldWatch's *State of the World 2002* points out that we have "hunger amid plenty" and that adequate food is available but not adequately distributed (WorldWatch, 57). **The deaths result from lack of purchasing power.** The food exists; the hungry cannot buy it. In other words, poverty kills. Poverty is often written off with the saying "the poor will always be with us," but when poverty is understood as the result of political failure of the institutions we have created, it can be seen as a form of structural exploitation and genocide.

Our parlor Monopoly game reveals the dynamics of competition, where the rules of the game show how progressive inequality occurs. The rules involve competition but no principle of equality of outcome, so when one wins and the others are in poverty, the game comes to a triumphant conclusion for the winner. In the real world, the game's elements are more dynamic. The number of players changes, and the size of the pie changes as new technology is invented. But the distribution of **pieces of the pie will continue to be unequal if competition is the main basis for distribution**. In addition to "competition" as a central rule-system, private property ownership, political power and social stratification will amplify the inequality. So racism, social stratification, and concentrations of economic power among individuals, corporations, and nations make it certain that inequality will occur. And inequality is but another name for poverty. Minor inequality makes little difference. Major inequality, however, produces personal feelings of hopelessness and often high degrees of retaliatory violence on the part of those who have little or nothing to lose in the distribution game. High levels of inequality—absolute poverty—lead to disease and starvation, something common in many parts of the Third World.

Those who accept the current high level of violence usually rationalize that there are not enough resources to go around. This is not true. There is plenty of food and plenty of material for decent housing. The problem is that we have a system in which dominance is exercised by nations, corporations, and individuals who are able to control the rules that perpetuate the poverty. Cheap labor is the basis for much of the concentrated wealth. Attempts to change the rules are likely to be resisted by those who profit by the cheap labor and inequality. Resistance to exploitation is often opposed by the state, even involving killing those who try to organize the poor. This process was at the heart of American government support of the "Contras" in Central America in the 1980s. Or when smaller nations want independence and try to move away from the structure of dominance that perpetuates the world poverty system, dominant nations will invade, as seen in the U.S. action against Cuba in the 1951 Bay of Pigs invasion and in Central America during much of the twentieth century (Kenworthy 1995).

The United States in the twentieth century was a world leader in resisting political changes that might increase the power of the public over the global system of corporate capitalism. We need to help people read sources outside of the mass media to show how we have been part of the problem in Central and South America, Cuba, Southeast Asia, and Africa. Sources that take the reader beyond mass media include: *The Progressive, In These Times, The Multinational Monitor, Dissent, The Nation,* the *World Policy Journal,* the *World Press Review,* and the publications of Ocean Press and Common Courage Press.

In the name of "free trade," the United States has launched the global monopoly game, establishing corporate production worldwide with the use of cheap labor in nations that are often under the control of military dictatorships. When people revolt and try to replace an oligarchy with some form of democracy, the U.S. has often been ready to use the CIA to subvert the people's revolt or even to invade with American "national defense" forces to overcome the threat. **The real "threat" is that democracy will replace the oligarchy which protects American corporate interests.** The invasion is always undertaken in the "national interest." We also sell arms to these repressive governments that often pay for them from the exploitation of their country's natural resources. The subjugated people that survive inherit an increasingly depleted country.

INSTITUTIONS WHERE THE RULES NEED TO BE CHANGED

BUSINESS

Business corporations exist to make profits, and the chief executive and the board members are all dedicated to that goal. People who work for the corporation have little or no power over the policies. Their supervision is top-down with many of the characteristics of a military system, though usually not as rigid.

People working for a corporation gain their power, if they have any at all, when they have special expertise that is in demand by the corporation. Or, if they are organized into a union they can use collective bargaining to negotiate contracts and thereby achieve a modicum of bottom-up power. It is usually in the interests of corporations to prevent this from happening.

Occasionally corporations have employers who have strong paternalistic feelings of responsibility for those who work for them, and this occurs especially when there has been long-term stability and an opportunity to develop close personal relationships with workers. But as international "free trade" policies force competition to ensure survival of the business, these traditional paternalistic connections decrease. Such survival increasingly involves closing the plant and moving to another part of the country or to another nation, where labor is cheaper, government policies more lenient, and thus profits are higher.

Structural change in the business sector is most apparent in cooperatives. A "co-op" is organized more democratically, while a conventional business is autocratic. Co-ops have been formed in virtually every sector of the United States and are an example of workers and customers involved in the joint formation of their policies. Bowles and Gintis point out in *Democracy and Capitalism* that "precisely because workers lack ownership of capital to begin with, they will have to pay more to borrow what they need, thus further disadvantaging the worker cooperative in the competitive game (1986, 85)."

Therefore, co-ops have a hard time expanding to compete with conventional corporations because the corporations can attract large amounts of money through banks and through stocks and bonds. If corporations were drawing funds from the entire society, the system could provide widespread sharing of profits and avoid concentration of power. But in fact, most of the money invested in corporations is coming from and going to a very small percentage of the population who work closely with the corporate banking systems. The system is structured to favor the oligarchy.

PROFESSIONS

Professions have special educational requirements and are licensed to grant special power and autonomy to their members, who accept the obligation to use their expertise to benefit the public. Medicine, law, architecture, and teaching are examples of professions, and universities have been set up to provide them their special expertise through professional schools that are key parts of these institutions.

There is a strong tendency in all professions to develop exclusionary language that by excluding the general public increases power within the profession. Penetration of this professional power requires that language be modified for clarity. Democratization of language would help the public understand and engage in dialogue.

Added to the unnecessary complication of language is the excessive complication of concepts. The public should force demystification of all professions. Otherwise they will move increasingly toward "in-group" language that not only excludes the public, but also hinders development of the ideas and concepts on which the profession is based.

The combination of exclusionary language and control of fees for service has made medicine and law into professions that exploit the public by charging fees vastly higher than the hourly wage of the average person. Even worse, the medical profession has a long history of fighting against public sector control of medical fees. Medicare, when it was proposed, was treated as a "communist" intrusion into the rights of the medical profession (Corning 1969).

Professions rapidly forget that they exist at the behest of the public, through subsidized universities and public licensing. And the considerable autonomy of members of a profession to establish and enforce standards comes at the price of dedication of service to the public. Instead, law and medicine have usually wanted both the autonomy which protective law provides and also the profit which business provides. The result has been increasingly for professions to shift from public responsibility to private profit.

All professions need public scrutiny and clear standards of public expectation. This requires particularly that access to services be affordable. If professions refuse to cooperate, their autonomy should be reduced. The final power is in the hands of the public, for professional services can be regulated and even provided directly through the government if privatized professions are not publicly responsible.

SCHOOLS

Formal education is carried on largely through a public system in which teachers have little power compared to the power of practitioners of law and medicine. Teacher organizations lobby like any other constituency for high wages and better working conditions but they seldom exert the power of a strong union to strike for higher wages and to use organized power to establish intellectual standards. The decentralizing of control of public schools predetermines that standards and economic support will vary according to communities. Some communities have well paid teachers, good facilities, and small classes. But poor communities and inner cities create the kind of second rate education that reinforces the weakness of the community—part of the self-fulfilling prophesy by which more inequality is created.

A wage high enough to attract good teachers should be part of federal policy and standards such as maximum class size should be equally mandated at a federal level. Citizens of a country all need access to good education. Reliance on states and local communities simply replicates the inequality that undermines "equal opportunity for all."

MEDICINE

Medicine has largely avoided conducting research on the prevention of illness and instead focuses on the more profitable area of diagnosis and treatment. A twenty-first century commitment to the improved health of the public instead of only to medical care would make conventional medicine only a part of the plan to create environmental health—focusing on food, air quality, water quality, work-place environment, vaccines, and control of toxins.

During the twentieth century, medicine primarily used a private sector business model, which put profit ahead of public health and then relied on medicine, drugs, and surgery to mitigate ailments. Economic costs have moved up exponentially, exceeding the entire cost of the public school system, while the preventive approaches to public health, which are far less expensive and often much more effective, have been neglected. These preventive approaches, of course, provide little economic profit for the medical business and the pharmaceutical companies.

NECESSARY PRINCIPLES: ECOLOGY AND ETHICS

ECOLOGY AND THE PRECAUTIONARY PRINCIPLE

Institutions now are largely self-serving. Corporations strive to expand their wealth and power as do nations. Even professions such as law or medicine often make their public contributions only within the structure of control in which they retain special benefits, usually relating to wealth and power.

During the twentieth century, the power of all institutions expanded without regard for the carrying capacity of the earth. Now, however, we move into the twenty-first century with more sense of the need for an ecologically-sustained planet. But the creation of alternative institutions needed to achieve such a goal has yet to be undertaken. The dynamics of twentieth century institutions, especially growth-oriented capitalist economics, developed such momentum that it has been much like the Titanic moving at full speed toward an iceberg. There may not be enough time to slow down and turn before disaster strikes.

Whenever possible, *lead time* should now be instituted in all planning. When in doubt about dire ecological consequences, we need to hold off. This "precautionary" principle provides us with time to better understand whether going ahead or changing direction is really the right thing to do. In a world in which uncertainty is a major part of reality, the **avoidance of irreversibility** is crucial to our very survival.

The long-term political goal is clear: The life-support system of the planet must be sustained and even regenerated. And the short-term goal is the precautionary principle—if in doubt about an action that could commit the resources of the planet to irreversible change in the life-support system—don't do it!

ETHICS

But why sustain the planet? There are two ways to consider human beings: one is to use people instrumentally to contribute to institutions and to serve their leaders, the other is to treat people as "ends." **As ends, people are the purpose of the institution. As means they are instrumental grist for the institutional mill.** As ends, we have human rights and we should build our institutions throughout the world on the principle of the worth and dignity of the human person.

But this creed is a long way from being the deed. Means and ends have gotten reversed to form the "upside-down" world of the twentieth century. Currently schools increasingly prepare students to become marketable entities in a corporate-driven economy. Ethics-based education should help people participate as citizens in the needed transition by focusing on human and environmental issues and learning how to use cooperative power to effect social change. A major objective would be to have more public control of government and the public policies of the economic system. A democratic education should help people achieve this goal.

OBSTACLES TO PROGRESS: HUMAN NATURE MYTHS

INNATE SUPERIORITY

Most of the myths about human nature such as racial superiority and genetically superior intelligence have been used to support political inequality. In olden times myths about sovereign power removed personal responsibility from the king, in modern times from legislatures who often presume the public is not intelligent enough to understand public policy issues. And innate inequality beliefs continue. If poverty, intelligence, moral qualities, and even criminality are the result of genetics, then nature has supplied the basis for superiority and dominance, and everyone should keep his/her place in the hierarchy of natural inequality. Such desperate myth-making is still used to attempt to remove responsibility from the privileged, even though genetic criminality myths have been pulverized by sociological and anthropological evidence until only those who have been educationally deprived hold on to those fabrications.

Citing differences in intelligence as the cause of poverty still manages to surface as a genetic argument and continues to have some effect in defusing economic reform. A good geneticist knows that intelligence is not a function of a single gene but is polygenetic and therefore outside the province of current genetic science. Virtually all the heated arguments about intelligence fail to define different types of intelligence and usually confuse what one has learned with one's capacity to learn.

Even more importantly, economic justice and human needs have nothing to do with intelligence but with social ethics. Poor people have the same

needs as the rich, though not necessarily the same wants. When the wants of the rich cut into the needs of the poor, the ruling class must find some way to avoid responsibility. Blaming human nature is still worth some political points. Like many arguments that should involve science and ethics, we find that ideology and social class are likely to undermine clear thought when the power of an established oligarchy is at stake. The "natural superiority" ideology is useful in the media, for it plays well to common prejudices and the latent social Darwinism which has often been used to justify competitive capitalism. (See Boyer and Walsh, "Are Children Born Unequal" in *Saturday Review*, October 19, 1968 for a widely published analysis).

THE NICHELESS ANIMAL

One major reason why we destroy the life support system of the planet is that we **lack** genetic programming that would tell us what we ought to do. Inadvertently, we destroy the ecology because we are **nicheless**. We are the unique nicheless animal. We do not set out deliberately to destroy the environment, we destroy environment because we have not been programmed through evolution to fit into an ecological niche.

The long evolution of natural ecological systems consists of flora and fauna of all types that have genetically-derived behaviors and which interact with each other to form a whole system. Animals survived because of the niche they filled in the ecosystem. They had no intellectual understanding of what they were doing, but each provided some use to the total natural system and helped produce stability. This stability was in turn a flexible entity which continued to evolve and readjust as the system changed, often by death and trauma.

But we are not an integral part of the natural ecological systems. **We affect ecological systems but we have no genetically driven programming to tell us what to do and what niche to fit into.** We use and we exploit, and as nomads we often depleted an area and moved on. When we returned, the environment may have recovered enough that we could again exceed the sustainable carrying capacity of that region. We had no special understanding of the ecosystem, but at least until now we lacked the technology to completely destroy it.

No creature except humans has to understand how natural systems work in order to survive. Since natural systems are enormously complex it is exceedingly likely that what people will do will be the **wrong** thing. If you live in the tropics and can pick fruit and grow yams to survive you may not yet be consciously in tune with the life-support system, but you may not upset the natural stability enough to make a difference. Bring in a corporation with bulldozers, chain saws, and opportunity to make money from the exploitation of nature and all that is changed.

Human nature does involve tool making and tool use. Some other animals make and use tools, but human ingenuity is incredibly greater. When applied to technology and worldwide economic activity the genetically-driven human capacity to develop complex language can have a powerful effect on the planet. So the fact that we have no instinctual, genetically-programmed niche means that unless human intelligence and social learning rise to the point of getting collective human behavior to work with natural systems, we will probably do the wrong things—and with the use of computers with expanding population, and with increasingly intensive energy use, we will do the wrong things at an accelerating rate.

THE PERNICIOUS SELF-INTEREST MYTH

It is commonly believed in western civilization that economic systems merely reflect human nature in that everyone is simply "pursuing his or her own natural self interest." When each pursues this "natural self-interest" in turn, there is cumulatively a driving force for production and for creating an economy that provides good for everyone.

Two assumptions are typically involved: one is that self-interest is part of human nature; the other is that greed is acceptable as a driving cultural value. The society that results is therefore "me" centered rather than "us" centered, and is based on competition, not on cooperation.

This "self-interest" belief is held deeply in the minds of Americans. It is both their view of human nature and their rationalization for an economy based on self-interest.

A simple analysis of this belief reveals that the **"self-interest" notion confuses the "self" as the subject of the interest with the object of the interest. Of course each person is the source of the interest, but the interest does not need to be directed only to one's self.** Much human action comes from interest in what is presumed to produce personal advantages, but mothers do love their children and people sacrifice themselves to protect others. And some societies (such as Cubans) and cultures (such as the Hopi) play down personal self-interest in favor of an interest in the welfare of the community. Esthetic experience focused on objects of beauty can only occur when the object of experience is **outside** the person.

A "self with an interest" is the key to the optimistic side of human nature, to education, to mental health, and even to collective survival. The overriding collective interest has always been for the group's survival. But now it is crucial for economics, politics, and education to develop appropriate institutions and learn what is necessary to connect people with society, community, and even natural systems. As long as the only personal question is "What can I get out of it, and what will it do for me?" people turn into egomaniacs who never discover the outside world, and therefore never develop their own remarkable potentialities to relate to it. Paradoxically, we must discover ourselves not by focusing on ourselves but by losing ourselves in the larger world.

Since we are nicheless we need to compensate for having no pre-given direction to our remarkable capacity to learn. We need to learn what natural ecosystems are and how to use them and work with them. We need to connect with people of other cultures and races to build new institutions to control the violence we inflict on each other and on nature, and in so doing to build community rather than isolated individualism. The self-interest myth is destructive to community and to human development. It is part of the metaphysics of industrial capitalism. We need to think of ourselves as "people" not as "individuals." Any view of ourselves that prevents connections with people and the planet is dangerous and obsolete. The old idea of "self-interest" as the defining human characteristic leads us into a trap that prevents the design of community and a cooperative future.

MIND TRAPS

TECHNOFANATICISM

People are tool-makers and inventors. Building and creating come natural to us. In the last 200 years we have seen an overwhelming concentration of energy directed toward inventing technology that has been invested with a kind of religion—the belief that "technology will solve our problems." New devices such as automobiles, airplanes, and a vast array of other things have resulted. The latest is the computer, which promises a "communication revolution" that will solve all our problems.

We often believe that "whatever is technologically possible ought to be done." Technology then becomes both means and ends. For example, without considering costs and the full range of priorities, including human needs, we rush into outer space because it is possible. Once NASA was born, it had its own life and momentum. ICBMs, nuclear power plants and atom bombs gained justification independent of their usefulness as our technotoys, for they were the essence of the meaning of the twentieth century. And now we rush head-long into biotechnology and genetic engineering with little or no sense of the way we might be playing roulette with established ecosystems by creating plants and microbes that have never been part of the evolutionary process.

The contributions of technology should not be disregarded, for people's lives clearly have benefited from many inventions—appliances, air condi-tioners, telephones, and improved medical treatment. But technology is always connected to a system of production and distribution that is tied pri-marily to the power of dominant institutions. Despite what we often hear, in a capitalist world it is not likely that democratic control will come from people having their own computers. People may use computers to fight exploitative legislation more effectively, but the computers of multination-als can move speculative capital around the world at a much faster rate—adding to their profits and power. The twentieth century's economic game rules and power structure will have to be shifted from the global casino to more public control in order for technology to serve ethical goals that focus on the worth and dignity of people.

Institutional reinvention requires more understanding of both the uses and limits of technology. Technofanaticism is a powerful ideology, placing exces-sive faith in the ability of "technofix" to solve problems. **Technofanaticism depoliticizes people** by distracting them from an understanding of the fun-damental issues of political and economic power that underlie the technolo-gies they are using. The 2 percent or so of the people of the world who have most of the wealth and power need public myths to prevent revolution. They therefore have a lot at stake in buying and controlling media. In January 2000, the largest computer network (AOL) combined with the largest mag-azine-television media corporation (Time-Warner), thus creating the poten-tial for consolidating information power to serve their private interests (Bagdikian 1997).

Television, newspapers, and magazines have a vested interest in keeping the necessary myths intact since they are controlled by corporate advertising and corporate ownership. People are offered the vague and deceptive hope that technology (especially computer technology) will expand communication possibilities and provide greater human freedoms without changing institu-tions and political power. That is, however, not possible!

The Y2K phenomenon will go down in history as the supreme example of technological vulnerability and dependence. A science fiction story based on the scenario of a world crisis resulting from a programming error built into all computers which **caused them to fail to extend the calendar** would be treated as absurd. Yet this happened in the real world.

There was the uncertainty of effects on banks and utilities. Nuclear missiles in the United States and Russia had their triggering cloaked in secrecy, so worldwide deprogramming was needed to provide reasonable assurance of safety at the end of 1999. Even after the United States spent $100 *billion* on deprogramming, the computer experts had misgivings. But on January 1, the year 2000 arrived with no major catastrophe. The Y2K event illuminated the way we have become vulnerable to accident and terrorism in a worldwide computer system that is a fragile web of micro chips. When and where will the next crisis be?

A central principle needed for planning the twentieth century is to understand the inherent characteristics of mechanistic systems versus ecological systems. **The more complicated a mechanistic system, the more likely it will fail. But the more complicated an ecological system is the more likely it will not fail, for the ecological system gains stability based on diversity**. So communication systems that are mechanistic fail to communicate when they are too complicated. That is why conflicts between nations are often resolved by human beings sitting down together, as at Camp David under President Carter. When messages move second hand, third hand, fourth hand, and then through a mechanistic system which has some built in failure probabilities, the result is likely to be high distortion. Technological dependence and remoteness of social links have made *misunderstanding* more likely. During the cold war the United States came close to launching a nuclear exchange with the Soviet Union when geese on a radar screen were interpreted as incoming nuclear missiles.

A major twenty-first century challenge will be to put technology in the service of all people. It is now obstructed by the religion of extreme technological faith. High risk "technofix" efforts such as "missile defense" crowd out considerations of the how the power of nations and corporations must be changed to solve major world problems.

Students are often led to treat computers as a substitute for libraries and to substitute "communication" systems for structural understanding of the world system..

Most schools are so lacking in philosophy that they have fallen for computers as essential to learning. Arthur Pearl summarizes the effect of the computer "revolution" in schools as follows:

There is a crafting of illusion that something marvelous is happening when nothing of substance occurs. Stripped to its essentials, computer literacy is less than cook book literacy, and much, much less than Volkswagen repair literacy. Schools outdid themselves in a mad rush to install such devices in the classroom. They came instead of more teachers, higher salaries, art and music programs (Pearl-Cooperstein, 21).

TELEVISION: THE SUPREME OPIATE OF THE MASSES

The political power of television is enormous and now eclipses religion as the true "opiate of the masses." It represents the ultimate in "deflection politics." Appealing to the worst part of human nature, programs have provided enough violence, sensationalism, and silliness to keep people attentive even during repeated soporific commercials that try to turn them into unthinking consumers. It is an example of technology in the service of the corporate system, providing symbols that show us that (1) people are fools and willing to behave stupidly in commercials, (2) that the system is willing to engage in any manner of deceit to obtain profits, and (3) that putting balls into hoops is central to the meaning of life.

One channel, public television, has been reserved to serve an educational role and to help create an informed citizenry. In its early days, it was exemplary. In the 1980s, the Reagan administration reduced the budget and forced PBS to use commercial sponsors. Within 20 years, public television has gone largely in the direction of commercial television. A safe group of commentators is repeatedly used to respond to a safe set of questions. However, nature and cultural films (including good music) are available through corporate sponsorship because they are non-controversial. Programming on politics, history, and economics, however, is usually so weak that it provides little basis for developing an informed public. *Wall Street Week* and *The Nightly Business Report*, appropriate only to commercial television, have been on public television for decades.

Legally and technically, however, the reform of television is far easier than the rehabilitation of the press. The **airways are public property** that is leased by corporations. The public has the legal power to impose any requirement for content or commercials. For the commercial stations to distort the political system during elections by becoming the most expensive element of campaigns is entirely unnecessary. Conditions of licensing should include free political time to candidates on both PBS and commercial TV.

PBS should be financed by public money and run by a board directly elected by the public. Statutory law could mandate Congress to allocate guaranteed funding and ensure that the standards for program content are guided by a statement of purpose to be followed by the elected board. Commercial television could be charged license fees high enough to support public television. The entire plan is simple and logical, but it first requires the public to know the truth about current public ownership of the airways.

The same principles apply to radio, which is at least as dismal on commercial stations that usually offer perpetual commercials in place of public education. But since radio is less costly, there is a greater variety of stations. Some have provided the most intellectually and politically useful information available to the public. The Pacifica Network stations are among the most well known. Some public radio stations are reaching out and broadcasting local lectures—an outstanding example is an organization called Alternative Radio (located in Boulder, Colorado) that supplies penetrating taped speeches, often recorded at universities. Many of these speeches have a strong social justice and anti-corporate emphasis—the kind of material that fits the social ethics goal that should be driving twenty-first century institutions in a transition from the twentieth century.

Low costs of transmission have allowed radio to achieve this desirable educational objective. Television is inherently expensive and uses the subsidy of public property rights through free licensing. The potential power of public ownership of the airways needs to be fully utilized to make sure that television actually serves the public interest. The public owns the airways and should control them. Radio and television models in other countries such as Germany, which have avoided much commercial corruption, should be examined for policy suggestions.

Obsolete Paradigms

We think and act within a view of the world that we can call a "paradigm." Unless we are aware of our particular way of thinking we are fated to act according to that view. Earlier civilizations such as the Greek, Roman, and Christian held a fixed, "block" universe conception of reality. The universe was believed to be essentially unchanging, and the highest form of knowledge was to know ultimate reality. For Christians, faith was the key to the knowledge of ultimate reality; for the Greeks, rationality was the basis for "true" understanding. Instead of depending exclusively on faith or rationality, Darwin turned outward to study directly the way that life forms of the earth developed, and his empirical studies of the evolutionary change in species from lower to higher levels of complexity destroyed the previous static, fixed universe conception. From then on a new paradigm has evolved, and it has produced a different way of conceiving reality and the human capacity to create reality.

Early astronomers considered the earth to be the center of the universe. The paradigm shift to the sun as the center was a drastic change, and people who advocated it—even offering astronomical evidence as Galileo did—were often persecuted and even killed for threatening the established order. But the new evidence won out, and the new paradigm prevailed until recent times. With newer information, the perception of the sun as the center has shifted to seeing "our universe" as the center, and now even this is giving way to the belief that "our known universe" is only one of many. Moreover, the old assumption that there was any meaning at all to the term "center" is itself under question as anthropocentric and unscientific.

William James and John Dewey took the next step: to focus on the consequences of action rather than the idea of knowledge of "independent" reality. Pragmatism—testing a proposition by its consequences—framed another new paradigm that redefined the very meaning of knowledge.

These illustrations of how basic worldviews have undergone fundamental change lead us to consider whether we are currently in need of other basic paradigm changes. Our belief system provides the basis for our goals, and in the modern world the application of technology to industrial-economic processes is guided by presumptions that have consequences, for better or worse. The modern world has made use of evolutionary processes with a vengeance. Change is presumed to be not only inevitable but virtually synonymous with progress. The word for supporting all change is "growth." Nations, cities, and businesses that "grow" are presumed to be on the right path. No goals are needed. Growth is considered to be inherently good.

But as "pragmatic" evidence accumulates, this modern paradigm is being challenged as have all other contemporary belief systems. Growth without recognition of limits now faces the real constraints of a finite planet with finite resources and a finite carrying capacity. The growth paradigm had served as a twentieth century religion, but this faith is no longer self-evident. For change and growth, driven by twentieth century market forces, had made use of only two aspects of science: applied physics and chemistry.

Rachel Carson and other biologists have seriously challenged the exclusive dominance of physics and chemistry that has been underlying the entire growth economics era. The building of dams and the control of forests, land, and sea have been accomplished through engineering based on physics and chemistry. An entire medical profession has also been based on these limited areas of science. But the **basic life-support system of the planet is biological-ecological.**

The new survival paradigm is tied to **limits** and to ecological systems. However, the momentum of the engineering-of-the-environment era is still dominant. As Emerson said over a hundred years ago, "Things are in the saddle and ride mankind."

Hard science is increasingly providing information on the consequences of the old short-range, engineering paradigm. The oceans are being depleted of marine life, the atmosphere of the planet is disintegrating. Our ultraviolet shield and temperature stabilizer and the forests and topsoil on which food and oxygen production depend are disappearing as a result of impacts of this short-sightedness that threatens our ecological life-support system.

A paradigm change is necessary not only to have real progress but even to survive. Paradigms provide conceptual organization and tunnel vision at the same time. Some common ways of perceiving the world are necessary in order to have cooperative civilization, but if those ways of thinking and believing lead to disaster because the real world of consequences is ignored, the paradigms are not merely obsolete but suicidal.

This most critical mission of education should be to evaluate the adequacy of current belief systems. Most current education is itself so much a part of the problem that it reinforces conventional belief rather than helps people reconsider.

Intelligence, science, and rationality applied to problem solving require a better way of first defining the real "problems." Next, the interrelationships between problems must be understood. Then, value-priorities must be taken into account. Economic goals should be means, not ends, and they should be secondary to the value of human life and the biosphere. Given a new way of thinking, we can then take steps to right the current "upside-down" society that is based on paradigms that no longer work.

In light of its long-stated commitment to upholding human rights at home and in its foreign policy, the U.S. government today poses a threat to the universality of human rights.

—Human Rights Watch 1999

There is a sense that the United States has become too arrogant, too dominant, too self-centered, proud of our wealth, believing that we deserve to be the richest and most powerful and influential nation in the world. I think they feel we don't really care about them, which is quite often true.

—Jimmy Carter 2002

RECLAIMING GOVERNMENT

What we have been calling a democratic government is not responsive to the needs of the public and the decline in political participation is one of the results. What is needed is restructuring of government to serve the public rather than corporate capitalism. Then the public will participate.

The frustration and cynicism that many people feel about government often leads them to want less government—or no government at all. Seldom is the structural obsolescence of government recognized, yet government in the United States and generally world-wide is structured to fail in the most important aspects.

The characteristics of the conventional model need close attention. First, it consists of the election of people to office. Second, it is based on representing constituencies, sub-parts of the larger society. Third, campaigns are driven largely by money to support candidates. What is omitted is significant: *The public never elects the goals which elected officials are to implement.* The main defacto goal therefore becomes whatever is the personal goal of the legislators—and that is, usually, to be re-elected.

Two things stand out: one is that there are no overriding public goals; and the other is that there is no basis for serving any real national interest. All interests are those of the supporting constituencies, those that provide the money and the votes. Fragmentation is inevitable, for the structure uses rules which pre-determine fragmentation. The vision of government is inevitably short-range. The legislature is mainly crisis-reactive. There is no mandate that governmental power will be used either to promote economic justice or to benefit future generations. The biosphere on which the life support system of the planet is based is considered irrelevant, for government is driven by the pressing economic goals of moneyed constituencies. The longer-range future is of secondary importance. Protection of the ecosystem is limited to emergency responses to dramatically publicized imminent crises.

This form of government makes planning in the public interest very unlikely. It is built around private interests, which are presumed to cumulatively form the public interest. Because of the lack of any basic principles of justice to guide legislation, each group—minorities, environmentalists, the poor, or the disabled—must fight hard to get their concerns enacted into law. Future generations, not being around to provide constituency power, are ignored.

People can either concentrate on the personalities of the people they are electing, or else vote for a political party. Electing more pleasant people does make a difference, but never a significant difference. The structure and the rules of government are what produce the major consequences.

Many judges, including U.S. Supreme Court justices, are appointed by the President and therefore ideology is transmitted into the courts. Corporations can be assured of many "correct" decisions if the judges are actually in their pocket, though the public thinks they are living under the "rule of law." The de-facto election of George W. Bush by the Supreme Court in the November 2000 election will be the classic case of abandonment of the rule of law.

HOW IT GOT THIS WAY

Some earlier tribal governments exhibited a model of direct democracy with shared decision-making, but during most history tyrannical control through military power dominated (Johnson 1997). British kings were hereditary sovereigns not democratically elected, who could do no wrong. The American colonists, once freed from British rule, wanted decentralization of political power to shift into the hands of the common person. They distrusted a strong central government.

The Enlightenment and the Protestant Reformation had produced a new concept of personal worth and individualism. Yet, most people lived in small communities, so early American government was largely conducted through town meetings, a direct form of local democracy. But when the U.S. Constitution was written, it was created by the wealthy land owning class whose major purpose was to protect the wealthy minority from the poorer majority. (Zinn, 1997b, 75) These founding fathers saw no need for a bill of rights, but support from the poorer majority, mostly rural farming classes, required its inclusion. The Constitution then came to have two elements—the protection of property (the special interest of the aristocratic landowners) and a bill of rights to protect the public from excessive coercion by government.

Charles Beard, in *An Economic Interpretation of the Constitution*, pointed out that "the rules" designed by the dominant classes were to "control the organs of government." As Howard Zinn has shown, the Constitution was not simply the work of wise men but of "certain groups trying to maintain their privileges, while giving just enough rights and liberties to enough people to ensure popular support (1997b)." Expanding each right has required an enormous struggle at every point. Women's groups trying to obtain the right to vote were beaten and harassed. Workers trying to unionize were beaten and even killed, a pattern for virtually all minorities striving to achieve basic rights. Power was never voluntarily relinquished; it was always taken through counter power, sometimes violently, sometimes nonviolently. Democracy and free speech were the main instruments for non-violent change. Yet democracy and speech have often been controlled through concentrated economic power, which has obstructed democracy, thus raising the odds for violence.

In a land of enormous natural resources, the U.S. government has been an instrument for establishing the rules for allocating these resources. But instead of basing decisions on principles of social justice, the politics of private property established by the early wealthy landowners has often dominated. Inequality of results were beneficial to the wealthy classes, so **competition between unequals has been the main rule for allocating natural resources**. In the nineteenth century, the economic control of government had made the allocation of railway rights and public land a windfall for the rich and powerful. Many acres of land on each side of the tracks were part of the massive corporate windfall and were sold at a tremendous profit. The 1872 mining law continues as a massive giveaway of public land to mining companies for pennies an acre—and they pay no taxes on the property. In the twentieth century the licensing of commercial radio and television stations to use the publicly owned airwaves has shifted wealth and information power to major corporations that were controlled by the wealthiest citizens.

From the nineteenth century "robber barons" to the twentieth century multinational corporations, the rules have provided their intended results. Now that the model is being cast globally as "free trade" (again, competition between unequals) with no constraints to protect workers or the environment, corporations are like computer "pac-men" chewing away at the very fabric of the natural life-support system of the planet.

The rules of institutions largely determine their outcome. In the United States what is called political democracy is based on (1) checks and balances of government structures and (2) the use of constituencies to influence basic public policy.

The early purpose of the checks and balances, using three branches of government, was to prevent tyranny of government. To achieve this, the three branches were created which can not only balance, but even nullify each other's actions. While this system may help to prevent the tyranny of any one branch of government, it does not prevent the development of **corporate** tyranny, for government is without goals and weak in relation to the driving force of economic institutions to increase their profits.

Constituencies, which pressure for their piece of public policy and the economic "pie," gain influence largely through the uses of their economic power. Financing of candidates through media-based elections means that the rich and powerful corporations have disproportionate power. Such power will inevitably be used to enhance their own power instead of serving the public interest. In fact, **public interest becomes largely a fiction under this system.**

From Growth to Development

> Growth for the sake of growth is the ideology of the cancer cell.
> —Edward Abbey

The belief in unlimited growth dominates most business ideology, thus government in the United States does whatever it can to promote this ideology. Those who disagree are labeled anti-growth. This is intended to be a critical label. We often hear that "growth is inevitable."

But the word "growth" obscures thought rather than clarifying it. If it has any meaning, it is mainly that quantitative expansion is considered "growth." This is not the meaning of growth used in human development, for when a child is growing optimally, he/she is doing more than just expanding. We don't want Johnny to merely swell up, we want him to evolve—mentally, emotionally, and morally.

Some parts of the economy become better if they expand. A small town that lacks the population to support a good school or cultural events or to provide much employment might have reason to welcome some expansion, some growth. A town can be too small to provide the community interaction that produces cultural stimulation, and people may want to leave if life is boring.

But the indiscriminate and extreme growth ideology that has characterized America in the twentieth century has presumed that growth everywhere was a blessing. If a small town grew, it was presumed to be better off, until it became medium size. Then it would be better off if it grew until it became even larger. Such growth moves expansion in the direction of a city the size of Los Angeles with the attendant problems of pollution, congestion, crime, and alienation. If growth is always good categorically, it must not stop. Los Angeles then needs "growth" to become the size of Mexico City. This progression of the illogic of growth illuminates its lack of sustainable goals. Having lost a sense of survival and of quality of life, it has its own dynamics: the bigger the better!

Why the insanity? How did people get locked into such abdication of logic and even common sense? During the twentieth century we did not develop *either social or environmental goals.* There was no way to evaluate what we mean by getting "better," so we moved to quantitative indicators, of which the GNP, the Gross National Product, is the leading device. Once aggregate income expansion defines "progress," the entire world can be judged as to where it is on the ladder of "progress." The speed at which a nation's GNP "grows" determines its health. Nations showing the fastest growth are "progressing" faster than the others and serve as models to be emulated.

So what happens when other indicators signify that an area that is optimum by "growth" standards is becoming congested with traffic, threatening health with pollution, destroying prime top-soil, increasing crime and poverty and ignoring widespread responses from residents who say that life there is getting worse, not better? According to the mantra, this cannot be. But, of course, it increasingly is. The term "progress" needs to be clearly differentiated from the term "growth."

Serious planning for real human progress has yet to really take hold, though various local groups and some states have worked on what are sometimes called "benchmarks" tied to vision statements. These are good first-step conceptual exercises in showing that qualitative indicators are needed, but they have not as yet had the force of law to direct economic activity. They sometimes constrain excesses related to destruction of the environment, but growth ideology still dominates, always advocating stimulating the overall economy to expand and presumably to produce some trickle-down effects. This approach to economics often involves more bads than goods.

When the "bads" approach is used, the way to save the old system is to "mitigate" the bads—such as relying on technological quick fixes by putting emission devices on cars. When pollution gets intolerable, instead of planning a transportation system that is within environmental carrying capacity, more highways are built to respond to "demand." Short-run mitigation measures are very profitable to a segment of the community, namely the businesses and the shopping centers that depend on the highways. But the costs of land acquisition and construction of freeways, and the social effects as well, are transferred to the society as a whole as problems compound and become increasingly intractable. The growth system is expensive.

Integrated planning, guided by positive indicators would put long-range public needs in charge of economics and help turn the current obsolete world system right side up. The distinction between "growth" and "development" remains important, for a society needs to identify the changes necessary to provide a sustainable high common quality of life. And such changes need to be tied to human and community development, to the ways in which people connect with each other. Individualism and competition are part of the current cultural values that drive the "growth" paradigm, but they need to be contained and made secondary to overriding long range goals based on ecological sustainability and social justice.

Perhaps we should open up the issue to public debate by saying *no* to "growth" and *yes* to "development." This would help raise the question "Aren't they the same?"— which would provide an opportunity to draw the distinction. The idea of the-bigger-the-better is under stress, seen increasingly as threatening to the entire planetary environment. Various human rights need to be tied to principles of development, moving beyond civil liberties into such positive rights as the right to employment at a living wage, the right to a healthful environment, and the right of future generations to inherit sustained natural ecosystems.

All the old paradigm indicators of growth are paraded in the daily paper and treated as "progress"— GNP, number of houses built (with no indication of whether they are affordable), employment figures, etc. The goals tied to qualitative development and the specific indicators to measure movement toward these goals are what we need to see in twenty-first century newspapers in place of GNP figures, to show whether targets of "development" are being hit or missed. Such development indicators need the enforcement power of statutory and constitutional law.

Herman Daly and John Cobb worked out alternatives to GNP in their book *For the Common Good* (1989). They subtract the destructive factors in the economy from the sum of economic transactions. While the GNP has risen, the "sustainable welfare," which includes the subtraction of destructive factors, has *declined* during the last quarter of the twentieth century. "Progress" became *retrogression* when external costs were subtracted. The most powerful growth segments of society can dominate in the short run if the public and future generations continue to subsidize them. In the name of progress and "growth" the world is involved in a con game that relies on large scale ignorance to keep it going, for people would see they are shooting themselves in the foot if they really understood what they were doing.

It is time to take planning for "progress" seriously and to use knowledge and technology to provide more benefits and fewer costs. Development indicators could direct change toward actual progress where human development and common quality of life would serve present and future generations. This is a model of a world beyond the ideology of corporate capitalism.

The rules of the capitalistic game driven by the profit motive produce predictable consequences. American democracy, lacking positive human rights goals, has not evolved beyond voting for individuals who often represent the corporate oligarchy, the contemporary version of the robber barons.

The Universal Declaration of Human Rights unanimously adopted by the United Nations in 1948, has never been authorized or implemented by the American government. The principles extend beyond constituency politics into positive human rights, transforming people's needs into political entitlements. But the American government is tied to the power of constituencies, and effective constituencies are usually those with the economic power to control public opinion. The priorities of such constituencies do not usually include human rights.

The world political system is characterized by fragmentation and structural anarchy. There is neither a global federation nor any global government. So the world of sovereign states, varying in their respective power, has become a system with an economic and military hierarchy. Nation-state dominance is predictable. The top dogs will dominate the underdogs militarily and economically. Top dogs will remain on top and the underdogs will try to gain more military and economic strength to raise their status and reduce their domination. **In this system there will be no effective global planning to serve either human rights or the ecological integrity of the planet and underdogs will often revolt and be put down as "terrorists."**

HUMAN RIGHTS: NEGATIVE AND POSITIVE

When Americans refer to human rights they usually connect the meaning to the Bill of Rights, which consists mainly of "negative" rights involving **freedom from** government restrictions. The First Amendment is the prime example, providing freedom of speech, assembly, religion, etc. But in 1948, when the Universal Declaration of Human Rights was developed through the United Nations, the shift was made to include "positive" rights as well— rights to employment, education, housing, food, etc.—**freedom to, not just freedom from.**

The twenty-first century should incorporate both positive and negative rights. Socialist countries have chosen to stress positive rights more than negative rights (Frank 1993, 91). To move beyond the American concept of negative rights, we need to include the positive rights—the rights to jobs, medical care, housing, food.

This is an important area of investigation for students and is crucial to the design of twenty-first century policy. Clearly the combination of positive and negative rights should be a goal for the twenty-first century. There is really no system of human rights on this planet, in the sense of rights claimable by all humans. We need a universally enforced system.

THE NUREMBERG PRINCIPLES

After World War II the United States led in creating the Nuremberg Principles under which war criminals were tried and in many cases executed. The central principle was new and history-making. It included "crimes against humanity." No one would be excused for killing by claiming he had carried out state orders, and thus morality made an historic quantum leap, superseding national law and obedience to military commands.

However, in Vietnam the United States committed acts of mass murder of civilians that were clearly violations of the Nuremberg principles. But there were no war crimes trials for Americans, not even for dropping atom bombs on Japan. The victors held themselves above the very law they created. To become universally applicable, law must apply equally to both victors and vanquished.

The principles are not only an important area of inquiry for students, but a basis for twenty-first century world law in which global morality and protection of human life overrides national law.

The creation through international treaties of a permanent International Criminal Court in 1998 was a significant step toward implementing the Nuremberg principles. The ability to hold accountable people who have committed grave crimes, even if they are heads of state, is a positive development. However, the United States opposed the Court, raising questions about the actual American support for the rule of law (Roth 1998).

General Pinochet, the former dictator of Chile, was extradited from Britain to Spain in 1999 for his murder of Spanish citizens. Other nations were actively cooperating. This precedent may help move crime and punishment into an arena of world law where individuals could be held accountable under Nuremberg principles for murder and other crimes once rationalized as "national defense."

The Common Heritage

All land areas have some form of legal control. Even the Antarctic is under international treaty. But most of the world is ocean. The oceans represent the new frontiers of law—connected with rights of passage, access to mineral resources and fish, and also rights of future generations to these resources. This latter right gave rise during the 1960s and 1970s to the principle of the "common heritage," which is a far-reaching principle of equitable claim on ocean resources for all people, including current and future generations.

The objective of a common heritage requires new principles of management and a system of governance and enforcement. The proposed "ocean regime" calls for expansion of laws beyond nations to include the "law of the seas." The United States promoted the idea in the 1970s but voted against it in the 1980s under the Reagan administration. This unfinished frontier needs to be included as a subject area in a twenty-first century curriculum, to continue the momentum of the 1970s and provide solutions to the current tragedies of the ocean commons. The oceans under the traditional system of free use have become garbage dumps and cesspools, and the fish and minerals are being depleted as each nation and corporation takes what it can without obligations to future generations. The more powerful the nation the more it is able to exploit (Porter and Brown, 155).

UNITED NATIONS CHARTER REVISION

The United Nations is based on an "international" structure in which political power is nation-state power. It can act when there is a high level of agreement between states. The original veto power of the five leading members of the Security Council (winners in World War II) still remains, so action to stop international conflict is largely a reflection of the interests of these dominant states.

An effective twenty-first century peace keeping system requires structural changes, such as:

1. An internationally coordinated, standing peace keeping system to replace national military systems with phased national disarmament.
2. More control of the U.N. by the public through direct election of representatives.
3. Increased power of the World Court, with enforcement abilities with movement toward meaningful world law.
4. Enforcement power to prevent violations of human rights based on the Universal Declaration, with revisions to include environmental rights.
5. A global mandatory tax system to support the U.N.
6. Elimination of U.N. veto power by an individual nation.

WORLD ORDER MODELS PROJECTS

In conjunction with structural alternatives to the United Nations, the World Order Models Project should be examined. The World Law Fund created this remarkable examination of structural alternatives beginning in the 1960s. It involves many university centers and therefore includes regional perspectives in proposals for world order. All models must be directed toward social justice, war prevention, poverty reduction, and environmental sustainability.

This approach makes many "international studies" programs outdated. Their birth was largely in the post World War II era, before the idea of global humans rights and the rule of law was seriously considered. International studies programs are usually not problem solving, rather they are mainly descriptive avoiding ethical value considerations. The World Order Models Project, however, sets out from the very beginning to try to change the war system and increase social justice and ecological sustainability.

The World Order Models approach is basic to all planning. Whether piecemeal incremental muddling or basic systems change will be the dominant approach is crucial to the future. This book supports the latter, and my own work closely parallels and has been influenced by world order methodology. I worked with World Law Fund projects in the 1970s organizing teacher conferences, creating a peace studies library at the University of Hawaii, and writing a high school social studies text, *Alternative Futures, Designing Social Change* (1975).

LAND USE PLANNING

The way we use land in the United States has produced destruction of farm and forest land and also has created high costs tied to automobile-dependent transportation. Instead of zoning land on the basis of the highest and best long run public use, most land is put on the market to be sold for short run profit—as it was in the nineteenth century. Even more, the costs of the impacts on the public sector of this private profit system (expansion of roads, sewers, water, new schools) are seldom collected from the private developers. Growth pays for the developers at the expense of the larger public who pay higher taxes and suffer overloaded traffic and overcrowded schools. The result is a rapid movement toward sprawl and gridlock. The entire nation moves toward becoming one big Los Angeles while burdening the public with bonds and higher taxes to pay for the costs of growth. But some states have elements of structural change appropriate to the twenty-first century. Oregon and Hawaii instituted land use controls through zoning. Some land is zoned residential and commercial, but separate zoning for agriculture or forestland has tightly restricted use. In most states rural land is controlled by the market and available for uses other than farming and forestry. Typically, such land is converted to expanding urbanization to create outward sprawl.

In some states charges are made to developers for the public costs of such development—expansion of schools, roads, sewers, water systems, parks. If costs of development are not collected, the public subsidizes the public impacts and costs created by private developers. Hawaii had a critical need to preserve the high mountain areas in order to have control of water sources, so the watersheds are tightly zoned to restrict all development. In the 1970s the shoreline was put under zoning control to prevent continuation of the rapidly expanding shoreline sprawl.

The entire United States needs federal land use planning. The irreversible destruction of prime farm land, watersheds, and forests can be stopped only by designating, authorizing, and enforcing appropriate sustainable uses. Some states have taken positive initiatives. The Oregon model in particular needs to be studied and adapted to other states, for it uses centralized state goals for the protection of forest and farm land and restrictions on expansion of urban growth boundaries.

But these examples should simply be steps toward an ambitious twenty-first century planning process for land use. In the twenty-first century, **we will need global land use planning**. Europe already has some good models in place, particularly in the northern region—England, Holland, Germany, Denmark, Sweden, Finland, and Norway. But even in these countries the pressures to "privatize" all resources and turn all land into a market commodity are strong. Both statutory and constitutional law are needed to reverse the process.

Conversion of farm and forestland into houses and pavement puts some land into an irreversible use category, especially to the extent that the land involves prime top soil which is virtually non-renewable. It is dangerous to the food supply of the future and an immoral foreclosure of options for future generations when we shrink farm and forest land and convert it to sprawl. And it also greatly adds to costs and therefore the taxes of residents. Upzoning, in which developers capture the increased land value, has been a huge windfall and subsidy for the developers. The foot is on the growth accelerator as long as this form of unearned income is available to developers. The increased value should be taxed off so that funds are available to downzone, converting more land into parks and open spaces.

ENVIRONMENTAL RIGHTS

Socialist countries focus on positive rights, but no country provides "generational rights." These involve the rights of future generations to the natural heritage and to the social and political heritage developed by previous generations. Rights to the natural heritage involve sustaining non-renewable natural systems—forests, streams, mountains, clean air, and water. The life support system of the entire planet has been progressively degraded to the disadvantage of future generations, notably the forests, the biosphere, the atmospheric ozone layer. Future generations by definition are not here and cannot complain as their heritage is stolen from them. So we must speak for them and have the power to represent them.

The twenty-first century should use constitutional law to expand human rights. These need to include rights of future generations to the sustained benefit of natural systems, for natural systems are the basis for the support of all life. A nongovernmental organization in Oregon called Oregonians for

Environmental Rights, of which I am president, has plans for adding constitutional rights into the state constitution through the public initiative process. Twenty-two states have this initiative power and could follow the Oregon lead. Legislatures are not likely to introduce bills to institute such rights, for they give powers to citizens that supercede the statutory power of the legislature.

States cannot spearhead new rights such as a right to employment without inviting mass immigration from other states and causing the state to go bankrupt. But states can move ahead with rights that bear on the health and resources of the state, such as stream and forest protection. California has mandated, for example, that a certain percent of cars sold in the future have technology to raise fuel mileage and reduce pollution. States are appropriate frontiers for passing requirements for certain human rights that can then be copied at the federal level.

The proposed Oregon plan provides protection for future generations from human destruction of natural ecological systems by giving "use ownership" as distinguished from consumption rights to all future generations. Individuals and groups may be granted "standing" in court to represent future generations and protect these rights.

The right to a healthful environment shifts the burden of proof to the polluter to show that the pollution a person or corporation causes is not a threat to human health. (This formulation makes it useable in courts.) Both of these rights—to sustained natural systems and to a healthful environment—would be a major advancement in positive rights, extending the scope of the Universal Declaration of Human Rights.

A BIG JUMP—THE NO SMOKING STEP IN HUMAN RIGHTS

The social and institutional changes regarding smoking constitute a major step toward establishing global environmental rights. The movement to ban smoking in designated areas such as restaurants and offices was led by people in the United States supported by the mounting evidence of the health hazards of smoking tobacco. International airlines followed suit, prohibiting smoking even on long overseas flights, and public areas have increasingly been required by state law to be either smoke-free or to have separate areas for smokers. In 1997 California passed the most advanced no smoking laws, including all public areas, work places, and even bars.

This precedent sets the stage for a bolder claim to the right to a healthful environment such as the one planned in Oregon. It elevates health and personal survival to a higher level than the previous upside-down assumption of the "rights" of polluters. The question of whether there should be a smoke-free environment is no longer a matter to be decided by a majority vote in each restaurant or work place. It is a *human right* in which *everyone* has a right to clean air, as part of the right to life, thereby placing that right over a person's presumed right to smoke. The smoker with no right to pollute the public's air must find a way to contain the social effects of smoking, such as smoking in his own home or in separate smoking areas.

This principle now needs to be extended to the entire economic system so that work places such as textile mills and coal mines also have to conform to the prior right of all citizens to clean air. And clean air is only one element of the environment that we need for health; we need clean water and lower noise levels as well.

CONSTITUTIONAL CONVENTIONS

Through a unique provision, the Constitution of the State of Hawaii advanced the rights of minorities and the protection of the environment. Every ten years the public votes on whether to hold a constitutional convention to amend the constitution. The first vote was held in 1969 and created a new constitution. In 1979 the public voted for a convention and the constitution was revised. In 1989 the majority voted *not to hold* a constitutional convention.

This is an example of the way the public can have a more direct influence over law-making in addition to using state initiatives. Most states have neither device. Nor is there any provision for a federal constitutional initiative, a fact that deserves discussion and debate.

BUCKLEY VS. VALEO

Both of the ways of creating needed change are threatened when large amounts of money are used to influence elections. Corporations have increasingly been able to corrupt public judgment with political "messages" that often control the outcome of elections.

In 1976 a U.S. Supreme Court case, Buckley vs. Valeo, ruled that the first Amendment of the Constitution permits all forms of free speech and that the use of corporate money to influence elections is a legitimate example of "speech."

In 1886 the courts had ruled that corporations are entitled to the same First Amendment—freedom of speech—protection as real "natural" persons by ruling that corporations are also "persons." This personhood status has been used by corporations to defeat the votes of real people, for grass roots organizations are usually overwhelmed by massive and expensive disinformation campaigns that corrupt the democratic process.

In 1990, the Michigan legislature passed a law forbidding corporations from using their corporate funds for contributions to political candidates, but allowed them to solicit voluntary donations from their employees. The U.S. Supreme Court upheld this.

In 1998 activists in Montana designed a ballot measure which took the same principle that was used in the Michigan law and applied it to spending for initiative campaigns, and it passed in a state-wide election. But the corporations appealed it in 1999 and it was overruled by the State Court of Appeals.

The important goal of shifting power back to the public is tied largely to overthrowing Buckley vs. Valeo since this decision by the Supreme Court supports corporations in their use of funds as "free speech" to buy campaign ads on television and often control the outcome of an election. This distortion of "speech" means we have created "the best government money can buy." Movements that are developing to control this corporate power are examined in more detail in Chapter Ten.

The ways in which economics limits democracy in the United States must be understood by the public if the freedom of speech under the First Amendment of the Constitution is to be preserved and protected. High school social studies texts need to be written to help students understand this crucial issue.

A Fair Distribution Ratio

The distance between the lower and upper strata of society with respect to income and wealth is called the "distribution ratio." This ratio could be changed by public policy. It is the most taboo of all American topics, for it strikes at the heart of the concealment of economic alternatives from the people, a concealment central to sustaining American capitalism. The taboo constitutes an intellectual "iron curtain" in the United States and is used to control an American public that has been led to believe that the market will allocate wealth and income in a naturally fair manner. The myth is that those who work hard will get much, and those who are lazy will get little. In fact, wealth and income are mainly a function of institutional rules, particularly tax ratios. A change in the rules changes the outcomes. A dramatic regressive change in the ratio of wealth and income occurred in the 1980s under President Reagan as the result of a change in the tax policy.

I have never found students who have taken an economics class that posed the question: "What is a fair economic distribution ratio?" Yet that is the crucial value question that should be a central plank in political policy. Economics should be the technical means to achieve the goals of policies that serve the public good, but it is not.

The United States has the highest economic mal-distribution ratio of all industrial countries. Those in the top 20 percent of income in Japan make 4.3 times as much as those in bottom 20 percent. Those in the top 20 percent in the U.S. make 11 times as much as the bottom 20 percent. Countries such as Sweden and Finland have a distribution ratio about half as much as the U.S. Eighty percent of the nation's property is owned by 10 percent of the population. "Our 13,000 richest families possess a net worth equivalent to the assets owned by the country's 20 million poorest families" (Lapham 2003, 9).

To those who say, "But there is still inequality," it should be pointed out that a fair alternative is not absolute equality but a smaller gap between the top and the bottom so that no one at the lower level is deprived of basic economic needs (and dignity) and so that the economic difference between top and bottom groups in the society is much smaller than it is now. Then those with lower incomes would not be forced into exclusionary, ghettoized housing areas with a sense of being permanently in a hopeless underclass, as they were in the twentieth century.

Understanding the alternative should begin with recognition of the predetermined inequality resulting from the market models which conventional economic theory provides. Political control by corporations produces public policy that serves the rich by keeping distribution either through the market or through policies controlled by self-serving corporations. The tax changes made in the 1980s illustrated how a pro-corporate policy can create inequality. The Reagan administration shifted tax relief to the rich and accelerated the established inequality so greatly that it gave rise to the term "reverse Robin Hood economics."

The average (median) real income in 1998 was about the same as in 1973, yet the numbers of millionaires and even billionaires rose exponentially. Distribution at any given time is largely zero-sum, meaning when some get a lot, others get little.

World Economic Instability

What evidence is needed to prove that the world system is bankrupt and that Band-Aids or a quick fix will not do the job? Consider the following: By 1998, Thailand, Indonesia, Japan, and Korea were in a combination of depression and economic chaos. Currency was out of control and the banking system was broke. The American experience with savings and loan companies in the 1980s was replicated in the entire economic and political system of these nations, and the daily press was watching to see if Brazil and much of South America would go the same way. In 2002 Argentina became virtually bankrupt. The response of remaining capitalist nations was to rush in with money to try to prevent the banking collapse, but this quick fix seemed insufficient. The patient didn't have just a cold; he had advanced cancer.

Interestingly, Alan Greenspan, Chairman of the Federal Reserve Board, was so committed to pure capitalism that he took the position that no country should be saved from itself if it engaged in unwise economic policies. Instead, the market should do the cleansing. (But he agreed to the usual subsidy when large, very wealthy speculators faced bankruptcy.)

The more common view of the Asian countries was that these countries were too big to be permitted to fail. This was the view taken of the American Savings and Loan companies' collapse which resulted in public bail-out of huge individual and corporate debt. Small investors, however, could be permitted to fail.

Percent Change in After-tax Income, 1977-1994

Source: Congressional Budget Office

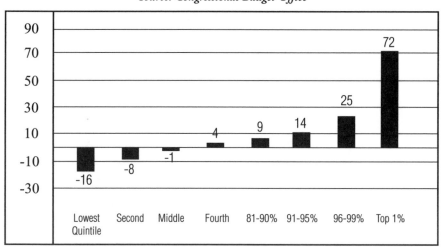

Greenspan's alleged capitalist philosophy seems in conflict with his actions. For either the capitalistic system in the private sector will be self-healing or it does not deserve the autonomy and independence from government that underlies capitalist ideology. So if we are asked to bail them out, we should have a say in how they are run in the first place to prevent the need for a bail out. But if the system is not really broke and will self-heal, it should be left largely to do so. If the system collapses, one of two things is likely—control and paternalism from the outside countries, or revolution from within.

By the end of the twentieth century the world economic and political picture was one of considerable instability, and the nations themselves showed many signs of obsolescence as summarized in these statements:.

1. The prosperity of the 1990s was largely a Ponzi game in which about 90 percent of the expansion in the value of capital came through money chasing after money, without producing any real economic value. The speculative bubbles led to a crash.

2. The world capitalist system was making use of American "trickle down" ideology, but very little economic value was trickling down, and so extreme poverty remained.

3. But global corporations looking for cheap labor considered this an advantage. It produced wealth for corporations but misery and starvation for millions.

4. Nuclear proliferation in India and Pakistan revealed that the world's nation-state system was still a war system in which anarchy and free trade of war material (mainly from the United States) continued much the same as it had since World War II. Russia was in a state of incipient anarchy, with 6,000 nuclear missiles increasingly left unguarded and vulnerable to theft and sale by the Russian Mafia. Six thousand Intercontinental Missiles were aimed at the United States and the computer systems were deteriorating. (The U.S. was aiming the same number and the computer systems were crash prone.)

5. Free trade had taken precedence over ecological management of the global environment, forests were destroyed, CO_2 emissions caused global warming, topsoil was increasingly lost depleting the land for future generations, and fisheries were in rapid decline worldwide.

Can all this be "fixed" or do we need to redesign a new world system? The term "new world order" became a facade in recent years to cover up the old order and give the appearance of progress. Nations, following corporations, needed to mollify the public with a new image for the same old reality.

By the end of the century, Europe had taken some of the largest steps forward, with plans for creating a new European currency (the Euro) that would likely affect the shape of a new Europe. But most American action was reaction in the form of short range mitigation measures that provided a facade for leadership while the focus was on the next election.

Public money, moving through government and private banks, was sent to economically collapsing nations to stave off revolutions. Though stability throughout the world became more and more precarious, the "growth" mantra tied to corporate power continued.

Instead of the present GNP indicators we need to identify indicators which contribute to the common well being of all people, giving priority to the basics: food, clothing, housing, medical care, and jobs. These indicators should be created by law, possibly through public initiatives so that economic policies will be directed to serve the public. Unless ecological sustainability and human rights are the overriding values that drive a new politics, we will continue to accelerate in the wrong direction at enormous human and monetary costs.

FROM CIVIL LIBERTIES TO HUMAN RIGHTS

If there is to be real progress in the twenty-first century it needs to be led by advances in human rights. Educational programs that hope to do more than create more technicians to reinforce the old order also need to focus on human rights.

The United States originally provided leadership in civil liberties through the Bill of Rights. These civil liberties helped protect individuals from the tyranny of government—providing individual freedoms, which Americans have treated as the highest value. "Unrestricted" individuals could then compete in the market, the core concept of American free enterprise. But the opportunity for unequals to compete provided a social Darwinian model, which resulted in revolt, of blacks in particular. The entire movement of the 1960s, tied to Martin Luther King Jr.'s leadership, drew in a wide segment of American society to promote greater equality for minorities, the disabled, Latinos, and women. This movement gives recognition to a new level of rights beyond the individualism underlying competition. It now needs to take into account the shift to positive rights that the United States supported in helping create the Universal Declaration of Human Rights in 1946 (though Congress failed to ratify it). A new political strategy based on universal human rights should become the driving force of twenty-first century politics.

The concept of "sovereignty" needs reconsideration. If nations are "sovereign," they can do what they please with their own citizens. If cultures are "sovereign," the values of the culture dictate the behavior of citizens. Both conceptions of "sovereignty" provide the basis for totalitarianism. Unless the people within a democratic community are the basis for sovereignty, nations and traditions (culture) have the rights and people must conform.

The nation-culture sovereignty system has meant that torture, aggressive military action, denial of free speech, mutilation of the genitals of girls through clitorectomy, and imposition of prayer and religious dress are all requirements enforced in some countries.

But a world law system opened a window in a different direction in 1998 through the creation of a criminal court that follows the authority of supranational principles developed under Nuremberg law, which placed humanity at a higher level than the state. "Murder" has been a legal definition tied to the laws of every country. So previously "Thou shall not kill" was a moral precept that said you could not kill anyone except under special circumstance such as self-defense. But it was not "murder" if you killed someone in another country under the orders of your state. This lack of a universal definition of "murder" permits war and the use of military power without holding the killers responsible.

The International Criminal Court, established in the Hague in 1998 has obtained international support for trying those who commit crimes against humanity, including extraditing heads of state. Slobodan Milosevic, Yugoslav President during the ethnic cleansing in Bosnia, was indicted by the Court in 2001 for war crimes, the first time a sitting leader has been charged with war crimes while the crimes are still going on. The Yugoslavian Kosovo war produced many war criminals and the courts began trying some by the end of 1999.

Suddenly new issues of law arise. If acknowledged tyrants such as Idi Amin or Haiti's "Baby Doc" Duvalier were subject to indictment for murder, what of people such as former British Prime Minister Margaret Thatcher (for the sinking of an Argentine cruiser) or President Clinton (for the bombing of a Sudanese factory)? Might they also qualify as murderers?

A universal definition for murder to protect every person's right to life would propel the human race to a new level of progress. People, wherever they live, are important, and to kill people except in necessary defense is to commit murder. Responsibility would take on new meaning. The only defensible form of war would be when it is clearly defensive. Generals would not be able to give orders to "take the hill and kill the enemy" without being subject to indictment for murder.

The rules of capitalism are driven by the profit motive and not by human rights. Human rights principles go beyond national constituency politics by which all people's basic needs are political entitlements. But the American government under the old structure is tied to the power of constituencies, not to human rights principles. Effective constituencies are usually those with the economic power to control public opinion and gain power and their priorities do not usually include human rights.

As world rule increasingly shifts to global corporations, people become cynical about government because they think that government is the problem. Obsolete government is indeed a major part of the problem, but the institution of government itself is the only viable tool we have to control the power of the corporate elite. **The alternative to the use of government to serve the public is to accelerate the concentration of power in wealth to individuals or powerful corporations. New democratic public power through restructured government is the only alternative to continued oligarchy.**

CENTRAL ISSUES FOR A NEW POLITICS

1. Currently, the human race has no rights upon which each person can depend. Some governments exploit children, torture, and kill with impunity. The most serious results of such actions are reported through organizations such as Amnesty International and the United Nations, but they are without power to enforce human rights.

2. There is no global system to sustain non-renewable resources. As a result, each country and the multinationals diminish the world supply of natural forests, plants, and animal species. The current world is liquidating all natural systems. Minerals such as petroleum are being burned up. Hard minerals are being irretrievably scattered. Water sources and watersheds are diminishing.

3. There is no global system for the designation of standards for a clean environment. Therefore, air, water, and land pollution in most parts of the world is on the increase.

4. There is no system of sovereignty larger than nations. Military power is therefore used between nations to serve the purposes of nations. As a result, wars continue.

5. Nations have power over each other in proportion to their economic and military power. The large dominate the small, forming more of a structural hierarchy rather than a democracy of nations.

6. The culture of technological and economic commercialization dominates nearly all other forms of culture.

7. The economic needs of people are not the first priority within world systems. Free trade and the priorities of rich nations and the richest people within rich nations maintain their wealth and power and have first priority.

8. The petroleum supply on which most production is based is running out. It is finite and heading toward exhaustion.

9. National economic systems have short-range goals based largely on exploiting cheap labor and using up basic finite resources, the capital of nature. Pollution and its costs and dangers are passed on to future generations. Monetary debt is added to pollution and resource depletion.

A TWENTY-FIRST CENTURY POLITICAL AGENDA REQUIRES:

1. Globally enforced human rights.

2. Sustained non-renewable resources such as topsoil, old growth forests, genes of species, etc., which will require world political enforcement.

3. Enforceable employment opportunities.

4. Standards from military power to enforceable world law; the use of police forces (not military forces) to prevent violence.

5. A global confederation of states and localities with representative power in a world system, replacing national dominance with global democracy.

6. Encouragement of cultural diversity consistent with respect for human rights.

7. Economic priorities in the world system, putting needs first and wants second.

8. Economic transition to an environmentally benign and sustainable energy base.

9. Rights of future generations to: (a) the use but not the depletion of non-renewables, (b) sustained natural systems, (c) a healthful environment, and (d) monetary costs paid by each current generation with no passing on of debt.

RECLAIMING THE MARKETPLACE THROUGH ECONOMIC DEMOCRACY

Democracy is needed not only for government but also for the economic system. Regulated market economics can thrive under democratic government but not under the control of corporate oligarchy.

The twentieth century was shark time. Capitalistic economics was sustained by the public belief in supply and demand and market forces, when in fact the very rich and the corporations, not the market, controlled most of the wealth and most of the politics on which special interest policy was formed. The common people's share of the economic pie in the United States improved during World War II as full employment was created, and up through the 1950s and 1960s the gap between the rich and the poor narrowed slightly. But from the 1980s on, under the Reagan administration, those at the top zoomed upward, the middle class stagnated, and those at the bottom dropped farther down.

SOME EFFECTS OF REVERSE ROBIN HOOD ECONOMICS

"At the richest time in the nation's history, housing that the poor can afford is at an all-time low, fueling an increase in homelessness," according to the 1999 U.S. Conference of Mayors. "With complaints about beggars and bag ladies and mumbling, stumbling vagrants growing as well, cities are fighting as never before to move homeless people out of public spaces (New York Times News Service, November12, 1999).

67

Robert Reich, who served as Secretary of Labor under the Clinton Administration, points out that "in 1980, the typical chief executive of a large American company took home about forty times the annual earning of a typical worker; in 1990, the ratio rose to about eighty-five times. Between 1990 and the end of the century . . .*the increase averaged 419 times the earning of a typical production worker* (Reich 2002, 74-75)."

We are in a class war where income from the poorest fifth of Americans has actually gone down (.9 percent since 1979. The after tax incomes of the middle fifth of Americans are up 10 percent since 1979, and after tax incomes of the richest Americans are up 157 percent. (*See Too Much,* Summer 2001, a newsletter from The Council on International and Public Affairs.)

"More than 35 million Americans—one out of every seven of our fellow citizens—are officially poor.... Nearly all of America's economic growth has benefited the wealthiest among us, and the tiny slice of the pie allotted to the poor has actually gotten smaller (Wellstone 1997, 15-16)."

The game of economics can be played in many different ways. An economy consists of the production and distribution of goods and services. This leaves open the questions of what is to be produced and how it is to be distributed. The dominant twentieth century reply has been that what is produced is the result of "demand," as if demand were a natural force, when in fact demand is stimulated and created by massive advertising.

But we must first distinguish between people's *wants* and people's *needs.* In much of the twentieth century, people's needs were ignored, and wants in the market place were based on indications of capacity to purchase. Those with money who *wanted* a big house or a yacht created demand. Those who *needed* food or shelter but lacked the capacity to purchase were ignored. There was no "demand" by the poor for low cost housing; for "demand" in a capitalist economy is based on money.

Production and distribution were driven by the rules of the game. *The twentieth century rules in the United States excluded any right of people to (1) a job, (2) a fair wage, (3) housing, (4) food, (5) quality education, (6) clothing.* In the 1930s, after a major depression threatened the political foundations of laissez-faire capitalism, some concessions were made, and what has since been called liberalism began to presume that government had some responsibility for the welfare of people. Before then, the poor were presumed to be charity cases to be taken care of mainly by churches and private humanitarian groups.

Throughout the twentieth century the obvious lesson, when you have competition between unequals, is that you can predict which groups will win and which will lose. The history of the United States consists of competition between unequals with only minor mitigation of effects. Those on the bottom are promised "equal opportunity" but the odds are against them unless the rules of the game are changed to alter the structure of power within the political system. Our "democracy" is a facade that keeps power where it is to continue control and dominance by the corporations and the wealthy. Minority political parties in the United States, unlike most European nations, are excluded from power by a winner take all political system. Changing to proportional representation by political parties would be a step toward greater democracy and at least would shift power and increase political debate.

The twentieth century was actually a "welfare" century, not for the majority of the people, however, but for corporations and the oligarchy. At the beginning of the twentieth century the country was largely owned and run by a few people—the Rockefellers, the Mellons, and the Carnegies. They created and owned the corporations that became the oil, the steel, and the railway companies. People as workers were part of the supply and demand process, bought on the market like commodities. High unemployment helped keep labor prices down and corporate profits up, and it was World War I that produced a break in the market system as government needed to create a form of state socialism with command control over the economy. Waging war required it (Zinn 1997b, 266).

The economic results were beneficial for the working people, even though the product—armament—was not a contribution to the needs of the people. The stimulating effects persisted after the war and the 1920s were a time of prosperity until the bubble of capitalist speculation burst in 1929. The collapsed house of cards produced unemployment and disillusionment, and the attempts of working people to organize into labor unions often resulted in beatings and even assassinations of labor leaders by mobsters hired by industry and usually supported by the local police.

Political pressures, however, led to the Wagner Labor Act, which made union organizing legal (Zinn 1997b, 291). Wages increased as collective bargaining began to empower the working class, and the Roosevelt administration increasingly used government power to regulate banks and provide jobs. Yet much of the Depression continued until WW II introduced another huge military intervention into the economy. The military economy saved capitalism. The spillover effects from the 1940s and pent-up demand for consumer goods that had been unfulfilled during the World War II and the Korean War economy kept the 1950s economy moving and then the Vietnam war expenditures in the 1960s stimulated the economy once again (Phillips 2002, 74-75).

But the Vietnam war was so unpopular that it was financed with debt to be paid later in the 1970s, which put the 1970s into another slump. When the OPEC nations that controlled much of the world's oil showed they could control oil prices and keep them high, the oil-dependent and vulnerable U.S. economy was hit even harder.

The 1980s, however, were a time of deregulation of business, laissez-faire capitalism, and high military spending under the Reagan administration. Concentration of wealth by the very rich and high national debt resulted at an unprecedented rate. The United States reversed its role as an international creditor to become a net debtor.

A new Republican political strategy was developed and was revealed by Senator Moynihan and David Stockman, Reagan's head of the Bureau of the Budget. It involved trying to *increase the national debt* so that when Democrats took over, the interest on the debt would be so high that it would be difficult to provide social programs. It was a strategy that served the Republican ideology very well, producing military stimulus during the 1980s and a tight restriction on social spending in the 1990s. But Republican President Bush was caught in the wake of this strategy, which had been set up with the presumption that a Democratic congress would take over when Reagan left office. A summary of the massive shift of government programs to the corporate private sector and the Pentagon was covered in *America: Who Stole the Dream?*, by Bartlett and Steele (*Philadelphia Inquirer*, October 20, 1991).

By the end of the century the U.S. became a nation tightening up spending in the public sector and shifting wealth to the private sector. It was the only developed nation without universal medical benefits and with comparatively large numbers of homeless people. By the end of the century unemployment figures were down to the mid-4 percent figure, but many jobs paid such low wages that it was increasingly common for people to hold two or more jobs just to pay their bills. Borrowing through banks and credit cards used future income as a way to support survival, resulting in high personal bankruptcy.

Schools became overcrowded and the railway transportation system became the worst of the developed nations. Relative poverty (high inequality) and absolute poverty (actual starvation) increased, and many cities decayed from lack of funds. Yet military spending, supported by both parties, continued full-speed ahead. The national military policy which was developed during the 1990s *required that the Pentagon have the capacity to carry on two full-scale wars at the same time* (*New York Times,* May 22, 1997). Such a policy provided a secure military-industrial complex budget while deflecting priorities away from social needs. President Eisenhower warned of a runaway Pentagon military-industrial complex in the 1950s. But members of Congress perpetuated this system by accepting re-election campaign funds from corporations vying for military weapons contracts and by buying votes from local citizens for keeping military bases in local communities even when unneeded by the military. This permanent war economy lives on.

TWENTY-FIRST CENTURY ECONOMICS

If economics is to serve human needs and also sustain ecological systems, it must be transformed from the twentieth century model. In an ethical society basic needs to sustain people come before wants. Ecological sustainability becomes a higher priority than corporate profit, and impact costs to society are paid by those who produce the costs.

We have not required the producer to pay for the full costs of production, so this is part of the massive subsidy process that built deception into twentieth century indicators. If real costs were deducted the total GNP for the last 100 years would slope **down** rather than **up**. Costs of water and fishery decline and the loss of forests and top-soil have been enormous but have not been included in the continuing quantitative calculations of the old economics.

The enormity of this might be illustrated by the subsidy involved in selling old growth trees from our public national forests. Trees are sold at *current market value,* never at *replacement value.* Replacement would mean that the tree would be valued at the cost to replant it and then wait, say 200 years, for a typical old growth tree to regrow. This is an easy business figure to calculate: assume that each tree costs $1 to replant and that this money is borrowed at 8% with the interest compounded for 200 years, waiting for the delayed return. *The tree would cost over 4.8 million dollars.* (Many old growth trees are 300 or 400 years old and would have to be valued in the *billions,* Try running these figures for a redwood tree over a thousand years old. They exceed the GNP of the **world** for one tree.)

Trees of over 100 years probably could not be cut if the replacement costs were charged for each tree sold. Also, if these costs were calculated as deductible costs in the total GNP cost-benefit calculations, the twentieth century would show a steep decline and therefore retrogression instead of "progress." National policy is needed to require that any trees sold on public land must at least receive real replacement cost in the business terms listed above. Old growth logging would cease unless it continued to be subsidized.*

There are two excellent sources for the kinds of economic indicators that are needed, and the new economics should be focused on a shift in indicators. Daly and Cobb have a detailed Index of Sustainable Economic Welfare (1989, 401-455). When the full range of external costs are deducted from the short-range economic benefits, the real progress indicators turn out to be the opposite from the usual GNP and Per Capita Income graphs. It gives one the feeling that we live in Alice's Wonderland.

Hazel Henderson's *Paradigms in Progress* has an entire chapter on "The Indicators Crisis (1995, 147-192)" which also reveals how the politics of economics adjusts indicators to serve particular groups while exploiting others. No serious proposals for "development" should be undertaken without shifting to real cost/benefit calculations that include *human and environmental costs* (often not convertible into monetary terms) and also taking account of short and long-range effects.

Our Common Future (World Commission on Environment and Development, 1987) sometimes called the Brundtland Report, was a major attempt of the United Nations to balance the needs of poor countries with planetary ecological sustainability. It defined "sustainable development" as that which "meets the needs of the present without compromising the ability of future generations to meet their own needs (43)."

WorldWatch's 1987 publication of *State of the World*, released the same year the Brundtland book was published, provided reliable information on the world environment and at the same time proposed policies that would revise world economics. The central contribution was to show that poverty cannot be tolerated morally or pragmatically if economies are to convert to sustainability. But the political contributors to the Brundtland study were the rich nations that were not about to let go of their unequal advantages and their control of global institutions. Ecological sustainability would require that over consumption in the northern rich nations be reduced, but that would conflict with the driving growth principle of capitalist economics. So the Brundtland Report became merely an enlightened wish list resisted by the economic structure of global capitalism. Any socialist system that also

---

* This proposal is not intended to suggest using economic costs to determine management policy for natural systems.

embraced growth economics would be in the same unsustainable trap. The Soviet Union was not capitalist, but it was also ecologically unsustainable.

In 1990, a companion report to the Brundtland book, called *Challenge to the South*, shifted the perspective to the Third World. The wasteful mass consumption of the Western nations was recognized as an impossible model, and the policies of the International Monetary Fund and the World Bank were rejected as merely top down, capitalist models that have focused on GNP rather than on human needs and the common quality of life. This Third World perspective had been conveniently ignored in The Brundtland Report.

It is now well known that **poverty is the most compelling force for overpopulation** in the same way that corporate capitalism is the most compelling force for concentration of wealth and therefore poverty. This insight is seldom emphasized in the corporate "free press," but the concept is central to thoughtful studies of the problems of the Third World.

An overlooked feature of western capitalism is the role of the stock market, which appears to be a wonderful, open, participatory economic institution— a kind of magic money machine. But even a brief inspection of the actual function of stock markets gives a picture of what really happens.

> "Stocks have reached what looks like a permanently high plateau."
>
> —Irving Fisher, Yale Economist, October 17 1929

Is The Stock Market A Grand Hoax?

When Gershwin wrote the song, "I got plenty of nothing," was he referring to stocks? Probably not. Yet analyzing a stock reveals that people actually own nearly nothing except the hope that someone will come along and will want to pay more for their stock than **they** paid. Anyone who pays more will do so on the assumption that someone else will pay more than they paid—and on and on, known as the Greater Fool Theory.

Real property provides profits through rent or business production and provides a claim on the profit as a result of ownership, but a share of stock in a corporation provides no claim on any of the profits. Let us assume that you "own" such a share. At the behest of the board of directors, you may be offered a dividend that usually represents a lower return than the interest on a safe investment in a local bank savings account. In reality, a stock certificate offers no substantive claim for anything. There is a substantive claim in a bond, for that is a loan with a stated level of interest. People can buy your bond and expect that rate of return. People who buy your stock can only expect the small dividend (which can be eliminated). The stock is held on the assumption that, if the company prospers, people will pay more for the stock. But why should they? Your stock is almost as disconnected from the corporations as your used Ford is disconnected from the Ford Motor Company.

But you might say you have "ownership" because you can vote at the annual stockholders' meeting. An ordinary investor will soon find that for typical corporations this is entirely meaningless, as the agenda of the meetings and the proxy questions are carefully controlled by the corporate board and the CEO, and are often contrived to be unintelligible to anyone without a law degree. Stock "owned" via mutual funds even eliminates any direct proxy claim, and pension plans using 401K disconnect control even further.

You can, after all, make money on a chain letter too, if you can keep it going and bail out before others do. The well-known Ponzi game and the chain letter have nothing substantive to offer except the hope that a great many people will fall for it before it collapses. When people put their money into stock already circulating they depend on the psychological effects on the public of reports of growth for the company. Large amounts of capital are circulated that are doing nothing—they are not productive and they serve no real economic or social need. Jobs are created in the "securities" business as people buy and sell stock and try to stimulate a bigger speculative bubble. The more people who have stock, the more optimism about growth must be created to keep the house of cards from collapsing. CEOs want their stock to stay high when they bail out, so they commonly release distorted figures to encourage public buying of their stock. Ultimately, the value of the stock depends on a shared illusion, that something with the label of a corporation but disconnected from the corporation has value. It is really a sham.

When illusory wealth is created that has not produced anything substantive, it becomes a zero-sum game, providing nothing except a transfer of "wealth" from one person to another. Stocks are only useful to the economy initially, at the time they are issued by a corporation in the initial public offering. The corporation uses the funds for whatever it produces. Most stocks are traded after they are issued in secondary markets and provide wealth to those who buy low and sell high, but to do this others must buy high and sell low. No real national wealth is created, it is only transferred between people. The net result is to provide **no** wealth to the society, **no** aggregate wealth whatsoever. The axiom that there is no such thing as a free lunch still applies to economics. The stock market is largely a zero sum game. The main wealth is in the "friction" of charges made by brokers during transactions.

But why would people play this game? John Cassidy details the stock market of the 1990s in *Dot Con. The Greatest Story Ever Sold.* "To be willing to take a risk, people needed to see others doing the same thing—and see them making money doing this." Based on this psychology "a rising stock market turns into a speculative bubble (2002, 4)." Within this mob psychology people can lose all connection to reality. "The peak of a speculative mania is a sight to behold. In the scramble to cash in before it is too late, all prior reasoning, sentiment, and knowledge count for naught. No one is satisfied with even exorbitant gains, but everyone thirsts for more, and all this is founded upon a machine of paper credit supported only by imagination (191)."

John Kenneth Galbraith referred to the same psychology in the September 1929 speculative bubble, saying with his usual irony that if there must be madness, something may be said for having it on a heroic scale.

In the 1990s a dream world of a "new economy" was becoming fashionable. Many people believed that companies that had nothing to sell but a faith based plan based on an "information" economy created by computers, was the best place to "invest." Billions went to Silicon Valley internet companies that had nothing to sell except hope. Their initial public offerings were bought up at inflated prices and resold on the stock market at even higher prices. The standard of "price/earnings ratios" disappeared because there were no earnings in most dot coms. People followed others into this wonderful world of rising dot com stock prices. Reality inevitably superseded faith and illusion, and the bubble broke, leaving millions with losses.

People put real money into stocks and therefore shifted their wealth into financial speculation in which money moves around doing nothing useful but rather deprives society of the real development that should have occurred—getting rid of slums and decay in inner cities, replanting forests, building schools, cleaning up toxic dumps, etc. Instead they get only a symbolic piece of paper with the name of a corporation. This diversion of public capital from socially useful purposes is an indication of why our social legacy is so meager. The dot com bubble at the end of the 1990s produced a social shock, but not enough to examine the assumptions on which the entire stock system is based.

The social effects of this game, which is really a form of gambling in the name of "investment," had tragic effects in the 1930s. Many people with stocks were left in a state of starvation when the stock market crashed, while those who had taken out their money often bought mansions and yachts. In 1998, much of Asia had a crisis depression because the economy was tied to speculation not only in property but in money chasing after money and stocks. In the same year, the Long-Term Capital Management Hedge fund in New York produced such huge losses by basing their business hedging on speculating on speculative capital that the U.S. Federal Reserve provided $3.6 billion in public money to subsidize the survival of the company. It was so integrally tied to banks and wealthy individuals that the secretary of the Federal Reserve Board considered it to be "too big to fail." Little businesses were permitted to fail without help, of course. They get the "free market" while big business gets corporate welfare.

If excessive money is printed and distributed by government, dollars lose value in inflation. When stocks are treated as wealth they also create inflation by adding to the total money supply. But when stocks themselves inflate it is claimed to be "wealth" creation. Stocks are therefore speculative games that create a bubble that can burst at any time. **In 1987, sudden stock deflation produced investor loss of one trillion dollars in one day. This would have been enough, as David Korten points out, to feed the entire world for two years** (1998, 53-55).

In one week in April 2000 the loss exceeded two trillion dollars as the stock market produced a highly predictable crash. But most stockholders stayed in, buoyed by the constantly rising values and ignoring the realities of stocks—that they are not true wealth but only paper wealth in which myths and fantasies have been created, and that something cannot be created out of nothing.

The productive capacities of the companies from which the stock was issued did not change. The market speculation had created the illusion of wealth and played on the hopes of people. While giving them a feeling of security in fact the stock game makes their future unnecessarily precarious.

Is the stock market necessary? New stock issues provided only 4 percent of the capital of U.S. corporations, according to the 1993 Federal Reserve figures, which indicate that U.S. non-financial firms raised 82 percent of their financing internally, 12 percent from borrowing.

David Korten points out that up to 1994 "corporations paid out more to buy back their own shares than they received from new stock issues. In early 1998, what is loosely called *investment capital* was flowing from corporations to the stock market at an annual rate of 110 billion (1998, 54)."

End of the century economic crashes occurred in Asia where financial markets including banks were unregulated (except China, which isolates its financial system). In the twenty-first century global financial markets will need to be regulated while production of goods might do with less regulation. Regulation of stocks is particularly needed since they are the least stable form of pseudo-investment and can destroy a nation's economy and the lives of people who have relied on stocks for security. Pension plans and other sources of security for people (such as Social Security) should never be tied to stocks.

The Enron crash illustrated this lesson, even as the Bush administration touted a plan to have people shift some of the secure social security plan into the insecure stock market.

TURNING THE ECONOMIC SYSTEM INTO A LEARNING SYSTEM

In the mid-1980s I was in Yugoslavia and remember an illustration of how economics can be tied to democracy, citizenship, and learning. The clerk at the desk of a hotel was getting ready for one of their meetings through which employees of the particular group of hotels in which she worked would make important decisions. They, the employees, would evaluate the performance of the managers they had hired and decide on their salaries. They would also decide on what portion of the profits should be put back into improvements of the hotel. Failure to hire good managers and pay them enough, and failure to put the profits back into hotel improvements, could affect the competitive position of the hotel and the profits to the employees.

This hotel was one of the best I have been in from every standpoint. Later I stayed in another Yugoslavian hotel that was very poorly run. The employee-controllers in this latter hotel surely experienced the results of this poorly-run hotel as business slackened and, as in any business, they could learn that bad decisions are costly or even fatal. Their wages were tied to the collective decisions of their particular cluster of hotels.

The democratization of the hotels meant that there was a direct interest in the success of the hotel by *everyone working there*. They were the *owners*. They had to calculate investment advantages. These employees didn't need an MBA. They were involved in the real education of economic decision making and had a much more direct interest in the industry they were part of than do typical American employees. This model put the workers into an ownership-managership position, differing from the American model of pseudo public "ownership" through stock, but without any real control. (Except in hostile takeovers by other corporations.)

Economics in the twentieth century divides the working public into those who are constantly learning (the managers) and those who are performing often boring and repetitious jobs (the workers). Those who have the learning jobs get a double payoff—an interesting job and higher pay. Those with the more dehumanizing jobs get the double penalty—an uninteresting job and lower pay. When ethical principles are incorporated into economics, new purposes are required and *human development* becomes a major objective. A democracy is crippled by having two separate classes of people—one group "dumbed down" and another stimulated upward.

A really new economics is needed in the twenty-first century that uses human abilities to improve business world-wide while creating a human development-learning environment for everyone involved in the economy. Short of basic restructuring, there are ways to modify capitalism incrementally such as Germany's practice of requiring union members on corporate boards and American businesses that are already based on profit sharing such as Hewlett-Packard and Johnson's Wax.

But the big structural change would need to move from an essentially autocratic, top-down economic system to one incorporating principles of democracy and human rights. In twentieth century America the term democracy was usually applied only to political democracy, but not to *economic democracy*. Some of the most successful American industries have incorporated employee participation, still this has not progressed to the point where employees have the power to decide on the salaries of the top managers or the power to participate in setting basic goals for the industry.

American industries are still run mainly by rich white CEO males and boards of directors who use the old system of interlocking directorates to concentrate power and wealth and use their power to serve their own interests. If the economic system is to serve the public interest and extend democracy, it should empower those who contribute their labor to the industry so that all workers have reason to believe they are "insiders" and are an integral part of the organization. They are now too often just objects to be bought and sold by corporations that will willingly abandon communities and their employees if more money can be made elsewhere, as seen through successions of plant closings and relocations. The other "controllers" should be the public that is affected by the corporation. Any movement in this direction shifts toward economic democracy.

STRUCTURAL ALTERNATIVES FOR INDUSTRY

There are four structural models of industry. One is the old autocratic model with virtually no employee power. A second allows unions to create countervailing power through negotiation and the threat of strikes. A third is employee ownership and operation. And a fourth is government regulated, by which control can be either through a dictatorial government or by support of workers' rights through a democratic government.

From the 1980s on, the American worker actually lost power and worker rights. The Reagan administration was anti-union, and global corporations provided worldwide examples of dominance over labor and moved closer to the old autocratic model in which corporations can use the threat of job loss to keep wages down since they can move to another area of the world where labor is very cheap. This became known as job blackmail, "and was rationalized by the need for competitive downsizing (Boyer 1984, 83-84)."

The most rapidly expanding retail business, Wal-Mart, has kept unions out and discharged people who expressed pro-union views. This has worked well for the bottom line by keeping labor costs low. It has also depressed the quality of life of the employees. An inside look at this system is detailed by Ehrenreich in *Nickel and Dimed*, (2001) who worked at Wal-Mart in order to understand how it dealt with employees. (See also the article "Wal-Mart Values" by Featherstone (2002, 11-13).)

The use of Reaganomics for keeping inflation low during the 1990s was admitted by Alan Greenspan, Chairman of the Federal Reserve Board. He pointed out at various times in hearings in the years 1999 to 2002 that the good news was that inflation was being held down by the unwillingness of labor to press for higher wages because of the *fear of job loss. The insecurity of workers was needed to provide inflation control benefits to the capitalist economy. Corporate profit was the overriding value.* As Chomsky points out, "The Federal Reserve has been basically anti-inflation. . . They want unemployment to go up, basically. So unemployment goes up, the labor costs go down. There's less pressure for wage increases (Chomsky 1996, 103)." (See also Cockburn 1997.)

Foreign governments have cooperated in using direct action to put down unions. David Korten points out that in 1987 "in the midst of a bitter two-month strike in Mexico, Ford Motor Company tore up its union contract, fired 3,400 workers, and cut wages by 45 percent. When the workers rallied around dissident labor leaders, gunmen hired by the official government-dominated union shot workers at random in the factory." (1995, 129) Top-down, autocratic corporations working hand in hand with governments become essentially fascist when state violence is used to control the work force.

But it would be a mistake to assume that the United States has been simply embarking on a replication of nineteenth century state imperialism. As the historian William Appleman Williams points out, the idea of an economic "open door" became the new dominant theme of American foreign policy in the twentieth century. "Businessmen, intellectuals, and politicians who opposed traditional colonialism advocated instead a policy of an open door through which America's preponderant economic strength would enter and dominate all underdeveloped areas of the world (Zinn 1997b, 294)." This strategy has in more recent times become known as "free trade" and has been developed through treaties such as NAFTA the North American Trade Agreements), GATT (General Agreement on Tariffs and Trade), and MAI (the Multilateral Agreement on Investment.)

A humane economy of the twenty-first century would move beyond fear and insecurity as the basis for participation in the work force and would have new guarantees of economic human rights. The right to employment in a socially useful job at a living wage can become a major new right in the future, but it will come about in the United States only by demand and the development of political power—not as a gift from industry. Victories in the campaign for a better world, whether it be for workers' rights or women's right to vote, have usually come about through lengthy, dangerous struggles and often loss of life. Those with power and property make concessions only when they have no choice, sometimes in the face of revolution. Yet non-violent democratic power is the most humane method, requiring support from the larger public. Education must play the crucial role of counteracting the misinformation and distortion that is necessary for those wishing to retain political and economic dominance. Widespread education is needed to provide the understanding necessary for democratic based social change to occur without violence (Boyer 1984, 27). Article 23 of the Universal Declaration of Human Rights "recognizes the right of everyone to work, to free choice of employment, to just and favorable conditions of work, to protection against unemployment and to equal pay for equal work (Laqueur and Rubin 1989, 324-325)."

THE EDUCATIONAL EFFECT OF THE ECONOMIC SYSTEM

Most of the "education" people receive in the modern world comes from the many hours they spend working for a living. Workers' environments are usually monotonous and repetitious, while the experience of business managers is usually more challenging and stimulating. So "education" in industrial societies is tied to social class, which tends to create two different kinds of people.

Adam Smith, often considered the "Father of Capitalist Theory," was able to see how humbling routines would grind down rather than free the worker. He said that the laborer:

> whose whole life is spent in performing a few simple operations, of which the effects are perhaps always the same, or very nearly the same, has no occasion to exert his understanding or to exercise his invention in finding out expedients for removing difficulties which never occur. He naturally loses, therefore, the habit of such exertion, and generally becomes as stupid and ignorant as it is possible for a human creature to become (Smith 1937).

We now have considerable evidence from social psychology that people are largely changed by what they are required do (Aronson 1972, 27-35). This means that "unless government takes some pains to prevent it," as Smith advocated, the economy will be "productive" only at the cost of human development. People should not serve the economy; the economy should serve the people, or else a high GNP would be gained at the cost of the people it is presumed to serve, whereas a high GNP is now interpreted as the proof of an improved standard of living.

Since economies are inventions, they can also be reinvented. Some reinvention has occurred since the time of Adam Smith, but most of the people of the world—even in this period of history—are working under conditions that are still much as Smith describes. A friend of mine in Thailand interviewed a number of young boys for jobs and said he was shocked that they were all so puny, so he tried to identify the problem. They had all spent working hours stooped in front of a computer, contributing to the third world "information revolution"—and at the same time apparently contributing to their physical detriment.

People live in class enclaves in the United States. Robert Reich says the rich and the middle class live in parallel universes, and the poor are almost invisible. These tend to become separate worlds, socio-economic enclaves that undermine democracy and integration. The pattern is similar world-wide in capitalistic countries, but is more extreme in the United States.

Economic insecurity is on the increase, especially since the Enron-Anderson collapse and the stock market decline. And the "race to the bottom" to compete with the lowest wages world wide by multinational corporations has reduced job security in the lives of millions of people as CEOs have improved the profits of their corporation by discharging employees, moving to other parts of the world, and withholding these plans from the people who work there.

This top fifth separates itself through private health clubs, golf clubs, and gated communities and secure apartment buildings. The bottom four-fifths are in jobs which are tedious and repetitive. And the children of the top group are generally separated, either through private schools or, more often, through the suburban clusters where few blue-collar workers reside. The separation between the rich and the poor worldwide is much the same, with a controlling elite even in poor countries who live much like Robert Reich's "symbolic analysts" in the United States. And with "free trade" and computer-directed flow of funds, the world model is directed and designed mainly by multinational corporations that care neither about the people nor the planet.

Not only are the people who manage and control the symbolic processes the controllers of most of the wealth and income, but they too are creatures of the corporate system with little real freedom. They are moved at the behest of the corporation and must carry out policies that are often destructive to the workers and the environment.

Charlie Chaplin's classic movie "Modern Times" showed workers in factories becoming literal cogs in the industrial wheels. Instead of selling one's soul to the company store it is now the corporation that owns one's soul. The absurd semi-totalitarian national obsession with the "drug war" even puts many people in the humiliating position of having to urinate in a bottle to confirm their qualifications as employees.

We need a fundamental shift in how we evaluate an economic system. Our evaluation should include the educational effect it has on people. Quality-of-life indicators have begun to take some account of the environmental consequences of economics. We also need to evaluate "progress" through social indicators and the educational effects that different economic environments have on people.

The obsession with quantifiable efficiency is accelerating so that competitiveness continues to be based on monetary indicators of corporate profit as they appear in a global marketplace. However, an economy that is not maximally efficient and competitive may have a *high* score on environmental quality of life and may also provide interesting educational jobs and high levels of social interaction. It may reach a *higher* level of *real progress* than a higher GNP economy. People in Northern European countries often accept lower pay than in American corporations for the shorter work week and greater job security. They think, with their medical and employment benefits, that they have a higher level of "progress" than Americans have achieved.

We can have a better future if we realign the meaning of costs and benefits by using economic indicators that include more social and educational effects. **In the meantime, the economic system controls the public—the public does not control the economic system.** This unnecessary condition is at the core of a global pathology. The solution is to make economic activity an instrument of human development. This would require schools to change their approach to economic education, the nation to change the standards for "progress," and the daily paper to change the economic indicators which now ignore the impact on the people working within the economy.

CONSERVATIVE REPUBLICANS AND CONSERVATIVE DEMOCRATS

The two major political parties in the United States are largely instruments for keeping an oligarchy of the rich and powerful intact and supporting the ubiquitous propaganda required to obscure this fact. If the "bottom" four-fifths of the population understood what was happening, they would not likely continue to cooperate in supporting rules that concentrate economic power in a power elite.

The American public does not really provide intentional support for the rules that support the oligarchy. The rules and institutions are reinforced primarily by a public that has largely lost hope for a better government and sees no other alternatives. Elections in the United States attract only a minority of the electorate, and the common comment reflecting political apathy is that both political parties are essentially the same, so why vote?

This is a half-truth. Democrats use government to provide more public services than Republicans, but both parties are dedicated to keeping the power of the economic system under the control of corporate capitalism, which means the primary power is in the hands of large, increasingly global corporations. This is oligarchy—government by the rich and the economically powerful.

With a look at how the economic pie is divided, let us see what the results have been.

1. The total net worth of the top 1 percent of the population is equal to the total net worth of the bottom 90 percent of the population, and the rich are getting even richer. The wealth of the top 20 percent has increased while the

wealth of the bottom 80 percent has decreased. Under "Reaganomics" *from 1980 to 1987, the average net worth of the 400 wealthiest Americans tripled!* The Congressional Budget Office indicates that *the lowest fifth has declined in the last 20 years while the middle has stagnated.*

2. The two political parties have supported legislation that transfers public funds in various ways. When "welfare" is mentioned, it is usually assumed that welfare goes to the poor. The fact is, however, welfare to the rich is about three and a half times as large as the welfare to the poor, much of it being *corporate welfare.* Even the mainstream *Time* magazine ran a series on corporate welfare in early 1998. Pointing out that "during one of the most robust economic periods in our nation's history, the Federal Government shelled out $125 billion in corporate welfare, equivalent to all the income tax paid by 60 million individuals and families (Bartlett and Steele 1998, 36-37).

3. In 1950, corporations paid 26.5 percent of the federal government's general revenues. Now they pay about 10.2 percent (Phillips 2002, 149). Payroll taxes in 1950 were 6.9 percent, now they are over 31 percent. If businesses paid taxes at the same rate as 40 years ago, the federal deficit would soon disappear. The more "conservative" the political party, the more the argument is for lowering taxes on corporations and on individuals with high incomes. Lowering the tax rate for capital gains down to 20 percent has affected mainly the rich, and this has been at the center of conservative platforms for years.

4. Conglomerates are forming at an accelerating rate. Small corporations are bought up and become part of a giant corporation that increases its economic power and its influence over the political system. Even the press, which presumably is essential for democracy under the first Amendment of the Constitution, is now controlled by fewer and fewer corporations and wealthy individuals, and is used to serve the politics of its owners. Television is a key part of this oligarchy, shaping the ideas and messages conveyed to the public. It too is under more and more centralized control of a few giant corporations. For instance, General Electric, a leading producer of military weapons and nuclear power plants, owns NBC. What chance is there that programs on the dangers of nuclear power plants or on alternatives to the war system will show up on NBC? General Electric is involved in a basic conflict of interest with its control of a communication media (Grossman 2001, 218).

This form of corporate censorship is endemic in American media, but one might expect that public television would provide the needed alternative. Though funds for public television are controlled by Congress, a similar form of censorship exists. In the early 1970s an excellent PBS film on American imperialism called "Who Invited Us?" was shown. Congress chastised PBS and threatened budget retaliation. In the 1980s a friend of mine got PBS to agree to show a film he had made on the dangers of accidental nuclear war. The Pentagon heard about it and put pressure on PBS. The film was never shown. As PBS accepts more and more advertising from corporate sponsors, it is highly unlikely to broadcast any program that offers a fundamental critique of capitalism.

THE NOOSE TIGHTENS

As people lose more and more control over the economic system and mass media, the tendency has been either to become cynical or to shift to other areas such as actions toward increasing neighborhood power and gaining information through the use of new technology—mainly the computer. Computer communication between individuals and groups is rapidly expanding in the United States. It was an important factor in the 1997 public uprising in Belgrade, where control of mass media had fallen under the control of the oligarchy.

The two major American political parties claim that emphasis on computers and information technology will provide greater public access to wealth. But corporations make use of this technology to enhance their economic dominance, and concentration of power in the large corporation is not likely to be offset merely by increasing public access to information technology. The deceptive notion that "technology will save us" serves to depoliticize the public, and unless there is public education about how political power is used to produce our concentration of wealth and power, the corporate "black hole" will continue to suck in wealth and increase its power.

BEYOND THE COLD WAR

The end of the cold war with the Soviet Union put the United States in the command position in international politics. Pentagon military power and a network of corporations worldwide suggests that the twenty-first century will be the American Century. But the world economic system is very unstable and very unjust. Economic disruption such as a stock market crash, terrorism, and revolution by groups oppressed by First World dominance is likely and could cause serious dislocations. And, as the United States continues to be the leading manufacturer and distributor of military weapons, the world will become increasingly more dangerous, not safer.

The European nations are coming together as a federation—which can lessen American dominance—and public movements against the placement of U.S.

nuclear weapons in Europe have been growing. New political forces that see beyond the old order and work in more cooperative ways could come together to confront global problems such as atmosphere warming and weather disruption to help change world economic and financial rules.

SOME CHANGES ARE ENCOURAGING

Though serious root problems remain, the twentieth century has also seen encouraging changes. We should make sure that what has been gained is not lost. Many people who previously suffered from exploitation have improved their lives. My grandmother did not have the right to vote when she came to the United States, even after she had achieved citizenship. Women's right to vote was a great achievement of the early twentieth century, won after a long struggle. Because of this sacrifice we now have a heritage of greater gender equality. Women's access to equal treatment has increased in all areas, including sports. When I was in college the men played basketball for the audience while the sexily-dressed girls provided "pompom" dancing at half time. Now the girls are on the court, demonstrating athletic skills that girls in the past were presumed to lack because they were female.

Racism was widespread 50 years ago. When I was in graduate school in the 1950s a black graduate student in my class needed to have a string of friends in different states in order to travel cross country. Many hotels, motels, restaurants, and service stations refused service to blacks. After years of boycotts, sit-ins, marches, threats, beatings, and deaths, the Civil Rights Act of 1964 ended most overt institutionalized racism.

Wildlife is being viewed differently in recent years. Here in the west people who fish often release the fish unharmed, and many public streams require "catch and release." Hunting has declined as a "sport," and bison and wolves have been reintroduced to establish balances that occurred under conditions of ecological stability. Dams are starting to be removed because the negative effects on the ecology of rivers has often meant the loss of fish. The idea of "stewardship" is making headway with the public. (The George W. Bush administration has tried to reverse this progress.)

Recycling has become a public habit where it is coordinated with community planning. Vegetarian restaurants are growing in number, and vegetarian food is increasingly available in ordinary restaurants as well as in grocery stores. People now hesitate to buy and wear coats made of wild animal pelts. Young people are less and less inclined to want to kill wild animals in order to show their "manhood." The next stage is to learn to "shoot" with cameras, bringing back pictures of the animal while it continues to live. Young hikers are learning to "take only pictures and leave only footprints." They even collect trash that others have left.

Non-smoking public areas are common and increasingly required by law. The United States has taken such a lead on no-smoking areas that international flights have increasingly developed no-smoking rules. Recognition of the public's right to clean air is generating resistance to pollution caused by factories, and people are more frequently speaking out against all forms of pollution, pitting public groups against private polluters.

"Wigwam" burners in lumber mills have been phased out. Until the 1970s vast amounts of wood trimmings were burned, and the "wigwam" burners spewed smoke pollution in a haze over the western states. But no more. Instead, the old "wigwam" is a steel monument, a kind of historic sculpture that is now seen in rural towns.

The meaning of "property rights" is being contested, yet many people still want the absolute right to do anything they wish with land they own. When there was plenty of land and few people, that made some sense. But now it requires careful public planning to control land use so that the rural areas do not become merely extensions of urban sprawl. This means "limited ownership rights." For example, people may farm in rural areas but may *not* subdivide farmland for residential development. Those who say they "own" the land are expressing a view of "absolute" ownership, often suggesting that total land ownership is an American right. But land ownership has never been absolute. **This distinction between use rights and absolute control rights is increasing.**

It can be instructive to take a look at some models other than American Capitalism, which is the most unregulated economy in the advanced industrial nations. Norway, Sweden, and Finland have created a "Scandinavian model" which consists of welfare capitalism that keeps the essential structure of capitalism intact but provides public support for most social needs. The level of taxes is high but government services are generous. Distribution of income and wealth is much more equal than in the United States. Measurements of quality of life usually give these countries the top score.

Local cooperatives such as farmers, savings and loan organizations, electric distribution systems and food cooperatives have created small scale connections between democracy and economics in many parts of the world. But the only one that became virtually a nation unto itself is the Mondragon experiment in northern Spain.

A complex of companies in the Basque region has over 30,000 workers and six billion dollars in annual sales—complete with their own bank, a university, and a productive economy that engages in international trade. Workers and customers are the owners and they have control over the co-ops and the business policies. One policy is that the highest paid members should not have more than six times the pay of the lowest. This ratio is similar to that in Finland, whereas the United States has no stipulated distribution policy. This economy, based mainly on cooperation rather than competition, has stimulated movement toward democratic and egalitarian economics. And it can certainly provide a model for the development of similar movements in other parts of the world. Cuban socialism has taken its own road away from American capitalism. It is a model that has been neglected in most schools but deserves attention.

Some Lessons: American Capitalism and Cuban Socialism

"Let me say directly to Fidel Castro: You're finished"

—Ronald Reagan, May 17, 1990

The United States represents a model of advanced capitalism, while Cuba is probably a good example of (a particular) kind of socialism. By the end of the twentieth century, the U.S. model dominated the world. Yet the United States had shown such fear of the attractiveness of the Cuban model to other countries that it tried invasion, assassination attempts on Castro, an embargo, and then a blockade in an (unsuccessful) attempt to destroy Cuban socialism.

People need to understand the difference between these two political-economic systems to help identify some alternatives for the twenty-first century. The core differences are: (1) in the U.S., the economy is owned privately under a market system, while in Cuba, the economy is controlled by the government; (2) the U.S. system focuses on maximizing the gross national product while the Cuban system focuses on human development; (3) the U.S. system focuses on the growth of the national product to respond to the wants of people as they make purchases through the market. This is a "wants first" system. The Cuban system, on the other hand, focuses on people's basic needs, such as food, housing, medical care, and education. This is a "needs first" system. While the U.S. is stronger on speech and political rights, Cuba is strongest on economic rights.

The following brief comparison illustrates contrasts between the U.S. and Cuba:

	CUBA	UNITED STATES
Gambling legal	No	Yes
A drug problem	No	Yes
Personal taxes	No	Yes
Right to housing	Yes	No
Free education grades 1-12	Yes	Yes
Free medical care	Yes	No (except for elderly)
Low infant mortality	Yes	Yes
Birth control	Yes	Yes
Food guarantee	Yes	No
Multiparty system	No	Yes (for capitalist parties)
Democratic voting	Yes	Yes
Uncontrolled press	No	Yes
Economic equality	Yes	No
Money in elections	No	Yes
Forty-hour week	Yes	Yes—often more

On one of my trips to Cuba an American philosophy professor was on the bus with me, and I asked him if he had been here before. He said he comes every couple of years because it raised his "spirits." He thought the *ethical* values in Cuban society were superior to those in the United States. He thought the focus on cooperation and community was a higher value than individualism and competition.

When the United States controlled Cuba's industry and politics before the 1959 revolution, Cuba was a resort for the rich. It was controlled by a dictator (Batista) who worked with the Mafia which controlled gambling and prostitution. Industries such as the United Fruit Co. enjoyed the cheap labor that suited the interests of the wealthy.

Castro tried to work cooperatively with the United States after his successful revolution but was turned down by the Eisenhower administration. Alan Toffler has written that he "can recall Castro's triumphant visit to Washington and his speech at the National Press Club. I still wonder what shape Cuba might have today if the decision-makers in Washington had offered him economic support rather than unremitting hostility (1983, 216)."

American refineries in Cuba refused to process petroleum, so Castro nationalized them and converted them from private to government ownership and control. President Eisenhower saw Castro as a threat to American corporations and encouraged his assassination through the CIA. He set in motion an invasion at the Bay of Pigs which the Cuban expatriates carried out under President Kennedy, but which failed. Kennedy continued the assassination attempts and established an embargo to cripple the Cuban economy, hoping that Castro and the new government would be overthrown by its own people. It was a strategy similar to that used in the westward expansion of the U.S., where buffalo were killed in large numbers to starve the Indians.

With the survival of Cuba threatened, Castro asked the Soviet Union for assistance. It was granted, and under this cooperative arrangement Cuba became one of the most progressive of the Third World countries. When the Soviet Union collapsed in the 1980s the loss of Soviet aid greatly impacted the Cuban economy. In 1996 The United States instituted the Helms/Burton Act to punish other countries and corporations who traded with Cuba.

In spite of this de-facto state of war, Cuba has progressed. People are far healthier than in Puerto Rico, the American Caribbean showcase country. Susan Eckstein points out "that infant survival rates, like life expectancy rates, came to compare quite favorably with those of the more industrial countries. In 1990 the children's death rate in Havana was about half that of Washington D.C. (Eckstein 1993, 136-138)." The Cuban people's basic needs are satisfied by a national planning system and a highly developed local democracy.

One of the most compelling reasons for Americans to learn about Cuba is to discover the extent to which the American press has deceived the public, often with the help of the U.S. State Department. I found that American reporters in Cuba could get their material published in American papers if they said something negative about Cuba, but that the reports were usually rejected if they said something positive.

Americans rely on the First Amendment right to freedom of the press. But when our group of students and professors understood the difference between American press reports and the truth about Cuba, they saw that corporate ownership of American media helped explain why the American press has so often been a propaganda instrument to protect corporate capitalism.

Cuba is the only country in the western hemisphere that the United States has not controlled, conquered, or at least opened up for American corporate investment. We invaded in the Spanish-American war and kept the option to interfere if need be and we retained the Guantanamo military base. The Monroe Doctrine of 1823 was a declaration that no foreign country should have control in the western hemisphere. It turned into an excuse to put the United States in control of the western hemisphere, driving out governments (often democratic) that were independent of American power.

A long line of countries in Latin America—Mexico, Chile, Panama, Honduras, Grenada, Nicaragua, Puerto Rico, Haiti, and the Dominican Republic—fell to combinations of CIA manipulation of internal politics, Marine invasions, economic support of dictatorships, control of the press, embargoes, and assassinations of heads of state. Cuba is the hold-out.

To understand the United States it is useful to understand Cuba. American claims of exporting "freedom" and "democracy" can then be seen as a deception to cover up the meaning of capitalist "freedom." The United States has wanted Latin American countries to be safe (free) for American corporate investment. Because she won't cooperate, Cuba is the pariah—a haven for the poor, out of bounds for rich investors.

But Cuba's survival strategy under the crushing embargo since 1962 and the end of the Soviet Union's support has been to create a tourist industry, using the joint investments of Europeans, Canadians, and Asians. Thus, in spite of all the punitive measures inflicted on Cuba by the U.S., Cuba has survived and the U.S. has failed. The U.S. also failed in Vietnam. These two failures have been important moral lessons of the twentieth century.

OTHER U.S. CUBA COMPARISONS

The valuable aspects of capitalism are the energy and motivation that come from self-interest and organizational efficiency. These forces have been unleashed in China, and the result has been a rapid economic expansion. But another result is economic inequality, the condition that led to the Communist revolution in China.

In the United States, the difference between the lowest paid worker of a company and the CEO of that company is over 500 to 1. In Cuba the figures are uncertain, but five to one would be a rough guess, about like Finland.

There are more homeless in any large American city than in all of Cuba. Trickle down in the U.S. leaves many with no trickle. In Cuba everyone has housing, however humble, for when the state owns your property it can't charge more than 9 percent of your income for rent. Rent is based on income, at whatever level it is. Actually, most Cubans own their homes in perpetuity, as a result of their choosing to make monthly ownership contributions—a process similar to the American way in which ownership is acquired from a bank over a period of time. After the Cuban revolution, many people decided they wanted to have this opportunity to own their homes. Now about 90 percent of the people have ownership, a higher percent than in the United States.

The more you look into Cuba's system the more you see that for most people it is a huge advancement over most third-world countries. That is probably why Chomsky thinks the main concern of the American government is the danger that Cuba might serve as a good example to the rest of the world.

> Cuba is one of the poorest countries in the world and it has approximately the same quality of life index, in terms of health and so on, that the United States has. That's really scary and that's an enemy. That's what they mean when they say. "We can't tolerate another Cuba. It is bad enough that there is one country that can serve as model for this kind of development. Suppose there were two, suppose there were three" (Chomsky 1999, 42).

The American response to Cuban survival has been to use violence. These violations of international law by the United States have been condemned repeatedly in the United Nations by every country except one or two client American states. But at international meetings the standard U.S. government speech still involves affirming the American commitment to the *rule of law*, illuminating American hypocrisy. The entire American relationship with Cuba has been driven by willingness to continue the imperialism of the last 200 years. The American public needs to put an end to this exploitation and to see that there are lessons Americans can learn from Cuba and from our treatment of people who are dedicated to a different form of economics.

As the United States has become the dominant military power of the twentieth century, American government, the multinational corporations, and the Pentagon have been essentially ruling the world. Increasingly, as David Korten points out, the corporations are the driving force. Democracy and human rights are the most "subversive" ideas for the twenty-first century, for they are the keys that can move the world away from dominance by nations, corporations, and oligarchies of the wealthy. Few Americans understand how they have been losing the future. Politics is the means of deciding who gets what in the game of economics. If you don't like the outcomes, the rules of the game can be changed. Those who profit by the outcomes consider changing the rules to be heresy—or worse, criminal disloyalty. The core of good education is to understand the alternatives and their ethical implications and then to act accordingly. An alternative to capitalism is economic democracy, and it can be created in a variety of different forms, yet in the United States students are rarely taught that there are other kinds of economics than capitalist economics. This is not a way of upholding the idea of "choice" which is claimed by most Americans to characterize the United States. Because capitalism is treated as a religion only the "right" form of economics is part of the dominant belief system.

6

Approximately 18,000 patients in hospitals die annually due to error and complications from using prescription drugs.

—David Lawrence, head of Kaiser Permanente

Why do we have such intense punishment for people who take drugs illegally while drug companies make billions of dollars in profits every year by selling mood altering drugs to millions of Americans, including children?

—Dr. Dean Ornish

FROM SICKNESS TO HEALTH

This chapter continues to explore ways in which corporate power dominates American life—in this case with our health and access to medicine. Profitable medical deceptions are identified and the obsolete assumptions underlying most medicine are contrasted with a theory of health. Political connections with sickness are compared with policies that could make greater future health possible at lower cost.

How much sickness is really inevitable? Do we want to continue the huge human and financial costs of the twentieth century? Shouldn't a major objective of the twenty-first century be to maximize human health for all people? We now fall far short of that goal. Let's begin with a look at a major scourge, the disease that kills more Americans than any other——heart disease.

According to current estimates from the American Heart Association, 58,800,000 Americans have one or more types of cardiovascular heart disease (CVD).

Number one	High blood pressure	50,000,000
Number two	Coronary heart disease	12,000,000
Number three	Myocardial infarction	7,000,000
Number four	Angina pectoris	6,200,000

- Since 1900, CVD has been the number one killer in the United States in every year but one: 1918.

- More than 2,600 Americans die each day of CVD; an average of one death every 33 seconds.

- *CVD claims more lives each year than the next seven leading causes of death combined.*

- About one-sixth of people killed by CVD are under age 65.

- 1996 CVD mortality: male deaths — 453,297 (47.3 percent of deaths from CVD); female deaths — 505,930 (52.7 percent of deaths from CVD).

- In 1996, 35 percent of deaths from CVD occurred prematurely (i.e., before age 75, the average life expectancy in that year).

- Next three major causes of death in 1996: cancer 539,533; accidents 94,948; HIV (AIDS) 31,130.

- *If all forms of major CVD were eliminated, life expectancy would rise by almost 10 years. If all forms of cancer were eliminated, the gain would be three years.*

- From 1979 to 1996 the number of Americans discharged from short-stay hospitals with CVD as the first listed diagnosis increased 25 percent.

- In 1996 CVD ranked first among all disease categories in numbers of hospital discharges.

According to data from the Health Care Financing Administration (HCFA), in 1995 Medicare beneficiaries whose cardiovascular stays involved a surgical procedure received $16.4 billion in payments. That amounted to $11,746 per discharge.

Every year, half a million Americans die of heart disease. Every year more than a million undergo coronary bypass surgery or angioplasty to enlarge the openings in closed or partially closed arteries. The cost: $15.6 billion for the two procedures alone. The cost in pain and suffering: incalculable. Most people are told "You have to have a bypass or you're going to die" says Dr. Dean Ornish, a physician and clinical professor of medicine at the University of California, San Francisco. "That's not usually true. For most people, diet and lifestyle changes can be a safe alternative at a fraction of the cost and without the risks of trauma of going through surgery. In other words, they can halt— or even reverse—heart disease (June 1999, 1)."

Dr. Dean Ornish, in a 1998 study published in the *Journal of the American Medical Association* and the British journal *Lancet*, reported that "77% of people who were eligible for by-pass surgery or angioplasty were able to avoid it safely by changing diet and life styles, saving almost $30,000 per patient."

Dr. John McDougall, a physician who helped pioneer diet as prevention, has told people for years that, based on the evidence, people should simply say NO to by-pass. He shows that the evidence indicates that those who say *no* usually live as long as those who say *yes*, since by-pass, except in unusual cases, merely reduces pain which can be reduced by non-surgical means (1990).

The Heart Bypass Scam

In the early part of the twentieth century doctors routinely took out people's appendixes. It was virtually a fad to do so. Later (during my era) they took out tonsils and adenoids. Presumably, nature had no reason to put an appendix, tonsils, or adenoids in people. Organs could be removed like ornamental parts on a car. Next came hysterectomies. They were popular in the 1960s. If a woman's menstrual period was too irregular or she had problems around menopause, the doctor removed half of her sexual organs.

Fees for these medical procedures were increasing according to the demand, but the big jump came with by-pass heart surgery. Such surgery became possible and therefore it became desired by both the patient and the doctor. As Dr. McDougall used to tell surgeons—There is only one reason to do a bypass: you want $20,000 (1983, 68-9). This infuriated many until he revealed the evidence that, except in rare cases, those who had bypass did not live any longer than those who refused. The operation can also diminish a person mentally. According to Dr. McDougall, the blood-circulating machine congealed platelets which could hamper some areas of the brain.

Over the years the $20,000 fee for bypass surgery has gone up and also, therefore, the incentive to recommend that people have this operation. The procedure consists of having one's chest cut open and then a vein taken out of one's leg and then attached to the heart. There can be double, triple, or even quadruple bypass.

Bypass relieves angina—the pain of a heart trying to get enough oxygen. Relief of the pain is the main reason for doing the procedure. Yet with the proper diet and certain medication, the pain can be rapidly diminished. Within a few weeks of a low fat, high starch diet, there is often some reversal of the clogged arteries and the symptoms that caused the angina. Unless there is structural damage, continued correct diet can produce basic reversal of the entire problem.

U.S. medical costs as a percentage of the GNP are the highest of any nation, and we also have the lowest level of insurance coverage of any industrialized nation. A significant cost is bypass surgery, which is unnecessary except in unusual cases. But the popularity of bypass surgery is driven by three factors: 1. It is very profitable for the surgeon; 2. It is paid for, in most cases, by private or public medical coverage; and 3. It seems logical in a culture that has faith in mechanical pseudo-science and mechanistic paradigms which ignore the ecological approach of working with the body as a biological organism rather than merely as a machine.

These huge expenditures steal funding from other purposes, such as public schooling. They also keep corporate medicine tied to pharmaceutical corporations that often have monopoly control of their products, even when public funds are used to pay for the research. The result is a black hole that sucks up the wealth of the nation.

DIET AND THE AMERICAN WAY OF DEATH

The aristocracy of the Middle Ages demonstrated behavior that continues to be the world pattern—wealth then as now encourages people to eat high on the food chain. Roast lamb was preferred over potatoes. Meat costs more, and so it was associated with higher social class. The wealthy aristocracy saw no connection between their eating habits and their high levels of gout, heart failure, diabetes, and cancer. But the connection was there.

This connection came to light after World War II, when the German people were discovered to have very low levels of heart problems while the liberating Americans had very high levels. If stress was the main cause of heart problems, how could this be? The German people had been under very high levels of stress for years throughout the war, during which they survived on meager meals based largely on potatoes, grain, and black bread. The liberating Americans, on the other hand, ate high on the food chain—beef, eggs, and dairy food.

Scientists soon could see the strong connection between diet and heart problems. Called epidemiological research, this comparing of groups to identify causes of disease began to supersede the older anecdotal method. Doctors had previously used their patient's records as a way of determining cause and effect, usually with small samples (sometimes only single cases) and they were usually not trained to conduct statistical research. Medical ideology, moreover, explained away many diseases as genetically caused.

Groups such as the Seventh Day Adventists became prime study groups, because they are composed of two groups who each follow a strict diet—one eats everything except meat, and the other excludes meat and all other animal products such as eggs and dairy foods. This provided three large, measurable groups: 1) the average American group that eats all animal products plus some fruits and vegetables, 2) the minimal vegetarian Seventh Day Adventists who refrain from meat but eat other animal products, and 3) the Adventists who consume no animal products (also known as a vegan diet).

Research findings were distinct. For heart failure, cancer, and diabetes, the average American sample had the highest rate. Seventh Day Adventists who consumed dairy products and eggs but ate no meat had a much lower rate. And the "vegans" who ate no animal products had the lowest rates of these diseases which had previously been called "degenerative" as though they were caused mainly by old age. Widespread epidemiological research has since been used for nations, cultures, social classes, and working groups. This has permitted testing the older beliefs that these diseases resided in certain cultures, genes, races, etc.

The research showed what happened when these groups moved from their home area to another part of the world where eating habits were different. Results have been dramatic. Each group took on the diseases (or lack of them) associated with the eating habits of its new home. For example, women from rural Japan had exceedingly low levels of heart disease, but when they moved to urban Japan and had higher incomes, their levels of heart disease increased. When they moved to the United States, they had even higher levels, and their children had virtually the same pattern of high "degenerative" disease exhibited by other Americans—for they had usually abandoned their parents' eating habits. Genetics was, therefore, not the cause. The irony is that the poor of the world generally eat a more healthy diet than the rich, when they have access to sufficient food. They are forced to eat low on the food chain. Their high death rates are usually connected to infectious disease caused by the pollution and contamination of their food and environment, or by actual starvation.

This knowledge has important implications for what we call "progress." Americans consider themselves to be part of an advanced, progressive nation. Yet the number of heart bypass operations is the highest in the world. Even more ironically, these enormously expensive operations provide virtually the same survival rates as occur with those who refuse the operations. People who focus on the cause of heart attacks and eat low on the food chain rarely have heart attacks.

The most definitive research, the Framingham study conducted by the American Heart Association, began in 1948 and is still continuing. It has provided strong research evidence for a virtually direct relationship between cholesterol levels and heart attacks. Industries that produce cholesterol, such as beef and dairy companies, saw the need for public deception and spent many millions of dollars on public misinformation which ranged from individual testimonials to "bought" MDs who tried to confuse the public by suggesting that "more research is needed."

The first deception was that vegetarianism created health risks because of certain nutritional deficiencies. But the evidence shows the reverse. Vegetarians, especially those that avoid *all* animal products, have the *highest* health levels. Starches like pasta, rice, and potatoes have become the favorites of long-distance runners and many other athletes who require a lot of strength and stamina, though lots of starch is not necessary for people who exercise less. And people do *not* suffer calcium loss from vegetarianism, for vegetables, especially leafy greens such as collards, mustard cabbage and turnip tops provide plenty of calcium. The calcium in milk after all comes from cows that graze on green vegetation. The loss occurs when lots of meats and dairy products and other high proteins are consumed, which causes calcium leaching. Protein excess is a major cause of osteoporosis.

A Harvard School of Public Health study of 70,000 American nurses found that women with the *highest* calcium consumption from dairy products have *more* fractures than those who drank less milk!

MEDICAL MYOPIA: THE ASPIRIN STUDY

The medical profession has often failed to understand that what is statistically normal can be pathological. This is well illustrated in the famed aspirin study which has done more to increase aspirin sales than any sales promotion.

In 1988, a long-term study was published in the *New England Journal of Medicine;* it was called the Physicians Health Study (Heanekens 1978) and it had attempted to determine what effect, if any, aspirin would have on heart disease. The study was carefully controlled. Two groups were used for the classical control/experimental double blind model. One was given aspirin each day, the other was given a placebo. No one knew what they were given. The results drew worldwide attention. Those who took the aspirin had 33 percent lower incidence of myocardial infarction (a heart disease). This impressive result has contributed to the greater use of aspirin since then.

The interpretation of this study has crucial limitations, however, for the two groups that were studied consisted of random groupings of American men. What was ignored is that each group, by definition, consisted of people who are on a high fat diet, for that is what the average American eats. We therefore can conclude from the study that: If you are going to eat a normal, unhealthy diet, then you will have a lower risk of a non-fatal heart attack if you take one 325 mg. aspirin every other day. A normal American diet without aspirin results in about 50 percent of the men having heart attacks.

- No conclusion was drawn in this study of whether the aspirin takers would be better off or worse off if they had switched to a healthy diet, for this consideration was omitted;

- No follow up study was done to see if the overall effect of the study was that people would continue to eat an unhealthy diet and compensate by taking aspirin.

The fact that more than 22,000 doctors participated in this study suggests that the medical model is so strongly tied to mechanistic-chemical health treatments that the medical profession and the advice of such doctors is affected by this bias.

There is no evidence that the study was in any way supported or proposed by aspirin industries, but Bristol-Myers provided the monthly calendar packs to help doctors keep track of their records. The results of this study, however, were predictable, based on the common knowledge that aspirin thins the blood. However, it also causes stomach bleeding. In fact every chemical given to people which is not part of the natural production of the body produces some negative side effects, and many of them are not even known. When more than one pill is taken they can interact and produce unpredictable synergistic effects making unpredictability and negative side effects even more likely.

Doctors I have consulted who focus on preventative medicine (John McDougall, M.D. was one) commonly have patients come to them with long-standing ailments that other doctors are not curing but are instead treating with one drug on top of another. These patients are often taking as many as eight to ten pills daily. McDougall said he frequently could not even diagnose such people until the unpredictable synergistic effects of all these chemical pills were reduced and people shifted over to a healthy diet. Once they were chemically clean, a diagnosis could be made—but the ailments often disappeared by then. A healthier diet without drugs "cured" these people.

Extreme reliance on technology that I call "technofanaticism" reigns in the field of medicine (as well as in activities related to NASA, computers, dams, highways, and all the Pentagon conceptions of national defense). Did the doctors in the aspirin study think that the human body had developed a need for aspirin during the course of evolution? *When health theory takes account of inner and outer ecology the mechanistic trap is more likely to be avoided.* But such considerations are usually ignored when food is grown with the application of exotic pesticides and defoliants, when people eat a variety of chemical preservatives, and when the human body is challenged by substances that were never part of the evolutionary life support system. Combinations of synthetic drugs not only stress the human body but stress it in unpredictable ways. Ordinarily, people continue to take the drugs unless there are clear symptoms of intolerance. But effects on the body, especially in the case of cancer and liver illness, can take years to show up. Short-term advantages are then traded for possible long-term sickness.

MASKING SYMPTOMS

When people try to avoid pain, they often fall into a trap. Pain is a signal—part of the feedback of the human body, telling us that something is wrong. If the pain is extreme, taking some drug might make one feel better. But if the drug merely masks the pain, the pain message is ignored, and the warning signal transmitted by the body goes unheeded.

Millions of anti-pain drugs, many approximating aspirin, are taken every day. The heavy advertising in the mass media appeals to people on the premise that pain is bad and getting rid of pain is good. But it is the *cause* of the pain that is bad and the most-needed response is *diagnosis*. And in many cases, better diet, clean air, exercise, rest, and stress reduction will eliminate the symptoms. Yet the typical medical response may be a prescription to eliminate pain that might be quite tolerable and might even present a good reminder that a search for the cause should begin. The medical paradigm usually wins out for those who submit blindly and do, as the ads say "what your doctor advises."

GETTING THE RIGHT BALANCE

A healthy society in the twenty-first century will still need some medications, operations, and research on drugs to treat certain ailments, but these tools should be given second priority to the *prevention* of ailments. The two approaches are not now in balance. Many operations would not be necessary if sickness were avoided by focusing on improving people's health. Although smoking and high-fat foods are at the top of the list as sickness producers, there are two basic *institutional* factors which are causal. One is that food production in the United States is profit-driven. The other is that the medical/pharmaceutical complex is dominated by a mechanistic theory of health.

Leading pediatricians such as Dr. Spock (1998 139) have advised that children after the age of two should not ordinarily drink cows' milk. Mothers who nurse their children (with ecologically based nutrition) increase their brain development and later intellectual development, and improve their immunological systems and overall health.

The motive of the food industry in a capitalistic society is not to create a healthy nation but to sell products and make as much profit as possible. The food industry's power is felt in their legislative lobbying, their deceptive advertising, and the chemical-laced processed foods that substitute taste and convenience for nutrition, while packaging provides as little real information as possible on obscure lists of ingredients that few people can understand.

Producers operate on the profit-first, health-second creed. Chickens in overcrowded factory farms are fed pellets that contain antibiotics so that the maximum number of chickens can be raised in crowded areas that cause disease. When the bodies of the chickens are sterilized through antibiotics so that harmful bacteria will die, the fowl can be raised profitably in congested, contaminated areas. The consumer pays in serious ways. The bacteria increasingly become resistant to the antibiotics and the resistant bacteria are passed on to the people who eat the chickens. Thus there is a considerable trade-off in health resulting from a method by which producers can make more money and consumers can have cheaper chicken. The public would be better off from a health standpoint eating no chicken at all. Even uncontaminated chicken provides undesirable cholesterol and excess protein.

But with all this chemical sterilization, how much chicken sold to the public is uncontaminated? *Consumer Reports* in March 1998 presented the most comprehensive study of store bought chickens. They said, "70 percent were contaminated with campylobacter, the leading cause of food poisoning. The U.S. Centers for Disease Control reported that between 1988 and 1992, outbreaks of disease caused by eating chicken rose threefold, mostly from salmonella. In the largest published study of store-bought chickens we found harmful bacteria in 71 percent. Some generic E. coli (in fecal matter) is present on virtually *every* chicken on the market."

The Reagan administration's goal of keeping government off the back of industry led to the coveted USDA inspection label on chickens becoming a "poke and sniff" inspection. Slaughtering plants must conduct only one test per 22,000 chickens for E.Coli. It's like betting on the lottery that your chicken will be the lucky one to get the test.

Beef producers also have their ploys to maximize profit. Cattle often are given steroids to make them heavier, and these are then passed on to people consuming the beef. Most European nations have prohibited importation of American beef because their standards are higher. Of the different kinds of meat, beef has the highest level of negative health effects with a significant correlation with colon cancer. When beef is smoked or barbecued, the cancer-causing chemicals increase dramatically. Yet there is no movement to label the danger of such foods in the way cigarettes are labeled. Yale professor Kelly Brownell argues for such labeling. Garner and Halweil in a *World Watch* publication asks: "Is Ronald McDonald really so different from Joe Camel (March 2000, 52)?"

The very food sources that are the worst for people's health are also the worst for the environment. The run-off from the processing of chickens, beef, and dairy cattle is a major source of pollution in many American rivers. Cattle are a major destroyer of riparian areas as they use streams for drinking water and pollute them with defecation. Salmon spawning areas in western states have been heavily impacted by cattle, and the land itself is degraded by grazing. The consumption of plants by wild animals and their environmental impacts usually produces ecological balance, while domestic animals are invariably destroyers of natural ecosystems.

Jeremy Rifkin's *Beyond Beef* is one of the best books describing the world cattle culture from the beginning of recorded time. He shows how "cattle raising is a primary factor in the destruction of the world's remaining tropical rain forests...and for much of the spreading desertification in the sub-Sahara of Africa." In the United States, "organic run-off from feedlots is now a major cause of organic pollution of our nation's groundwater (1992, 2-3)."

While the rich countries complain of overpopulation and food scarcity Rifkin claims that: cattle and other livestock consume over 70 percent of all the grain produced in the United States. About one-third of the world's total grain harvest is fed to cattle and other livestock while as many as one billion people suffer chronic hunger and malnutrition. Yet millions more in the industrial world die from diseases caused by an excess of grain-fed animal flesh. *Cattle production and beef consumption now rank among the gravest threats to the future well-being of the earth and its human population.* Dismantling the global cattle complex and eliminating beef from the diet of the human race is an essential task of the coming decades if we are to have any hope of restoring our planet to health and feeding a growing human population (Rifkin 1992, 2).

Food economist Francis Moore Lappe has shown how much of our good food is fed to cattle instead of meeting the nutritional needs of the poor of the world. Raising cattle, as she points out, is an example of maximum waste and inefficiency: An acre of cereal can produce five times more protein than an acre devoted to meat production. Legumes (beans, peas, lentils) can produce ten times more, and leafy vegetables, fifteen times more... spinach can produce up to twenty-six times more protein per acre than can beef (1982, 69).

A market distribution system for food in a world of unequal wealth makes these inefficiencies inevitable. Only planning that takes account of topsoil limits, sustainable farming, and human nutritional needs can serve as an ethics-based, survival-based, policy for the twenty-first century.

INNER ECOLOGY AND OUTER ECOLOGY—THE KEY TO HEALTH THEORY

In the twentieth century, principles of physics and chemistry rather than principles of ecology were used to connect us to the outer world. The same point of view applied to the inside of people. The food we fed to babies was often a concoction of chemicals made by a corporation, and the quick lunches we invented for ourselves were much like the chemicals we put on plants— non-organic and outside of the principles of ecology or even biology. Chemicals have been combined to eliminate sugar, when weight loss is the overriding goal—trusting that the chemical companies would not threaten our health.

But the insides of people are as much an ecosystem as the outside world. Our life depends on a highly complicated connection between our digestive, circulatory, nervous, and endocrine systems that includes a balance of cells and microbes. The combination and interaction constitutes an ecological system that has been worked out over hundreds of thousands of years of evolution as people received their nutrition directly from plants and animals. As a result we are here. We have survived. And the complexity of the life-giving world within us is as great as the life giving world outside of us—the air, water, land, plants, animals, and bacteria.

But we have yet to treat our inner selves or the outer world as sets of life-giving ecological systems. Relying on the old mechanistic model will ruin both ourselves and the earth. The costs even in economic terms alone will be staggering, as fisheries are exhausted, topsoil is depleted, and as bypass surgery is performed to correct a threat to life that is caused by ignoring inner ecology. We need to look closely at the food we eat and to devise a national health policy which helps correct our obsolete habits and institutions. When the Clinton administration drafted legislation for "health care" in the 1990s, it was not surprising to find that it was all about medical care rather than about health care. The objective was to make medical care available to more people. The goal was good and necessary, but *it did not suggest that a nation of healthier people should be the overriding* goal. The achievements of modern medicine are very important, and access to medical care should be a human right, as the Universal Declaration of Human Rights has indicated. However, eating the wrong food, smoking, working in unhealthy environments, and being exposed to polluted air and water produce sickness that is **preventable**. Many of these ailments which lead to human suffering and premature death could be addressed in a properly developed national "health" policy which would improve the quality of life of people and greatly reduce the nation's number one economic cost—medical care.

The American economy is a vast conflict-of-interest system which promotes the very consumption habits that provide profit to industries and to the medical establishment. Milk is sold by showing movie stars with milk mustaches, but the contributions of milk to heart failure (from the fat) and osteoporosis (from the excess protein) is never mentioned. Meat is promoted by the beef industry and tied to macho behavior, and a variety of industries vie for the contracts for school lunches which typically help hook students to unhealthful foods at an early age in the same way that tobacco companies try to hook teenagers to become cigarette addicts.

But unhealthy food is not merely the result of industry promotion—much is cultural. It has deep roots which as noted earlier are often tied to social class. The unhealthful food is expensive, therefore eating it is a sign of status—the 16 ounce steak has a different meaning than the salad bar. People have only started to appreciate what "ecology" means, but these complex biological systems that support life within us and outside of us need to be in harmony if we are to have both a healthy environment and personal health. If the purpose of "medicine" is really to heal, it needs to shift from the narrow mechanistic model to the reality of how life actually fits together.

THE MECHANISTIC MODEL

The mechanistic model is ingrained in the entire conventional food processing system and in the medical approach to "health." The reason that food high on the food chain causes so many illnesses is that it is not very compatible with inner ecology. Good health requires foods that do not "pollute" us.

Pollution is not merely a matter of breathing carbon monoxide and other chemicals, it is a matter of bringing into the body anything that does not fit into the human ecological system. Ingesting cyanide produces rapid incompatibility so that life stops in a matter of minutes. But small cumulative amounts of pollutants cause us to break down slowly, and some people with strong bodies take much longer to break down.

We can discover what constitutes a pollutant when we see what happens to people who breathe or eat certain chemicals. If they breathe carbon monoxide in large amounts they die. But gradual amounts of pollutants reduce a person's health and increase the risk of succumbing to various kinds of sicknesses. Foods such as rice or potatoes have such perfect compatibility with the human body that no case can be made that these pollute us. By contrast, beef, milk (even "nonfat" milk), and most oils are incremental "pollutants" which cannot be consumed in quantity for a sustained period of time without cumulative impacts on the human body, which can lead to serious sickness or even death.

This is obvious with tobacco. It is also the case with many other substances such as pesticides. Lead in gasoline was cumulative in the body and had serious effects on American health so it was finally eliminated by federal law. Arsenic in wells and water supplies has a dangerous cumulative effect on people—and it is a major cause of sickness in Bangladesh. However, President Bush in 2001 resisted proposals to reduce arsenic in public water supplies, because of the added costs to industry but gave in after a public outcry.

It is fortunate that the foods most compatible with our inner ecosystem are also the most compatible with the planetary life support system. Our current state is lose-lose, both for our personal health and for the health of the natural systems on which life depends. In the name of progress we have created a pathological system, but by understanding what is wrong we have the basis for setting it right and creating a win-win situation.

The field of medicine is part of this obsolete mechanistic paradigm. When doctors give us chemicals to make us feel better, they have virtually no understanding of the actual bio-chemical effects on the cells of the human body. They usually base their judgments of the chemicals they give on the symptomatic effects of drugs, often with research information provided by pharmaceutical companies that are authorized to test *their own products*. The drug company's overriding objective is of course to maximize profits, so they wine and dine doctors at conventions and pass out PR material to get doctors to prescribe their medicines. In turn, the doctors are often part of a medical system that works in a clinic or hospital to maximize profit. This interferes with decisions on whether an operation is necessary and whether an x-ray is necessary. When doctors have their own (expensive) x-ray machines there is a strong temptation to keep the x-ray machine in operation.

So there is the problem of domination by a mechanistic paradigm, but in addition, there is often conflict-of-interest. The most hopeful medicine— preventive medicine—is not as profitable, so it has fewer practitioners. Eugene Robin, a distinguished Stanford University physician, wrote a balanced critique of medicine in *Matters of Life and Death: Risks vs. Benefits of Medical Care*. He gives specific recommendations for reducing the harm caused by medicine from risks of a simple blood test to a major operation. His information on unnecessary surgery includes the "hysterectomy" fad. He points out that "the amount of surgery increases as the number of surgeons increases, "especially in a fee-for-service system (1984, 95)."

THE ECONOMICS OF MEDICINE

The national debt is connected to the medical black hole. Anyone who has spent a day or two in a hospital is likely to have been shocked by the bill. Many people are faced with liquidation of their entire savings after a couple of days in the hospital. Though the United States is a wealthy, modern country and spends the most of the industrialized countries on medical care—over 14 percent of GNP—it has the smallest percentage of people with medical coverage. More than 41 million lack medical coverage. The U.S. has the lowest percentage of its population with coverage compared to other industrial nations, and even Greece, Korea, and Mexico surpass the U.S. in coverage (Anderson 1997).

Profits for pharmaceutical companies have, by far, exceeded increases in the average person's income and are much higher than in most other industries. Doctors' salaries have also risen rapidly so that they are one of the highest paid professional groups.

Unnecessary costs are connected to the system of private medical insurance. Administrative cost of the Medicare system is much less than the administrative cost of private insurance systems. Keeping track of costs and collecting insurance is often more time consuming than the actual medical treatment. This may be a major reason why the single-payer Canadian system can provide coverage to the entire population for about thirty percent less. The American system is highly privatized, with HMOs reaping huge profits, while the Canadian system uses government as the collection and payment agency. Older Americans already have such a system through Medicare, but it has not been extended to the entire population. Such a change would probably be the most desirable of the various proposals.

NATIONAL HEALTH CARE VS. NATIONAL MEDICAL CARE

The United States has the highest costs for medical care of any nation in the world. By the end of the twentieth century costs had reached about 14 percent of the GNP. But our health level is not nearly as high as that of many other nations. The costs of medical care have increased at a much more rapid rate than the GNP, a trend that is not sustainable. Some of this relates to the demographic shift to an older population, to higher drug costs, and to increases in hospital and medical fees. But when President Clinton called for a "national health plan" it was a semantic trap from the very beginning, for it was not a health plan, and only when the focus is really on health will costs go down and health levels go up. *We need a National Health Plan, not a National Medical Plan that is called a Health Plan.* The difference is very great. A healthy nation has lower medical costs. A nation with a strong medical plan could certainly help more people who are sick, but it would make little contribution to the health of the nation. Nationally and globally health should be the overriding goal and medical care should be only a part of it.

IATROGENIC (MEDICALLY CAUSED) ILLNESS

Iatrogenic is a term that is used to describe illness that is actually caused by the medical treatment process, that is by hospitals, doctors, and medications. To cite personal examples, my wife's mother was given the wrong pill while in the hospital which caused her heart to stop and she died; my wife had a life threatening mis-diagnosis, and I have had two major misdiagnoses that could have led to serious problems.

The National Academy of Science's Institute of Medicine released a large scale national study in 1999 declaring that *medical errors in U.S. hospitals kill between 44,000 and 98,000 people each year.* What are these medical errors? They include pharmacies providing the wrong drugs, doctors removing the wrong organs, doctors making the wrong diagnoses, and—it is not a joke—doctors writing so poorly that, as the report says: "Did the doctor order 10 milligrams or 10 micrograms? Does the prescription call for the hormone replacement Premarin or the antibiotic Primaxin?"

A study at one of the leading hospitals in Honolulu revealed that about 25 percent of the patients' illnesses were caused by the medical profession. If all the unnecessary operations—excessive bypasses, hysterectomies, and caesarean sections, for example—are added together, the number adds up to a very large amount of sickness and death that results from the unintended effects of invasive and chemically-based medicine.

REFUSING TO DEAL WITH THE CAUSES OF CANCER

Cancer has been the disease least subject to medical cures, and there are limited tools available to doctors. Even when a course of treatment is recommended, (chemotherapy, for example) the choice may offer only the same odds for success as from flipping a coin, and the side effects may make a person feel miserable.

The American Cancer Society has provided extensive PR that gives people a sense of unwarranted optimism about cancer cures. This strategy has been exceedingly profitable. What is almost never mentioned is that most cancer is caused by environmental factors. The American Cancer Society will tell people not to smoke but will not take aggressive action for control of nicotine as a narcotic. In a real sense, much cancer is caused by bad politics. Placing emphasis on personal responsibility rather than public policy is often a way to keep power in the hands of corporations, such as the tobacco, dairy and beef industries, that profit from a product that can increase one's chances of ending up with cancer and/or heart attacks (Zepernick 2001, 181-182).

Dr. Samuel Epstein has been in a 30-year fight against the cancer establishment, especially the American Cancer Society. In the *International Journal of Health Services* (Vol. 29, No. 3) he has an article titled "The American Cancer Society: The World's Wealthiest 'Non-profit' Institution." He says the American Cancer Society and the National Cancer Institute have "incestuous conflicts of interest" with chemical and pharmaceutical companies and, therefore, spend huge sums of money on the treatment of cancer instead of on prevention.

He blames our cancer epidemic on the poisoning of the planet. He says the overwhelming emphasis is on damage control— on diagnosis and treatment rather than on prevention. "You don't just expose people to carcinogens and then repair the damage by giving them a pill." Epstein's *The Politics of Cancer* describes the prioritizing of economics and politics over health and shows how cancer has now become profitable. But he also shows how cancer can be prevented (1978, 1998).

SELF-DEFENSE

Information available now on the Internet and at hospital libraries can be used before people submit to what might be irreversible damage to their bodies. Second and third opinions should be obtained and a good set of questions prepared for doctors such as, "What is the evidence for your recommendation?" When people begin to ask the right questions and do some of their own research, they will find that the best doctors are glad to cooperate and are unlikely to present themselves as infallible (McDougall 1990).

A book titled *Prescription for Disaster*, by Thomas Moore, (1998) points out that you are ten times more likely to be hospitalized as a result of adverse reaction to a prescription drug than by an automobile accident. Some of the other stunning findings in his book include the following:

- "One-third of pharmacies checked filled a prescription for two drugs with a dangerous interaction without warning the consumer."
- "Rhode Island doctors reported to the FDA only 11 of 26,000 adverse effects they observed."
- "43% of recently approved drugs caused cancer in animals, often at or near the human dose."
- "Prozac was linked to more adverse reactions reported to the FDA than any other drug in America."

Many people pride themselves on being informed consumers when they buy a car or computer. Certainly they also need to become informed on medical and drug information that has life and death consequences, particularly in a country where the Food and Drug Administration continues to be subject to political pressures that often serve the corporations.

WE ARE ALL "DOWNWIND"

Over half of the people working in California are dealing with toxic material on a daily basis, and some of it is radioactive. Development of atomic bombs and atomic energy advanced without our having any way of knowing what could be done to dispose of the waste materials, yet some such as plutonium have a 24,000 year half-life. During World War II our government focused so entirely on military power to win the war that health considerations were ignored, and the deadly results will affect generations to come.

Hanford, a government nuclear processing facility in Washington, made large continuous releases of I-131 (radioactive iodine) which is taken directly into the thyroid and causes cancer. Unlike plutonium it has a half-life of eight days. As the I-131 falls on fields and is ingested by cows, it concentrates in the milk. This is the main way in which people acquire thyroid cancer in areas of nuclear production. Many people received thyroid cancer from Hanford releases, which were the highest in 1946.

In 1949, in a project called the "Green Run," intentional releases of radioactive iodine were made from Hanford to test its effects on the public, reminiscent of the experiments by German scientists in World War II. The only lessons learned from this uncontrolled "experiment" are that uncontrolled "national defense" can be dangerous to our health and that the American government is quite capable of behaving like a totalitarian country.

THE TRAGEDY OF NUCLEAR POWER

The Hanford I-131 releases and the nuclear bomb testing in Nevada, which caused the death of sheep in Utah and cancers in people, should be a lesson about the dangers of nuclear materials. This information needs to be conveyed to those who now live in the vicinity of nuclear power plants. These plants were previously thought to be defensible as a profitable business, but fortunately, they have not been economic. Four were built in the state of Washington and three went into bankruptcy. None have been ordered in the United States since 1979 (the time of the Three Mile Island semi-meltdown), but American corporations make considerable profit by constructing nuclear power plants in other parts of the world.. Now that the Cold War with the Soviet Union is over the production of nuclear bombs is more irrational than ever. This is the optimum historical time to put the genie back in the bottle.

The Chernobyl disaster produced a wave of resistance to nuclear power plants, but smaller versions continue to be designed. While nuclear fusion is still in the experimental stage, it may emerge in the twenty-first century as a process that produces far less radioactive material than fission reactors. Yet no form of nuclear power is a responsible technology that protects future generations from its deadly contamination.

Our fission reactors continue to produce large amounts of highly radioactive waste, even though there is no known safe way to dispose of these dangerous materials that will present a serious threat to human health for over 100,000 years. Even transporting them places the public at risk. Our current generation operates with unspeakable arrogance when it disregards all future generations. The failure to convert to safe energy involves playing roulette with human civilization. The George W. Bush administration has supported more nuclear plants, **but corporations, that claim they are safe, will not invest in**

them unless the Price-Anderson act is reenacted by congress, for it protects the industries from large liability payments in case of an accident.

Because the only safe and renewable energy sources are from geothermal, tidal, and the various kinds of direct and indirect uses of solar energy (wind, photovoltaic, bio-mass, hydro) we can shift the twenty-first century away from the "permanent" nuclear cancer legacy. Current energy use is very inefficient and waste is more often subsidized than conservation, so a reduction of 50 percent of our current waste is equal to a 50 percent increase in available energy. Reliance on petroleum and coal is also a direct threat to human health through air pollution and the resulting global climate change.

Health in the twenty-first century is therefore tied not only to diet, smoking, and the working environment, but also to the shift away from petroleum and nuclear energy to a sustainable, renewable, solar-based energy system. By the end of the twentieth century there was little effort to make this conversion, mainly because global corporations tied to a petroleum economy were in the driver's seat.

OUR CHILDREN AS GUINEA PIGS

Even if people eat the most healthful selection of foods—fruits and vegetables—they have a problem obtaining uncontaminated food. American agriculture is based on the anti-ecological, mechanistic capitalist model, so the farming methods selected are those that achieve maximum profit regardless of the impact on the public. Chemical rather than organic fertilizer is applied to the soil and there is a constant war against harmful insects. Not that we want harmful insects, but our weapons in that war are dangerous.

Most farms are monocultural—the same crop is grown over large areas. This farming approach actually gives insects the maximum advantage, but through the use of exotic chemicals as pesticides, they can often be temporarily controlled until they mutate and develop resistance to the pesticide. Then either a new pesticide is invented and applied or the old one is used in increasingly larger doses.

Many of these pesticides are organophosphates, an outcome of poison gas research during World War II. Though "organo" is part of their name, they have no organic connection with biological evolution or any of the chemical combinations that evolved on this planet. They produce new and unpredictable side effect changes in insects, birds, and bacterial ecology, and their effect on human health varies according to the kind of pesticide and the amount ingested. What is clear is that children are in the most danger. When they eat the fruit and vegetables they need to make them healthy, they also ingest pesticides, many of which have cumulative effects over a lifetime. They are often "systemic" pesticides that permeate crops and cannot be washed off.

The Environmental Protection Agency (EPA) is caught in the middle, with the politics of the farmers on the one hand and the politics of public health on the other. Pesticide-using farmers are represented by agribusiness and chemical companies that have powerful lobbies, so in nearly all cases amounts and kinds of pesticides actually exceed health standards. There are no legal priorities that place health for the public ahead of business profits. In 1999, the EPA admitted that Guthion (used on apples) and 39 other organophosphates pose an unacceptable risk to children, yet political pressures prevented it from acting to protect the public's health.

Organic farm products are becoming more available but they struggle to compete with products of the agribusiness corporations whose large scale operation producing cheaper chemically based food often undercuts the prices of organic foods. The important consideration here is that the market rather than the right of the citizens to food that is clean and healthful is controlling the health of the nation. Capitalism and profit are the primary considerations, and a sizable portion of the huge profits of agribusiness is used to influence legislation and legislators that keep the old system intact.

Those who grow or work with crops are also victims. Farming produces some of the highest health risks of the various occupations. I have known a number of apple growers in Washington who quit to protect their own health. The solution to that problem has usually been to hire Mexican migrant workers who are so desperate for work that they are willing to trade their health for the money they make.

PRICING MEDICINES OUT OF REACH

Poverty within the United States and in other countries produces sickness and low health levels. Yet a poor country such as Cuba that has a low per capita income but a high level of economic equality has one of the highest health levels in the world. Infant mortality in 2001 was 6.2 for 1000 live births, a lower infant mortality rate than the United States, which stands at 7. According to reports from the United Nations Children's Fund (UNICEF), Cuba tied with Canada and leads the Americas with the lowest death rate among children under the age of one year. Cuba has made lifetime medical care a constitutional right When poor people gain access to adequate food, housing, and shelter, the historic levels of sickness drop rapidly. Medical care in the United States is available for purchase but not as a life time right. It is largely a business, often operating under corporations.

The basic medicines that can cure diseases are priced too high for most of the people of the world to afford, and corporate capitalism puts profits above people in the pharmaceutical business as in any other. Control over patients and over the process of distribution of life-saving drugs takes priority over providing such drugs at reasonable prices. While many developed countries control drug prices to keep them affordable, the United States does the opposite. The result is that prices are about twice as high in the U.S. as in Europe and nearly four times higher than in Japan.

The global reach of American corporations affects the life and death of millions. The following case is an example: Taxol, a drug developed from certain yew trees, was discovered, tested, and manufactured by the National Cancer Institute with public money and then turned over to Bristol-Meyers Squibb for marketing. The company paid $.25 per milligram and sold it at $4.87 per milligram, making $1 billion annually. When African countries wanted to manufacture the drug to treat AIDS, Vice President Gore pressured South African officials to ban generic substitutes for Taxol. The poor people in Africa cannot afford the $15,000 a year that the drug company charges, yet 85 percen of all AIDS sufferers live in third world countries. Only 1 percent of new medicines brought to market by multinational drug companies were designed to treat the tropical diseases that kill millions in the third world countries. The profitable areas of drug company concentration have been in research on impotence, baldness, toenail fungus, wrinkles, and drugs for pets (Silverstein 1999).

In the twentieth century, American politics continued to be controlled by big money. But the public was becoming more and more aware of the need to regulate campaign financing, and hopefully an informed public can cause basic change in the twenty-first century. **The movement from having the best government money can buy in the twentieth century to the best government that democracy can produce in the twenty-first century is at the core of a revolution that would affect human health not only in the United States but worldwide.**

Agriculture for profit rather than health has corrupted agriculture world wide and contaminated the planet with chemicals. Some DDT still continues to be present in the breast milk of human mothers, but while this particular toxin is now finally in decline, it is being replaced by a wide variety of equally or even more dangerous, often untested chemicals. The slow development of cancer makes the discovery of the effects of new exotic chemicals very difficult to trace. The twentieth century was on the high-risk course; the twenty-first century needs to convert to the low-risk prevention policy of "if in doubt, don't." This may require government that makes public interest the top priority.

Health is the result of a combination of economic, political, and educational considerations, including scientific knowledge of specialists and awareness by the general public. If achieving good health and prevention of disease are considered as political goals, the combined forces can produce significant results. But if economic profit is the overriding goal, many people will perish as access to adequate health care becomes a privilege for the affluent rather than a right for all. Can we speak seriously of support for human rights unless medical services and a healthful planetary environment are made universally available?

The Sad State of American Health vs. Our Myth of Superiority

When American capitalism dominates public health, as it does, and when treatment and diagnosis dominates rather than prevention, the effects are that we have one of the world's worse health records, compared to other industrial nations.

The *Journal of the American Medical Association* documented the sad state of American health in July 2000 by ranking the health of countries. Of the 13 countries in the comparison, the United States ranks an average of **12th**. The best in order of ranking are Japan, Sweden, Canada, France, Australia, Spain, Finland, the Netherlands, the United Kingdom, Denmark, Belgium, and then the United States followed by Germany.

- United States is 13th for low birth-weight, 13th for neonatal mortality and infant overall mortality, 13th for years of potential life lost.
- The U.S. is 11th for post-neonatal mortality, and 11th for life expectancy for females.
- Life expectancy moves to third for people 65 years of age. Medicare may be the significant factor.

The dismal comparison is probably connected to the kind of American politics that treats medical care as mainly a market commodity while other nations presume that medical care is a *right* which is supported by national systems. Of the more advanced nations only the United States and South Africa do not have a universal system of medical care. Medical care in the

United States has always been mainly a business instead of a right. In our common claim of "having the best medical system in the world" we neglect to say that the best medical care goes to the wealthy and to the aged who are on Medicare. Forty million Americans have *no* health insurance. Moreover, we place too much emphasis on a mechanistic, chemical-drug, institutional approach to medicine rather than prevention. We kill about a quarter of a million people a year through medically caused deaths, the third leading cause of death in the United States, after heart disease and cancer.

In the November 2000 Presidential elections, neither the Republican nor the Democratic candidate proposed universal medical care. Only the Socialist candidate proposed such a radical change.

TWENTIETH CENTURY SICKNESS CHARACTERISTICS

The conditions that prevailed were the following:
1. Doctors focused on curing sickness through the use of drugs and surgery.
2. People ate high on the food chain.
3. Farmers grew food with much use of dangerous non-organic chemicals.
4. The government presumed that pesticides were innocent until proven guilty.
5. Polluters extended the use of dangerous chemicals whenever it was possible.
6. The government subsidized industries that made people sick and often killed them.
7. Most people lived a sedentary, inactive life.
8. Government policies and actions institutionalized inequality and poverty.
9. The health care system distributed life-saving medicine mainly to the rich.

TWENTY-FIRST CENTURY HEALTH REQUIREMENTS

The conditions that could prevail are the following:
1. Doctors will focus on preventing sickness and promoting health.
2. People will eat low on the food chain.
3. Farmers will grow food using renewable, organic materials.
4. The government will presume pesticides are guilty until proven innocent.
5. The right to a healthful environment will be a constitutional right.
6. The government will criminalize industries that make people sick.
7. Government policies and actions will help develop physically active people.
8. Government policies will eliminate extreme inequality and poverty.
9. The government will install a national single-payer health care system for all.

Propaganda is to democracy what violence is to totalitarianism.

—Noam Chomsky

BREAKING FREE FROM CORPORATE PROGRAMMING

This chapter tries to show how the normal socialization of Americans involves influences that guide their beliefs about the world. These influences are considered to be a form of propaganda that indoctrinates the public with a narrow ideology that supports oligarchy and economic inequality. The chapter suggests ways to reverse these influences to develop the critical thinking necessary to have a viable democracy.

Most students have been subjected to so much economic, religious, and political propaganda that they cannot begin to think critically until they are "deprogrammed." If deprogramming is successful, students will become more immune to propaganda, resistant to the seductions of advertising, aware of the ideological slant of mass media and conventional education— and thereby more capable of independent thinking. The process requires being aware of the ways in which we are ususally indoctrinated.

The influence of mass media and the curriculum of public and private schools combine to produce a population that is commonly ethnocentric and nationalistic. People are largely ignorant, for example, of the unethical history of the United States, such as the extermination of Indians, the theft of their land through broken treaties, and the domination of other nations through military power. The process of programming includes lies and distortions but mainly relies on selective omission, keeping away information that would dispel collective illusions from the public consciousness.

A teacher is often confronted by students who have tunnel vision—products of the narrow ideology and beliefs reinforced by the media, schools, families, and most civic organizations. Such students need help from a teacher to feel comfortable with unconventional frames of reference and new perspectives. Many feel threatened when they move from conventional indoctrination to education that involves critical analysis. A common initial response of students is to "shoot the messenger," which usually means to feel hostile toward the teacher.

The American propaganda system is not centrally programmed as it is in a totalitarian state. Instead it permeates the culture, the media, and the institutions. Individuals who point out unpleasant realities of current or past American behavior are often subjected to social pressures and treated as pariahs. They are disturbers of the dream. Yet such disturbance, if based on truth, is essential for real education to take place. Liberation from conventional mythology is a prerequisite to leadership and to the development of a citizenry less likely to tolerate the exploitation that was endemic in the institutional structures of the twentieth century.

In the United States truth is available even though it is not always visible to the average citizen. Books that help liberate people's thinking are sometimes used in college courses, and many are found in the larger libraries. It is not uncommon for parents to be horrified at what is happening to their children when they send them to college and find that they have been deprogrammed through the discovery of ideas and books which they have never encountered before. This necessary "disillusioning" process is not an inevitable result of going to college, even in the better colleges, but when it occurs it is most likely to occur in social sciences and humanities courses. Political science, sociology, philosophy, and some history classes are more likely to be productive of liberation from conventional mythology. On the other hand, economics, business, agriculture, mechanics, and engineering are the fields in which students are often kept in cocoons of conventional belief while increasing the skills they will use to serve institutions which perpetuate such beliefs—unless they are fortunate to have an unorthodox teacher who has questioned conventional beliefs.

The academic sub-cultures of the state land grant "agriculture and mechanics" colleges usually differ from those of the liberal arts universities. Universities have usually been based on liberal arts at the undergraduate level with professional areas such as law, medicine, and education at the graduate level, whereas an emphasis on applied technology was the province of the "A and M" colleges. There is often a self-selective difference in the students and faculties in these different institutions, with those in applied fields having the most conventional beliefs. But these differences are increasingly being reduced.

The trap, even for teachers of liberal arts subjects, is that text books are usually descriptive and not value centered. They are usually accurate in presenting facts but do not probe into ethical issues. But exceptional teachers are familiar with books that do probe such issues, and those books become important instruments in "deprogramming." *A People's History of the United States* by Howard Zinn has become a deprogramming favorite. And no one is better than Noam Chomsky for challenging conventional foreign policy myths, though his books are difficult for many readers. (The Odonian Press, however, offers brief, readable Chomsky.)

Teaching students about American imperialistic interventions in Cuba, Vietnam, Grenada, Panama, Nicaragua, and the Dominican Republic in the twentieth century is essential in deprogramming. The treatment of the American Indians and the murderous and exploitative role of Columbus in dealing with the people he encountered are now out of the closet, though "Columbus Day" is still celebrated. Vietnam is slowly becoming a useful and undeniable example of an unethical and misguided foreign policy that resulted in death, mutilation, and sickness on both sides and made use of Agent Orange and land mines. To understand the way in which mass media became a spokesman vehicle for the government and used "national security" and "American interests" in rationalizing that horrendous policy is an important and necessary part of reality therapy.

Americans often wonder why the German people engaged so long in denial of their murderous role in World War II—particularly in regard to the Jews in the infamous death camps such as Auschwitz and Dachau. But the American response to Vietnam was not all that different. The public believed the lies told by the government. True stories must be taught. But this will not occur if Vietnam and the entire Southeast Asia war is treated merely as a "mistake," as Robert McNamara, Kennedy's chief advisor has termed it. Vietnam was no more a technical "mistake" than was Hitler's holocaust. Both involved murder and human behavior at the lowest and most barbaric level. Most soldiers on the ground were trapped in their own defensive survival and rarely had the least understanding of what the war was really about. But some who gave orders each day to have B52s rain bombs on villages knew better. I know people working for the CIA who were required to give a list each week to the American Air Force telling them where to bomb military and civilian targets with B52s. These targets were often villages in Laos and Cambodia. Although they told the Generals that there was often no basis for their prescribing such targets, they were ordered to turn in bombing targets. The B52s needed targets. They got them—regardless.

The entire "anti-communism" ideology became a cover-up for mass murder. The sooner people confront the truth about this episode in American foreign policy, the better. This shame of American history is exhibit A as an antidote for American self-righteousness, which can be one of the most dangerous forces in the world if it continues to guide a nation with dominant world power.

In their book *Hiroshima in America: Fifty Years of Denial*, (1995) Robert Lifton and Greg Mitchell have shown how Americans have been in 50 years of denial about the bombing of Hiroshima. President Truman's lies, the government's extensive distortion of information, and the management of the news media have convinced most Americans that the atomic bombings were necessary to save American lives and end the war. Truman knew this was not true, for negotiations were well under way, leaving only the question of the retention of the Emperor. Then why were the bombs dropped? The bombs were dropped to demonstrate American power prior to Truman's negotiations with Stalin. The advice from the American military, such as Admiral Leahy, had been that "The Japanese were already defeated and ready to surrender." Leahy added that "we adopted an ethical standard common to the barbarians of the Dark Ages (Cousins 1987, 43)."

Yet, to this day it is commonplace in media and in the public mind to treat the atomic bombing as if it had been necessary to save American lives by shortening the war and making an invasion of Japan unnecessary. In fact we kept the Emperor in power even after dropping the bombs and President Truman did *not* get the concessions from Stalin he desired as a result of demonstrating American nuclear power. Blind patriotism has been kept intact by rewriting history to provide people with moral consolation and a psychological basis for denial (Alperovitz 1996).

TEXT BOOKS AS PROPAGANDA

Lies My Teacher Told Me by sociologist James Loewen is a study of American high school approved history texts which reveal omission, lies, and distortions that have been used to make the texts politically suitable to the political requirements of school boards and state education departments. The result is not only that history is boring, but it conceals from students many important truths about their country which perpetuates the belief and myths on which conventional politics is often based.

A People's History of the United States by Howard Zinn is an excellent selection as a standard high school or college history text to compensate for the usual omissions, for it includes most of what is left out of the commonly adopted texts. Typical public school texts are almost invariably the result of informal censorship by the publisher who hopes not to offend the Chamber of Commerce, the American Legion, the churches, the two major political parties, and schools boards of big states such as California and Texas. As a result they are heavily watered down and non-controversial. Getting Zinn's book on the approved list of the state may be no easy matter. The *Library Journal* says: "Zinn has written a brilliant and moving history of the American people from the point of view of those who have been exploited politically and economically and whose plight has been largely omitted from most histories." Zinn's book was reprinted in a paperback edition in 1997 and adapted for classroom teaching and published by The New Press, New York.

By the time an American student graduates from high school there are certain basics he should know, such as how the Monroe Doctrine (in 1823) put forth the American position that the western hemisphere was our sphere of influence. Zinn points out that for the rest of the nineteenth century Americans acted on this self-proclaimed doctrine with the following violations of other countries' rights in the western hemisphere. In the Harper and Row 1980 edition he lists interventions from a list given by the State Department as follows:

- 1852-53—Argentina. Marines were landed and maintained in Buenos Aires to protect American interests during revolution.

- 1853—Nicaragua—To protect American lives and interest during political disturbances.

- 1854—Nicaragua—San Juan del Norte. Greytown was destroyed to avenge an insult to the American Minister to Nicaragua.

- 1855—Uruguay—U.S. and European naval forces landed to protect American interests during an attempted revolution in Montevideo.

- 1893—Hawaii—Ostensibly to protect American lives and property, actually to promote a provisional government under Sanford B. Dole. This action was disavowed by the United States.

- 1894—Nicaragua—to protect American interests at Bluefiels following a revolution.

As Zinn states:

> "Thus by the1890s, there had been much experience in overseas probes and interventions. The ideology of expansion was widespread in the upper circles of military men, politicians, businessmen—and even among some of the leaders of farmers' movements who thought foreign markets would help them (1997a, 291)."

This list does not include U.S. incursions into Japanese territory, China, Africa, or Russia. There was so much U.S. intervention in the twentieth century that history text books need to make sure that at least the Latin American interventions following the issuance of the Monroe Doctrine are part of the public record. ("Intervention" is the nice word usually used for an invasion when we are the invaders.)

While America's students were given the impression that the United States invaded other countries as defenders of "freedom and democracy," the record, again as summarized by Zinn, is that the United States:

> Instigated a war with Mexico and took half of that country. It had pretended to help Cuba win freedom from Spain, and then plant-ed itself in Cuba with a military base, investments, and rights of intervention. It seized Hawaii, Puerto Rico, Guam, and fought a brutal war to subjugate the Filipinos. It "opened" Japan to its trade with gunboats and threats. It declared an "Open Door Policy" in China as a means of assuring that the United States would have opportunities equal to other imperial powers in exploiting China. It sent troops to Peking with other nations to assert Western supremacy in China, and kept them there for over thirty years (Zinn 1980, 399).

But since we had self-proclaimed rights to the western hemisphere, we insti-tuted a *closed* door policy, engineering a revolution against Colombia and put Panama under our control to build the Canal. Then we sent 5,000 marines to Nicaragua in 1926 to stop a revolution and remained there for seven years. In 1916 we intervened in the Dominican Republic for the fourth time and stayed with troops for eight years, while troops were kept in Haiti in a 1915 invasion for 19 years. As Zinn again points out:

> Between 1900 and 1933 the United States intervened in Cuba four times, in Nicaragua twice, and Panama six times, in Guatemala once, in Honduras seven times. By 1924 the finances of half of the twenty Latin American states were being directed to some extent by the United States. By 1935, over half of U.S. steel and cotton exports were being sold in Latin America (399).

When these invasions are brought to light, a programmed American will like-ly say they were justified by our desire to help democracy in other parts of the world. In truth, it was just the opposite. As Noam Chomsky's 1992 book *Deterring Democracy* points out in detail, the American government was making sure that democracy did not break out, for American business inter-ests and political and military power would then be jeopardized. Time after time, the United States put in dictators, trained their armies, and encouraged them to use violence and repression against their own people to prevent the rise of democracy.

Chomsky comes on too strong for most Americans who are in the first phase of deprogramming, such as credulous Americans who have been brought up on *Reader's Digest* and *Newsweek*. But after Zinn, some readers could be exposed to Chomsky's brutally honest material. Here he summarizes it:

> We overthrew Guatemala in 1954, and have maintained the rule of murderous gangsters ever since, ran by far the most extensive international terror operations in history against Cuba from the early 1960s and Nicaragua through the 1980s, sought to assassinate Lumumba and installed and maintained the brutal and corrupt Mobutu dictatorship, backed Trujillo, Somoza, Marcos, Duvalier, the generals of the southern cone, Suharto, the racist rulers of southern Africa, and a whole host of other major criminals (1992, 14).

He also points out, quoting Howard French (*New York Times,* May 8, 1990) in *Turning the Tide* that

> ...there had been no prior free elections (in the Dominican Republic) because of repeated U.S. interventions, including long support for the murderer and torturer Trujillo until he began to interfere with U.S. interests. But when Juan Bosch was elected it was claimed he was a Marxist, though he advocated policies similar to those of the Kennedy Democrats. The U.S. was then instrumental in undermining him and quickly backed the new military regime.

> When the populous arose to restore constitutional rule in 1965, the U.S. sent 23,000 troops on utterly fraudulent pretexts to avert the threat of democracy, establishing the standard regime of death squads, torture, repression, slave labor conditions, increase poverty and malnutrition, vast emigration, and wonderful opportunities for its own investors, and tolerating the 'free election' of 1966 only when the playing field had been leveled by ample terror (72).

My first book *Education for Annihilation* included some of this history when it was published in 1972, but more and more information is available now which puts the pieces together. In 1997, a book by Seymour Hersh, titled *The Dark Side of Camelot* (1997), documented the many times the U.S.— with the help of the CIA—had plotted and tried to assassinate Castro. At the end of the twentieth century Cuba was the only western hemisphere country to hold out against American domination even though the United States had used military invasion, blockade, embargo, and many assassination attempts.

Cuba and the United States are the supreme examples of David and Goliath. American legislators have visited Cuba with the hope of returning to the U.S. with reports that counter revolution is ripe. They have been quiet after visits, for most Cubans were found to be highly supportive of Castro and the revolution, and moreover, they live at a level far above the third world regimes the U.S. has previously targeted for "democracy," even after being subjected to 50 years of American strangulation.

How to Read a Newspaper

Educating students for democratic citizenship requires helping them learn to analyze the daily newspaper. Some of this can be done by simply comparing the more liberal to the more conservative papers. But an astute reader needs to be able to probe the underlying message. What is the hidden agenda? What is the editorial or the political column really getting at? How is "news" selected from the vast number of events that happen?

Begin by asking: What politics is being promoted? Whose future is being served? Is it those who have or those who do not? The educated citizen needs to understand newspapers first as businesses that rely primarily on revenue from advertising. That reliance means that they must attract a maximum number of customers as does commercial television. Therefore, they typically have no primary commitment to the education of readers. They seek rather to move the public into the same political belief system (ideology) as the advertisers and newspaper owners—usually part of a corporate conglomerate. They are involved in what some sociologists call the "social construction of reality."

In fact they usually have a commitment to "reverse education," for the best way to serve ideology and political propaganda is through *selective exclusion.* Much news coverage is about the stock market and new businesses, with much less on labor and labor unions, and very little about hardship in the lives of the poor or about environmental degradation. But when those topics are included, news coverage seldom probes into causes or solutions.

Moreover, when solutions are considered, they are rarely proposals to restructure the political or economic system, but instead typically call for "personal responsibility" as the main device to avoid basic systems change. Any radical proposal such as economic democracy is likely to be weakened by merely calling for more "local control" or "home rule."

The political columns in newspapers are where editors can feel free to allow political advocacy, so in making their selections, they usually claim to "balance" advocacy by including one column that is liberal-Democratic and another that is conservative-Republican. Such columns are actually expressive of only two different views of capitalism—one is capitalism with some social conscience, the other is capitalism based on self-interest and with minimum social conscience. Since both represent corporate capitalism neither advocates a basic shift in power or priorities.

The underlying issue in most political columns is *who should get what?* Liberals think that there should be some sharing of the wealth and that government should be involved in effecting it. Conservatives generally think that competition produces a natural order of distribution and that economic inequality is natural, normal, and acceptable.

Since a country such as Cuba constitutes an ideological threat to the U.S. it is most likely to get bad press. Newspaper reports about Cuba refer to "communist Cuba" whereas reports about the United States are never stated as "capitalistic United States."

Under capitalism, people's basic needs are supposed to be satisfied by the "trickle down" effect of the expanding wealth at the top. When trickle-down leaves people in poverty, liberals expect that public funds should mitigate the effects, while conservatives expect private charity to do the job. These are the alternatives offered by most newspapers.

The American press, operating in the name of "freedom" of the press under the First Amendment of the Constitution, is able to "educate" a public to have little or no idea of structural or systemic solutions for poverty or environmental degradation. With television and the press as the primary sources of information we can understand why people live in "windowless cocoons." Information comes through in disconnected, fragmented pieces, without helping the reader make connections. There is no connection of the "dots."

Newspaper reporters who are more liberal than its owners and editors may produce reports which reveal the structure of local politics and often find them to be edited or eliminated. The process is actually much like censorship in the state owned papers of dictatorial and communist countries. The power to include and exclude constitutes political power. Newspaper ownership is increasingly tied to a handful of national corporations that control papers throughout the country.

The newspaper should be thought of as a kind of lobby, except that the agenda of a lobby is up front. With the press, one must try to find the hidden agenda. This won't give a 100 percent interpretive track record but it will come close and permits rapid understanding of the groups—the rich, the poor, corporate power, etc.—that are really being supported. The *Wall Street Journal* is explicit about an ideological commitment to capitalism and is useful for seeing how propaganda can be transmitted with the appearance of objectivity, since the paper conveys a large amount of data.

Propaganda by omission is the most effective form of public control because it can include accurate facts, and if the facts are correct most people think they are getting reliable information. Selecting the facts to be used is a powerful form of politics: for it defines the knowable reality. Defining reality is a way to control alternatives and influence policy and perception and in effect to exert control over the future. The First Amendment of the Constitution, which provides for "freedom of the press," actually provides opportunity for a process called the *engineering of consent* by which people are manipulated to support policies while believing that they have made up their own mind.

THE STRATEGIC USE OF TRIVIA

How can we judge the responsibility of the press? Papers have various levels of reputation for good reporting, but the main standard of success from the point of view of most papers is not based on journalistic responsibility and achievement but on business success. Simply, is the paper profitable? If a public can be lulled into treating trivia as "news," a generation can be raised which will buy a paper to fill out the crossword puzzle and to read the horoscope. And as pages are turned, bits and pieces of reports, usually organized by a centralized news business agency (Associated Press, etc.), catch the eye with particular attention to what is shocking or sensational. As the reader is drawn into disaster stories, the paper serves a therapeutic role. How fortunate the reader feels, that he or she was not on that plane when it crashed or on the side of that volcano that has just erupted. Thus the stream of "information" in our "information society!" It presumes to represent progress, by making the modern citizen well informed.

The philosophy underlying the First Amendment was ostensibly to provide the foundation of a democratic society in which a self-governing people would have the information they need to govern and elect with intelligence. This momentous addition to human evolution has achieved some success, especially by opening the society to alternate media—newspapers, magazines, and radio—which are often highly informative. But the diet of mass media in the local grocery store, in most community libraries, and in the daily newspapers serves mainly what I call "deflection politics."

Yet people can break through conventional newspaper propaganda by using the following methods:

- Assume that the editorials and the columnists are always saying the same thing with respect to the political values they are supporting. New events are then simply new excuses to write yet another column or editorial supporting the same old ideology. For example, a conservative may consistently select news about government to encourage the reader to be anti-government.

- Be prepared for discussions about issues that appear to be unrelated to politics but are designed to draw you into the editor's view of life. Touting the bravery for a war time hero can metamorphose into support of the current Pentagon budget.

- Assume that most reporting is really about whether the oligarchy is being supported (by conservatives); whether social programs are advocated (by liberals), or whether basic change of the economic system is advocated (by socialists: though they are virtually non-existent in American mass media).

- Assume that virtually all the material in the mass media involves a kind of ping-pong game between conservatives and liberals. Do not expect "conservatives" to conserve—the term is more deflection politics.

Look for the corporations that own the paper. The board of directors may be in New York while your local newspaper, 2,000 miles away, is making a profit for them and exporting the profits made from your community. They are unlikely to care about local issues.

Here are some examples of how daily news can be interpreted:

George Will—Conservative, supports the oligarchy.

Method: Clever use of indirect topics using erudition and cynicism that are intended to convince the reader that the writer is brilliant therefore believable.

His writing is consistently anti-big government, pro-smaller government, and for a larger private sector which means more corporate power. He supports such issues as school vouchers for they move the public schools into the private (capitalistic) sector. He talks about baseball, so people will accept him as "one of theirs." Yet he derides unions and the politics that strengthen the working class. According to Will, "free trade" and the "market" are the gods which the public should learn to worship. Economic

inequality is a taboo topic. It is not a matter of ethical consideration but is presumed to be justified as the result of the wisdom of
the market, the natural order of social Darwinism, or the motivation to make people work hard.

Molly Ivins—-Liberal, criticizes conservatives; supports the
working class and the environment.

Method: uses humor and irony and argues in reverse of George
Will—for public schools, for unions, for minimum wages, for
greater income equality, against Pentagon spending, for use of
government to help people instead of subsidizing the rich. She
provides an offset to the predominant middle-to-the-right posi-
tioning of most columnists.

Other common columnists are usually found in one of these same positions
with respect to democracy versus the oligarchy. *The Wall Street Journal* and
Business Week are primary media vehicles for the business community and
multinational corporations. Unlike every other industrial country we have no
common American paper which represents labor. *The Nation* and *The
Progressive* are two established liberal/progressive magazines, but they are not
likely to be found in high school libraries. *Time* and *Newsweek* which **are** the
most likely to be in those libraries, give the appearance of being moderate but
are owned by and serve corporate interests. Most newspapers are captives of
the dominant industries of their state: Big oil in Texas—Big timber in
Oregon and Washington—Big mining in Colorado—Big Pentagon in
Georgia—Big real estate in Florida—Big high tech in California.

Economists are often used to tell "the truth" about the economy, but they
inevitably are taking a political position that constitutes ideology. For instance
Milton Friedman, an influential economist from the Chicago school, now at
the Hoover Institute, writes articles that try to justify inequality in the name
of "freedom." Thomas Sowell also in the Hoover Institute is nationally syndi-
cated to serve the same ideology. The political effect of such writers is to minimize public revolt against structural inequality. Their "think tank" receives
substantial funds from the wealthy economic class that they serve.

Schools that limit their objectives to literacy so that students can merely read
the words of a newspaper will be playing into the hands of the political mis-
sions of the newspapers, for students will not have the knowledge to de-code
the messages. Word literacy without political literacy encourages a *Reader's
Digest* level of awareness about the American way of life. Their reliance upon
the media will make them media fodder, which will prepare them to serve the
oligarchy. Or if they happen to develop some sense of social justice and

empathize with underdogs they may gravitate into liberal politics. However, they are not likely to know that both conservatism and liberalism in the United States are based only on slightly different views of the role of corporate capitalism. Democratic education would also include alternatives other than corporate capitalism.

DEFLECTION POLITICS

The dominant pattern of ideas, information, and beliefs to which Americans are exposed constitute what Chomsky calls the *necessary illusions.* These illusions permit the engineering of consent which empowers the ruling class (Herman and Chomsky 1988).

According to Michael Parenti the "free press" mainly serves: "to make the communication universe safe for corporate America, telling us what to think about the world before we have a chance to think about it ourselves. When we understand that news selectivity is likely to favor those who have power, position, and wealth, we may move from a liberal complaint about the press's sloppy performance to a radical analysis of how the media serve the ruling circles all too well with much skill and craft (1998, 157)."

The big leap in public consciousness comes when people see that they have been duped and put into an intellectual cage, a "windowless cocoon" that confines their thoughts and beliefs. People don't like to be duped and exploited—for self-respect is threatened when we are manipulated and not treated as a human being. Stage one in becoming politically literate democratic citizens is for people to be angry about how they have been duped.

For example when people have been intellectually straight jacketed in religious orthodoxy, their rebirth often requires some way of seeing what has happened to them—by comparing their religion with others or by understanding the way their religion has enslaved. This is why every attempt at having a cloistered child see what is happening to him is avoided, by restricting the social group, putting him/her in a private religious school, or even keeping him/her in home schooling to prevent contamination by unorthodox ideas. Effective personality programming comes with the early use of religious symbolism, stories, and songs that often resonate perpetually in the child's sub-consciousness. Faith based religions such as Islam and Christianity, because of absolutistic metaphysics, typically use practitioners of a form of "hypnosis" to manipulate belief. The motive may be to provide power to the practitioner but it is often the logical result of absolutism that treats particular beliefs as categorically right or wrong. This form of "politics" is contradictory to the rational process on which democracy must be based, and in the George W. Bush administration this faith based politics became a challenge to the rational standards of democratic philosophy. The same process is typically used in political and cultural indoctrination. Using consumerism, technology worship, nationalism, flag salutes, stories of the bravery of wartime heroes, is standard programming. But the far more subtle and pervasive influence is accomplished by the use of **trivia and distraction from uncomfortable truths**. Many people are mainly interested in the comfort of pleasant fantasy and place a low value on truth. This produces failure of democratic socialization in the values of reason, science, and logic.

The *fragmentation of reality* is also a powerful tool, used in mass media and much of what is called "education." Being provided with bits and pieces of information and data without ways to provide connecting coherence, people fail to gain intellectual power. Those who try to remember many things not worth remembering usually do not realize that they are treating their mind as a form of garbage can. This mind-set can then focus on irrelevant minutia for the rest of a person's life. It is one of the most useful attributes of technician training, for people learn not to ask why, not to wonder for what? A world cadre of detail-oriented, obedient technicians is just what is needed in a "brave new world" of corporate industrial power. People do not need to be directly controlled by a totalitarian state if they are intellectually paralyzed. The human mind can be crippled in the same way as the human body, and all forms of autocratic control, military training most notably, require conditioned responses so the dominator "owns" the behavior of the trainee. Mass commercial culture is a kind of shepherd controlling the sheep.

The magazines and newspapers at the corner supermarket are exhibit A. Sex, violence, romance, sports, how to fix things, and escape stories are paraded by the hundreds in the most attention-getting covers. All of these would be useful in a totalitarian state for they would provide the necessary distraction from the realities of the world and the failures of government.

Community surveys are a good place to begin deprogramming. Start in the magazine rack of the supermarket, in the selection of magazines in the local library, in school textbooks, in the local newspaper, in the radio and in local TV programs. **How much of what you see is trivia and distraction from the human condition?** When human suffering is illuminated, how much is mere sensationalism—selling the material, but not suggesting we do anything about it?

The trap which makes self-evaluation difficult is that a person cannot see what is omitted without some understanding of the problems, issues, and alternatives in the world. The teaching of history in the schools usually concentrates on trivia. But a good teacher has the tools of literature and the selection of other than authorized history books. As a high school teacher I used such novels as John Hersey's *Hiroshima*, Steinbeck's *Grapes of Wrath*, and Upton Sinclair's *The Jungle* to help students identify with the plight of people facing serious challenges and to stimulate social consciousness.

For the more advanced students the remarkable tapes available from Alternative Radio (see the bibliography) take people from the trivia of most textbooks and mass media into an analysis of our society by the top intellectuals of our time—the people usually excluded from appearing on mass media.

 The best teachers are likely to be those who are exceptional in moral qualities and courage, who for example may have been active in protesting violations of human rights. If they have done nothing as democratic citizens their qualifications to set an example are limited. And unconventional materials appearing in the newsletters of small organizations throughout the country may be good curriculum material in the sense that they often reveal the problems and issues covered up by the daily newspapers.

Tricks We Use on Ourselves: Consolation Politics

People commonly use self-deception to avoid the pain of confronting reality. When we are told all our lives that we live in the greatest nation in the world and which is also guided by God ("one nation under God") it is very difficult to avoid *self-righteousness nationalism*. Conventional myths protect us from facing up to the obvious. For example, the immoral, unlawful, murderous invasion of Vietnam where Americans were involved in genocide and in behavior much too similar to Hitler's—becomes difficult for programmed Americans to accept. Yet, in fact, the defeat of the United States in that war was a valuable moral lesson in that *no redeeming results would have occurred if the United States had won.* The lesson was later used by groups opposed to similar intervention in Central America in the 1980s. When the American government continued the Vietnam pattern by engineering the killing of villagers in Central America, activists used the Vietnam lesson to arouse massive protest which helped save Central American liberals, leftists, and villagers from full-scale slaughter.

Examples of consolation politics:

1. We blame the market: e.g., we tell ourselves that forests disappear because of market economics.

2. We blame supernatural deterministic forces: e.g. it's the will of God, or trends beyond human control.

3. We blame the Communists/or Liberals or other categories that serve as devils: e.g., in Germany in the 1930s Jews served this purpose. In the United States, government is categorically a devil for many people. This serves corporate power.

4. We shift responsibility to the "leader." We were just doing what we were told—obeying.

5. We seek out novels, entertainment, and recreation which can keep our attention on what is "pleasant." This becomes an addiction protecting us from reality.

6. We act as if the meaning of life is to produce and consume. When boredom occurs, we go shopping. When the bank account increases, we buy a new car. Such distraction avoids the unpleasantness of much of the poverty and exploitation of people throughout the world—often created by governments supported by our policies.

7. We fall back on a time-worn homily or a comforting cliché: "the poor are always with us," to avoid responsibility to do anything about poverty.

THE RESPONSIBILITY OF EDUCATORS

Education which serves the public and future generations helps people understand the forces that undermine democracy and human rights. Such teachers need to hold up a mirror that permits students to take a different look at themselves, to help them extricate themselves from the symbolic entrapments of corporate dominated culture so that they can provide leadership toward a better future. Terms such as *deflection politics* and *consolation politics* may be useful instruments for the analysis of experience and for defense against propaganda.

Social thinkers from Wells to Toynbee have repeatedly argued that global society is in a race between education and catastrophe.

—Paul Kennedy

I know of no country in which there is so little independence of mind and real freedom of discussion as in America.

—Alexis de Tocqueville

EDUCATION FOR DEMOCRACY

I consider this a book on "education" because understanding needs to precede political action. The tie between education and politics is inextricable and within it lies the potential for a transformed future. Education is formalized in schools, but the media and all informal contacts are part of our education. Radio, television, and the non-mainstream press are often more involved in issues-education than the schools. When this book refers to "education," that term encompasses schools plus all institutions that transmit information and ideas.

Democratic education should help people participate in the needed transition to assert democratic control over both the political and economic process. The inventions called institutions are now often used to control the minds of people so that they become followers, not democratic citizens. Redirection is needed for twenty-first century education.

Most twentieth century education:

- Trained people to become employable but not as democratic citizens
- Helped shift power to the corporations
- Ignored environmental issues
- Taught capitalist economics
- Ignored public planning
- Was nationalist and ethnocentric

Twenty-first Century Education Should:

- Educate people to become democratic citizens
- Shift power from corporations to people

- Teach ecological planning
- Teach humanistic economics
- Focus on long-range goals
- Shift to global perspectives

ROLES AND QUALITIES OF TEACHER

Howard Zinn has said, "The choice is between teaching and acting according to our most deeply felt values, whether or not it meets approval from those with power over us—or being dishonest with ourselves, censoring ourselves, in order to be safe (Zinn 1997a)."

The institutional pressures to conform to local beliefs are very great, and most people capitulate. The pressures are also strong to adopt the mores of communities, where orthodoxies tied to religion, politics, and economics brand people as accepted or as heretics, often affecting their ability to earn a living. Most people learn little by little to bend with the wind and do what is expected, even though "deeply felt values" and even common sense are violated incrementally until people hold few convictions of their own.

As a result the people called "leaders" often have sold themselves many times over to gain power and wealth, while the actual leaders are committed to uphold values that serve people. Such leaders are both honest and morally courageous. In the conformist world, courage is measured through physical acts such as climbing mountains. But courage needs to be tied to intellectual and moral courage—saying and doing what we strongly believe is right and are willing to defend even though we may be subjecting ourselves to criticism.

A teacher should have these qualities and try to cultivate these qualities in students—thinking critically and being willing to resist pressures from others. Democracy is not created by conformist consensus but by thoughtful consideration of diverse points of view. A superior teacher encourages students to ask questions about the meaning of life. Are we to just have fun and satisfy our desires, reproduce and then die, or do we want to become more human by living significantly and affecting some change in the historical process?

The difference is in being an object or in being a person. Economic institutions may turn us into commodities in order to create more commodities. People then become part of a treadmill and follow others who are themselves part of a collective treadmill in a state of perpetual motion. When we teach courses such as math, chemistry, and other natural sciences, they may be taught merely about facts, skills, and techniques. But the core of being a democratic citizen is about asserting ourselves as human beings and using knowledge in a socially valuable way, facilitating a process whereby others can also become persons rather than objects. Critical thinking, dissent, and questioning of authority provide the power for being a democratic citizen.

In our own society, we need to work against authoritarian institutions—cultivate those that enhance community well-being and include public policies that promote human rights and a healthful environment. Many of our institutions are anti-democratic and authoritarian, the military being the most obvious. But many businesses are also anti-democratic and authoritarian, and conservative churches are often structured to produce intellectual passivity.

The role of the teacher should be to encourage moral qualities in people to help them gain responsible power over authoritarian institutions. This is largely a way of defining democracy. It means that a teacher must not be the hired puppet of a school board, a principal, a superintendent or president of a corporation. A true educational role is served when the teacher is helping students learn intellectual processes and ethical social objectives. For a teacher to accept any other role would be like a doctor selling out the health of a patient in order to obey orders of a hospital administrator. The ethical connection between teacher and student is profound and must often be used to override the arbitrary power of those in charge of the institution.

Of course all of this has a larger purpose—namely, to help convert the arbitrary power of any institution into a system of governance that provides participatory power for those it serves. Twentieth century authoritarian institutions should be converted into democratic institutions in the twenty-first century, and it is the responsibility of the teacher to help facilitate this historic transition. What is at stake is **truth** and the rational process that must underlie democracy. A teacher must welcome and even encourage students who offer better arguments and information than the teacher does, for both profit by the knowledge. This rational dialogue is the foundation of democracy and anyone who does not want to participate in democracy building should not consider teaching in public schools.

The Objectivity Trap

"We're proud of being objective in our reporting," is a typical statement of a newspaper publisher. This word "objective" needs closer analysis.

It is easiest to begin by pointing out what "objective" is not. A story about an event which distorts facts to the point that witnesses can say, "That is not at all what really happened," can then be called non-objective. But if a report of an event has all the facts right, is it then "objective"?

A cluster of facts requires interpretation and explanation. At that point, what is the requirement for being "objective"? If someone was beaten up by the police should there be a **judgment** of wrongdoing? Or should it be said simply that the citizen was clubbed without suggesting the cruelty of the act? If it is reported as "cruel," a value judgment is attached. That judgment comes from an ethical principle, such as "people are important and should not be treated cruelly." This might be virtually the same as the assumption of the "worth and dignity of the human person," the most universal of ethical principles.

So this raises the question of whether there is an "obligation" to help a reader see that a moral or ethical issue is at stake. If so, then the idea of a report being "objective" would in many cases make the report "unethical" if it treated people as objects merely to be described without any value judgment, as though people existed in an ethical vacuum.

The logic of this argument is that facts should be accurate, but reporting about people should suggest whether human rights issues are involved, and give an indication of what the issue is. A description of the **effects on people** then becomes appropriate, and reporting, whether in newspapers or by academics, becomes a way of focusing on events that bear on the well-being of people.

An explanatory theory should use the same humanistic analysis. For instance it is commonplace to report unemployment in relation to labor supply and demand, but not dare to question the ethics of the explanation that treats people like commodities. Prices of goods are usually given the same "objective" and detached reporting as the unemployment of people—yet the unemployed, particularly those who are blocked from employment for institutional reasons, are being treated cruelly if unemployment is unnecessary. Capitalist supply and demand should not be treated as an accepted dogma, but rather evaluated on pragmatic consequences such as whether people are finding employment opportunities.

The myth of "objectivity" permits people to stand outside the real world, providing excuses to look in but to do nothing about the injustices they see. When people should be conveying some sense of outrage at an injustice, they often treat human events as mere data.

For publishing, teaching, writing, or broadcasting, responsible communication should indicate that people are affected and suggest whether their predicament is necessary or unnecessary. Even more, whenever possible the solution should be suggested. In the case of compulsory unemployment, there is no ethical excuse. A technical obstacle does not exist—only an ideological obstacle. In a society that calls itself advanced and progressive, we have not met the achievement of even the most "primitive" societies that always have work for everyone and a chance for all to participate in the productive process.

A fundamental error is to equate "objectivity" with "neutrality." We must be accurate with information, but being neutral about people and the institutions we have invented means we have failed to assign ethical values to them. By transferring the idea of "objective" science from the physical world to the social world, which is common in descriptive university publications, we often avoid ethics and human rights. Such belief and behavior are endemic in our current society. It undermines the potential of education to develop responsible connections between people.

Education should not be propaganda serving a particular ideology, nor should it be neutral. I have often seen sensitive and competent teachers who think "both sides" need to be brought in because "truth lies in the middle." One teacher always used both *Time* and *Newsweek* to reveal "both sides" and didn't see that this only duplicated the same ideology. The only reason to bring in different points of view is to get better information and better analysis of the ethical issues. There is no reason to think that truth is in the "middle" of the sides. Was the "truth" somewhere between Martin Luther King, Jr. and the Ku Klux Klan? Students should be learning to ask the kinds of questions that permit them to see through the propaganda, mythology, and distortion that lead most people to accept the beliefs and institutions that exploit people and destroy our planetary life-support system. The "objectivity" ploy is part of the problem.

STUDENT AS HISTORY CREATOR

We have no choice about whether or not to be a history creator, because whatever we do or whatever we fail to do, we will be determiners of some of the future. Those who believe they have chosen to be non-political do not understand the nature of political power. Since we can choose to participate in shaping public policy, the failure to participate simply shifts decision making to others, giving them greater power. The **failure** to use the power we have to vote, lobby, join interest groups, and run for office, is therefore a political "act." We **cannot** be non-political.

Since the institutions we have created in the past carry the power to shape the future, the assessment of institutions is crucial to our destiny. No institution is more important than the school for having the opportunity to help people understand where the current world is going, what the alternatives are, what our responsibilities are in choosing the best alternative, and how to be effective in participating in directing the future. **This knowledge is the substance of citizenship education.**

But the Catch 22 is that the schools like all other institutions in our society are rooted in traditions that were established before the new era developed. The focus has been on teaching the three R's, some principles of math and science, and a few skills such as typing (now computer skills). This permitted people to be employable and to meet the demands of everyday life.

A major educational challenge is to identify the kind of politics and economics that is appropriate for this new era of mandatory global cooperation between peoples and nations. **This means designing the future rather than merely adjusting to trends. It does not mean uprooting all traditions, for it is the current world that indiscriminately obliterates traditions for short range economic profit.** Rather, we now need to evaluate traditions so that we support those that are valuable and change those that threaten the well being of the human future.

The current world is rife with myths and self-fulfilling prophecies that keep the old order intact. Education should help students demystify and demythify. Among the leading contenders are beliefs such as "peace through strength," "growth equals progress," and "you can't stop progress."

ESSENTIAL KNOWLEDGE

THE TRAGEDY OF THE COMMONS

Garrett Hardin's "parable of the commons" (1968) is one of the most essential educational concepts, for it refers to competition within finite resources and how such expansion finally produces collapse when the carrying capacity is exceeded. Students should all understand why the collapse occurs and design alternatives to avoid collapse.

Specific modern-day situations that illustrate the concept include ocean conditions which have produced the collapse of the sardine fishery in California and Peru, the over fishing that has caused near-collapse of cod in the Atlantic, the use of the finite global biosphere for CO_2 disposal, the degradation which has resulted from the use of the Mississippi river by each separate community putting its sewage in the river, and the destruction of natural systems such as forests.

Solutions involve creating an enforceable method that will preserve or sustain the resources. This may mean shifting away from traditional geographic units to political units based on ecosystems. In the case of oceans, there is a need for a sustainable regulatory mechanism for the entire ocean. In the case of the Mississippi River, there is a need to have a political system that supersedes the geographical area of local communities. In the case of the global atmosphere, an enforceable system of world law needs to override the self-interest sovereignty of nations.

Systems Education

We are currently trapped by the old conception of knowledge which says that "facts" are what count. This leads us to treat "data" and "information" as knowledge.

The natural sciences make use of "systems" such as solar systems, the circulatory system of the body, the respiratory system, etc. Engineers use a systems approach to build bridges and make electronic components. But this is all within the principles of physics and mechanics. Engineers do not work with "ecosystems." They only work within ecosystems when they are required to do so. Biological systems and social systems are in a different domain.

We teach history as a description of the past, not as systems, yet the best approach to history teaching would probably be a systems approach, such as by asking "What international system was in place or what could have been in place that might have averted World War II?" Marxist history is systems history, but systems history does not need to be Marxist. A systems approach can help us design the future by seeing that if we had different economic and political systems in place in the past, war, poverty, and environmental degradation could have been avoided.

If we are to identify our major problems as retention of obsolete systems, we need to shift to a systems approach to design new systems. Education will then include ecological systems, political systems, and economic systems. If an obsolete economic system produces poverty we can either try to "fix" it by tinkering with it or take steps toward structural changes in the economic system. The fix currently used involves mitigative fixes to poverty. This is much like using an aspirin to cure cancer. It would, at best, merely mask symptoms. The current dominant method of treating major social diseases is to react to the symptoms. The result is that the basic causes of the problems continue. Since many factors influence social justice and even human survival, our error in failing to consider alternative systems is tragic.

Through years of teaching systems alternatives I have found that students learn these concepts easily. The human mind operates well to grasp concepts and ideas that in association produce whole clusters of meaningful information held together in a gestalt. The human mind seeks "meaning," while the computer is happy with data. The human mind directed toward solving vital issues and searching for systems alternatives may find the computer to be a useful tool. But when there is no **systematic** social direction, the computer program guides the human mind into technical computer logic.

The result is the failure to use human intelligence to control technology for human purposes, and even worse, **the crippling of mental potential by converting education into technical training**. The human mind then atrophies from a creative organ to a mechanistic robot programmed by computer logic. Hal, in the movie 2001: A Space Odyssey, suggested how this kind of mentality can be brilliant but dangerous. It does not care for the human consequences of what it does—only for technical efficiency. It is amoral.

NEGATIVE CAUSALITY

Since there are a variety of political "systems" which can influence historical events—the current nation-state system, the capitalist system, communist systems, etc.—we can move to a new level of causality by suggesting the possibility that a factor which was not present might be considered a *primary cause*. For instance, there was no world law or global peacekeeping system in the 1930s. Lack of any international structure to prevent war might then be considered a cause of war. In designing the future and looking at policy alternatives, we can take a new look at history and ask not only what antecedent events were in the system (positive causation) but also what may have been **lacking** which, if added in the future, might change the outcome. What was lacking can be called "negative causality."

After World War II, it was in fact precisely this logic that gave impetus to a new institution—The United Nations. It was expressly designed to help prevent the "scourge of war" in the future but adding something new that hadn't been there. But the UN system was not sufficiently "radical" for it largely retained the old nation-state and kept power in the nations that had emerged as the winners of World War II, providing them with the power to nullify creation of a supra-national system by authorizing veto power to members of the Security Council.

Negative causality opens human imagination to a new level of creativity and hope. Instead of "freedom" meaning only an individual's freedom to adapt to established institutions, it can also mean that people can redesign institutions and put them under control of the public.

People who call themselves "realists" reject basic changes in institutions and want to retain established international and national systems. This preserves the power of the status quo, largely the rich and the powerful. Since World War II such "realism" led to acceptance of the bi-polar power struggle between the Soviet Union and the United States and the nearly 50-year-long Cold War. With the demise of the Soviet Union, the realists have treated the dominance of the United States as the reality that prevails and must continue to prevail. American military superiority has permitted continuation of priorities based on the first consideration being continuation of the military-industrial complex instead of on social needs.

Marx provided a structural explanation of social conditions, treating capitalism as a "system" which produced predictable effects. To the extent that he was correct we can use the general approach of systems analysis to compare capitalism with other "systems" in order to identify the system that will produce the best outcomes. This applies some science to politics. Similarly we can compare the current system of the sovereignty of nations with a system of world law (supra-national representative law).

We can ask why we have unemployment, and the answer might be given in terms of recent interest rates and the vagaries of the international market. But all that is a way of explaining in relation to positive causality. If, however, we say "there is unemployment because of the lack of enforceable employment rights," we are using negative causality—namely that **what is not in the system is the main cause.** Then what could be added is a way to not only explain current unemployment but also to suggest what could be added to the political system to produce a desirable outcome.

Understanding different kinds of causality should be incorporated into twenty-first century education. Negative causality is a new concept that I have developed and is not found by that term in current educational materials. It may be one of the most useful educational tools for breaking through the tunnel vision of conventional thought and opening up alternatives which can be used to help solve our most serious problems.

THE ETHNOCENTRIC TRAP: GROWING UP ABSURD

Culture Against Man is the title of a 1968 book by Jules Henry, an anthropologist who broke away from the conventional view that human development should consist of passive enculturation by which we induct people into the habits and beliefs of society. He encouraged the "active" role of people involved in creating culture.

This insight is vital to bring in a new era in human evolution that would free the human spirit from dominance by myth and mysticism, used so often to colonize people. We think of "primitive" societies as those that have created many deceptions to give order and meaning to their way of life, but the modern world still inducts people into beliefs and habits that deprive people of control over their institutions.

When culture in the name of either religion or patriotism is dogmatic and absolutistic, it can turn into totalitarianism where people learn obedience rituals that make them controllable to serve either the purposes of a church or a state. The United States has struggled with the issues of church and state and has confused the constitutional separation by quoting on its currency "in God we trust." In countless communities in the United States people salute a flag—a compulsory loyalty oath—in which their nation is "under God," before they begin their deliberations. ("Under God" was slipped in during the Eisenhower administration.) The authority of "God" is invariably joined to the state to justify military invasions to advance the cause of "peace and freedom."

Narrow nationalism is on the decline in the more educated areas of the world, but the religious belief system that is embracing the entire world is "moneytheism." Most economic courses taught in universities treat capitalist economics as "truth" rather than as "belief"—not as merely a theoretical construct but often as a secular religion. Those who believe are being inducted into the prevailing business-economics "in-group." Harvey Cox, Professor of Divinity at Harvard University wrote the following in the *Atlantic Monthly:*

> At the apex of any theological system, of course, is its doctrine of God. In the new theology this celestial pinnacle is occupied by The Market, which I capitalize to signify both the mystery that enshrouds it and the reverence it inspires in business . . . The Market, we are assured, possesses these divine attributes; they are not always completely evident to mortals but must be trusted and affirmed by faith. "Further along," as another old gospel song says, "we'll understand why."

Most media and many institutions including the stock market are based on such "believers." In places where capitalist assumptions are questioned the American media have a chance to create another "devil." Military policies under George W. Bush authorize killing as part of a God-based American foreign policy.

Early indoctrination of children clearly has such deep life-long effects that concepts such as "God" often pervade people's minds for the rest of their lives. Any group that wants to control the minds of people tries to get the children indoctrinated at an early age so that beliefs are driven into the unconscious, thus controlling their thoughts without their awareness. The Pope knows that. Hitler knew that. The English with their "elite" schools for the aristocracy knew that. Prejudice against other races and ethnic groups often begins at an early age. The family is the common setting to implant racial and ethnic discrimination before children know what is happening to them.

The kind of education now needed is one that helps people understand how colonization and indoctrination works by blocking the ability to question. **Early indoctrination of beliefs that undermine people's later capacity to look openly at symbols and social systems should be considered a violation of the human rights of children**, a kind of lobotomy of their potentiality which violates their worth and dignity. Such "education" not only cripples the children but reduces the capacity of the society to rely on their intelligence to construct institutions which serve the common good. People become hollow.

> he came
> he went
> he made no difference
> left nothing, really
> except that he was known
> for saluting the flag and
> praising God

MOVING FROM ETHNOCENTRISM

Every child begins life in a geographical location and in a cultural context. Ethical behavior must first begin in this narrow world which is phase one of the child's developmental process. If the world never becomes larger than this local environment, the child will become highly ethnocentric and view the rest of the world through the values of this narrow local community.

There are usually some very decent values people share in this local community, and in earlier days of isolated groups, this pattern worked fairly well. Even then, however, the conflicts with nearby villages, tribes, and cultures could turn into killing, stemming often from absolute ethnocentric belief that "our way is the right way."

What is needed is to help people move psychologically into a larger geo-graphic and cultural world. Social policy can facilitate or hinder this process. Hierarchical societies ruled by a fixed elite inhibit mobility. Democracy, as John Dewey described it in *Democracy and Education*, (1916) connects people into an expanding community and can help us toward world community in the twenty-first century.

Huge differences in income and group discrimination produce stratification and dominance. The stratification of housing is seen in gated communities for the rich This is part of a process and a system which is anti-community, anti-empathy, and anti-human development. The need for jails and more police becomes predictable.

ETHICS AND EMPATHY

How can we develop ethical behavior in people? Empathy is the key, but more is involved. A child first needs the closeness and security of its mother and father. The anthropologist Ashley Montagu defined "love" as the "conferring of survival benefits," and when a child has an emotional attachment to its par-ents and good nutrition, preferably breastfeeding, it is off to a good start.

Then a process is needed to help develop ethical behavior at an early age. Kindness and acceptance displayed by the parents is the beginning of the right example for the child, rather than anger and rejection. When violence is part of the environment of the young child, including spankings and dis-plays of hostility, the child is being moved in the wrong direction, taking on those same behaviors as coping skills.

The lessons for the child need to involve extension of the self into the world of other people and animals, so that a child who is happy can empathize with others. A child who develops in a hostile world where images of violence are common may have little empathy for others. Social Darwinism, survival of the fittest, can easily become this child's view of reality if egocentric self-interest dominates the social environment.

What is crucial in this process is whether life is important for the child—is there joy in the child's life—is life increasingly the great opportunity to be alive and to help with others in the life-affirming process? If the child thinks that people hate him and if life has no joy, empathy can take on a reverse effect and produce sadism rather than compassion. If the child wants to injure and punish himself, he may also want to injure and punish others. This may be the beginning of a psychopathic personality.

Activities that model psychopathic behavior—killing in gangs, killing in the military, playing games that permit killing to be treated as the real thing—all deter the development of ethical behavior. Our capitalist television provides far more "food" for the psychopath than for the empathizer. There are some exceptions—programs that are humane and compassionate especially those with nature scenes that help people think of animals as having their own right to life. Killing and hunting and the old male macho ethos are in decline among the more civilized segments of society, yet violence and killing are used as a device for attracting attention to TV programs for the purpose of selling corporate products. In this case, the corporation is the anti-ethical teacher, playing a role in a system permitted by the public for the purpose of upholding the sacred ideology of "freedom of the market place."

The most important contribution to education is getting students to ask questions about the ethical issues that underlie society. This requires that the teacher initiate questions that students would never ordinarily hear, such as why some people are so rich and some so poor. And why we call the military system "defense" instead of a "war system," and why some are unable to find jobs even though there are many necessary kinds of work that need to be done.

Breaking the Vicious Circle

Though psychological and social processes are one side of the coin in the development of human behavior, the other side is the institutional structure. Developing good people and a good society needs to go beyond the cliché of the 1990s, which talked about "family values." To focus only on the family is a way of avoiding the institutional complicity that is destructive to families, such as unemployment and corporate control of mass media. Good public policy is one of the instruments to break up the vicious circle of anti-social behavior. For schools to concentrate on science and math and avoid the social experiences that would diminish ethnocentrism is also a way of stultifying human development. **The capitalist economic system hinders ethical development.** When people are used as instruments, bought and sold in the market-place to enhance the wealth of a minority, a mother raising her child properly will be turning that child out into a world that has forces which could easily supersede the good start she has provided. She therefore must be astute about politics and her model as a citizen. Parents provide a powerful example of what it means to be a citizen, and serve as a teacher to help bring about ethical political changes which can shape their child's future.

When schools now talk about twenty-first century education, they may refer to science and computer "literacy" as the characteristics of such future education. In fact the current institutions will simply be reinforced without education which gives ethical and ecological direction to change. Technofanaticism drives much of the kind of "science" we see in NASA and exotic military weapons. The vacuum in education is in ethics, which involves human rights.

As schools increasingly use achievement examinations for diplomas and qualification for college entrance, the content of those examinations should consist of the kinds of knowledge that are most important, for the content of standardized examinations has great influence on the curriculum. Instead of "neutral" information, students should be examined to see if they understand such crucial information as the difference between the comparative lack of human rights in the twentieth century and the needs for the twenty-first century. The Universal Declaration of Human Rights and the unwillingness of the United States during the twentieth century to support the positive economic rights of the Declaration should be basic subject matter, essential to democratic and liberal education and included in qualifying college entrance examinations. Math classes should show how exponential projections are basic to doubling time, which is necessary for population planning.

Good schools should make students resistant to propaganda, they should help deprogram them from conventional indoctrination.

Textbooks are part of the problem. High school textbooks, especially social studies texts such as American history are developed by profit making corporations. They seek to be "politically correct" and usually become propaganda through omission. For example, a nation wide history text first published in 1992, includes material on the United States relationship with Cuba, but **omits any mention of the embargo**. The embargo has consistently been condemned since it was instituted by President Kennedy in 1962 by nearly every member of the United Nations as a violation of international law, human rights, and a threat to the health and the economy of Cuba. If we found that current history texts used in Germany did not mention the holocaust, what would we say about the responsibility to truth and democracy? We expected that education would be planned propaganda in Stalin's Russia, but the cause of American propaganda is different. Since textbook publishing is a huge business for corporations in the United States we can understand why truth is second to ideology. School boards are responsive to political pressures by businesses, and professors who write these books must please the publisher. The lucrative writing contract can be fulfilled with a little selective amnesia.

I talked with a social studies teacher who considered most history texts to be corruptions of education, driven as he said "by money not by concern for truth." He has his students use the computer as a research tool to contact a variety of sources. This use of the computer is very different from creating student technicians who will be marketable to corporations. The computer may be used to reach out to libraries and information sources that corporate text books may choose to overlook (though the web is increasingly cluttered with commercial advertising). But without a good library of journals and books students will be deprived of the opportunity to take reading materials with them wherever they go.

Corporate influence on the schools has accelerated to the point where public reaction is developing. A national movement is underway to get school boards and state legislatures to oppose school commercialism. In September 1999 two state bills to halt commercialism in schools were passed in California. Social studies and science fields have been corrupted by corporate teaching units donated by lumber companies (timber "harvesting" companies) that provide films and pamphlets on environmental education which convey corporate ideology. Economics "education" is similarly well endowed with corporate curriculum.

A number of cities have opposed Channel One, a public affairs TV broadcast used exclusively for public schools. By bribing schools with free TV sets Channel One can provide some current events clippings followed by lucrative commercial advertising. The company claims to reach a captive teen market 50 times larger than MTV's. Coca Cola and Pepsi also buy their way into schools to "serve the needs of students."

LOCAL CONTROL AS LOCO CONTROL

When the American occupation after World War II imposed structural revisions on the Japanese political system, reform of the schools included mandatory shifting to local control. Americans had difficulty explaining why this was necessary, except to use the following logic: "The United States is a democracy—in the United States schools are under local control, therefore in order to create democracy in Japan the schools must be like they are in the United States." The Japanese then learned that the United States uses its own tradition as the standard of democracy.

During the early "Jeffersonian" days local communities had their own schools and their town meetings and there was little national community. As the nation developed politically and economically the early local control system failed to change, so it was necessary to give it a justification. Being "close to the people" was the rationalization but means and ends simply didn't connect. If schools were to help develop democratic citizens who participate in national elections, how could there be as many different meanings of "democratic" and good education as there are local communities? Since a citizen of Mississippi can vote for a national senator, should the quality of education be any different than for a citizen of California? Why would the decentralization of a nation's educational system improve the quality of education? It would surely provide variety, but is the transmission of local mores and political influences the way to understanding the increasingly complex world? When educational reform movements developed in the twentieth century they did not address the basic questions of authority and control. Rather, satellite TV systems were installed, math programs were changed, and computers substituted for typewriters.

Many local communities have decided to provide Jr. ROTC programs, taught and paid for by someone in the armed forces who follows the prescribed program from the Pentagon. I watched the high school graduation ceremonies in Hawaii where the Jr. ROTC students demonstrated their skills by throwing dummy hand grenades. Their admiring teacher had pride in a job well done. If a "democratic" education is defined as being the same as nationalistic and one suitable also for a "totalitarian" country, we have intellectual and moral anarchy. Local authority without adequate democratic theory is endemic.

Local descriptions of curriculum objectives invariably mention "critical thinking" as a general goal. In 1999 the Legislature in Oregon supported the American Legion request for compulsory flag salutes in schools even while "critical thinking" is listed as a state educational goal. When there are no real intellectual standards, political power of interest groups control educational goals. American education is vulnerable to the influence of special interest groups because there are no clear intellectual directions, no clear overriding theory to include and exclude goals to give meaning to "democratic."

The results are disastrous. There are some very good teachers in the schools, but without clear theory the arbitrary power of the administration and the local school boards usually prevails. Unless teachers unionize they have little protection from arbitrary action. But even if they unionize they are vulnerable to pressures from various religious and political groups who are often appeased by administrators who have little understanding of any concept of "democracy" but have considerable understanding of how to survive in a system of local control.

National corporate publishing houses that supply the textbooks know how the game is played. "Don't rock the local political boat." They provide a version of history that avoids the ire of local nationalistic and religious organizations. If the students graduate and go to a high quality college they may be subject to trauma when critical thinking is the norm, and where logic, reason, and evidence become the authority rather than the mores and traditions of a society.

Two basic considerations are involved in future planning of public schools. 1. What should be the financial and administrative unit? 2. What should be purpose of the institution? Hawaii provides a good example of an administrative unit that moved away from local control. There is only one school board for the state. The funds for maintenance, salary, and new buildings are provided by the legislature. This changes the behavior of the administrators, who in mainland states spend much of their time on budgets, not on program. In Hawaii all students throughout the state receive the same economic support, which overcomes the usual rural deficit. The model should be extended to the national level. Students in Mississippi should have the same level of school support as those in California. They are all American citizens with the same rights. It is clearly time to change the administrative and budgetary unit.

The second consideration is to recognize that to have a democracy the schools must consider the difference between a democratic and a totalitarian society. It is clear that a citizen in a democratic society is a participant who needs to understand social issues and how to join with others as a citizen in helping direct the course of the future. Totalitarian societies need obedient technicians to increase the power of the economic system and to reinforce the concentrated power of the state.

Democratic societies must provide an environment of equality between races, sexes, and social classes. The school then must perform a reconstructing role, for the larger society is white dominated and power is unequal since wealth and income are mal-distributed and concentrated. All the issues of what constitutes fairness in comparison with current society need to be on the table for discussion. When students graduate from high school they should be able to understand ethical issues in public policy and should have some experience in local and state government, if only through letters to the editor.

Conflict is normal in human society, but the method of resolution is crucial. Will it be overt violence through guns, violence though the exploitation of people and the environment, or will reason, debate, and evidence be the method? Will the rule of law be the rule of the power of corporations to control the law, or will law represent the public interest?

The democratic "process" is not merely participatory—voting etc.—but substantive requiring evidence and debate. When I ask students if we should "respect other people's opinions" they usually fall into the trap. We should respect other people's "*right* to have an opinion and to express it" but since many opinions are wrong, immoral, and absurd the important thing is to learn to use rational dialogue between people to improve our opinions, a process central to good education.

The twenty-first century should be the time to develop democratic citizens who can help design and create a better future. A new educational curriculum is needed to prepare people to reconsider alternatives and priorities rather than merely continue training people to fit into the market place and to simply reinforce the old order. For more on this, see my book *Education for the twenty-first century.*

FUTURES EDUCATION

A recent educational movement has shifted from study only of the past and the present to study of the future. By focusing on alternative futures, schools can help create public choice by illuminating directions for public policy. This becomes a new kind of political education that can shift from descriptive knowledge of the past and present into prescriptive policies that increase the power of the public to guide social change. Few schools at any level have as yet made use of futures education, yet it has important potential for democratic education.

Schools should be places for people not only to study the past and the future but to participate in creating the future. We all have goals or we wouldn't get through the day, but education should help people develop goals not only for themselves but for their society, locally and globally. Most current education is deflection politics, restricting people's capacity to participate in change because most schools have students looking into the rear view mirror to see where we have been (often as a propaganda picture), or being taught to fit in the current society. Whereas **the central question should be where are we going versus where ought we to be going**.

An example of the best in futures education I have seen was a class created at the University of Hawaii called Simulated Constitutional Convention. The public had voted to have another state constitutional convention in 1978, so this class consisted of people who studied issues and made proposals appropriate to a new state constitution. The process involved considerable disagreement and debate. The future of the state was being defined and there were naturally different views of what the state should be. But when the real public election occurred a number of these students were elected to the convention. Others were ready to participate as the proposals developed for the new constitution.

These students and the farsighted teachers who developed the class made a major impact on the new constitution that helped shape the future of the state. Some were elected as actual delegates; others shaped the agenda and concepts of the convention.

The same process is applicable to public schools throughout the country as comprehensive plans for cities and counties are developed. The students' visions of the kind of community they want can literally become part of the future as they discuss, persuade, argue, and conduct the research that can help shape vital documents, such as the comprehensive plans for their local communities. Arthur Pearl proposed a connection between school and the future as follows:

> Children learn to invent the future by inventing the future. From entrance to school until and after graduation, inventing futures and debating them is the primary activity of education. The inventions are not frivolous, they are solutions to pressing problems—peace, prosperity, justice, ecological balance, human institutions. They are not limited to large global issues, they touch on individual concerns—employment, politics, culture, leisure, intimate relations (1982).

MORAL INDIGNATION IS CRUCIAL

People especially want change when they find what is happening is not tolerable. Traffic congestion, noise, ugly development, continued unemployment—these experiences can set people in motion as they see that they are unnecessary. This gap between the real and the ideal is the basis for moral indignation. Injustices to people and abuse of the earth must be considered so revolting that they lead to democratic action to stop them. No one who accepts the world as it is can be considered "educated." They are *morally stunted.*

Futures education requires a shift from sterile information gathering and rote memorization to interaction between people, so that intellectual conflict and disagreement is normal. The goal is not conflict, but democracy requires the use of open expression of ideas and debate so that the best ideas will prevail. The goal is a social process in which all people are thinking better, acting better, and joining in the nonviolent process of using democratically based law to create the future. This is democratic "community"—a dynamic process very different from the imposed "order" we see in corporations or autocratic organizations. It is at the core of what should be called human development.

FUTURES HISTORY

Books about the future have a long history. Edward Bellamy's nineteenth century *Looking Backward* combined imagination and science fiction in trying to predict the future. The best known futures book in the 1960s was *Future Shock* by Alvin Toffler. In the 1970s, the World Futures Society and the World Futures Study Federation were formed, two organizations that have been entirely concerned with "futures" as a new academic area.

The World Futures Society meets annually in the United States. It is supported by major corporations and usually avoids discussion of the way political and economic power is used. Technology is usually seen as the key to "progress," and programs are largely oriented toward the business community to predict the future and to adjust to trends. The WFS operates one of the main bookstores for futures books.

The World Futures Study Federation is an international organization that has encouraged futures studies programs in universities. Both organizations lean heavily toward technological solutions, though the WFSF shows more courage to confront world poverty and show how capitalism and growth economics exploit the environment.

Most of the material that people read through "futures organizations" comes from well-intentioned liberals who want a better world but seldom identify the core ethical issues and rarely offer plausible structural solutions. They usually give the illusion of being involved in significant change by providing a form of romantic idealism that is intellectually safe and appears to be avant-garde. Unfortunately, what they generally provide is a form of deflection politics.

They make themselves "safe" for contributions and speaking engagements because they do not challenge power. They usually offer techno-fixes, suggesting that new technology will solve the problems. Much "futures" material is made up of projections of current trends, typically suggesting that people and businesses need to anticipate and adjust to these trends. But since many trends are pathological, the advice reinforces pathological institutions rather than transforming them.

The Foundation for the Future is a think tank that claims to be looking ahead into the future for the next 1,000 years. Seminars are held regularly and in the winter of 1999 the seminar topic was "the cultural impact of extraterrestrial contact." The published summary indicated that the seminar "opened by noting that there are a number of ways of searching for extraterrestrial intelligence and that any of these might be successful at any time in making an unequiv-ocal detection." The coordinator noted that the consequences "could have a profound effect on the evolution of our own civilization."

This is "deflection politics" at its best. Instead of planting both feet on the ground they have planted both firmly in the air. This also has a bonus effect for serving as "consolation politics," for it removes the participants from responsibility as they engage in super-speculation, shifting their energies to computers and expensive telescopes so they can gaze into the heavens. The "Foundation" is able to attract considerable funds from other foundations, which is often the case for think tanks that attract specialists who promise not to come up with any proposals that shake the current industrial order.

The futures studies field, however, in spite of these aberrations, has great potential value as an intellectual instrument to redirect education. I have been one of the pioneers since the 1960s. The approach I have developed is as follows: I assume that what is called knowledge in schools and academic studies is largely *descriptive* of the present and the past, lacking a basis for planning the future. So I stretch the area of inquiry into these steps:

1. What was

2. What is

3. What will be a likely future based on trends

4. What alternatives are feasible

5. What alternatives are most desirable

6. What steps are likely to lead to a desirable future

Step 5 involves values and ethics, and step 6 involves strategies for problem solving.

AN ALTERNATIVE FUTURES EXAMPLE WITH DIFFERENT KINDS OF WORK

The following matrix shows that 16 different kinds of employment are defin-able. On the left side is quantity of employment, on the right side the qual-ity (kinds) of employment.

1. Variable Unemployment, such as unplanned capitalism as in the 1920s and 1930s.

2. Planned Unemployment. The American Federal Reserve Board intentional-ly creates enough unemployment so that job insecurity will help hold down inflation.

3. Full Employment Opportunity. This principle has been given lip service but has not been established as a legal entitlement.

4. Compulsory Full Employment. This is often imposed by totalitarian governments to maximize the power of the state.

Questions:

1. What kinds of work are useful, useless, exploitative?

2. Which A-D represents market capitalism, welfare capitalism, socialism, totalitarianism?

3. Which best represents the combination used in China, U.S., Russia, Sweden?

4. Which is the best alternative (preferred future)?

5. What would be the transition steps that could produce the change from where we are to the preferred future?

This horizontal matrix indicates the kinds of work that can be done—such as a mix of useful, useless, and exploitative work. As we move to the right we can add social values, first socially useful, next ecologically valuable, and then a combination of both.

EMPLOYMENT ALTERNATIVES
Quantity & Quality

	KIND			
AMOUNT	1. A mix of useful, useless & exploitative work	2. Socially useful work–ecologically destructive	3. Ecologically responsible, but socially a mix, as in #1	4. Ecologically responsible & socially useful
A. VARIABLE UNEMPLOYMENT (UNPLANNED)				
B. PLANNED UNEMPLOYMENT W/GUARANTEED MINIMUM INCOME				
C. FULL EMPLOYMENT OPPORTUNITIES				
D. COMPULSORY FULL EMPLOYMENT				

Of the four quality levels, the first is what we see in the U.S: a mix of "useful, useless, and exploitative work." There are no social or ecological priorities to guide the American economy. A country may have socially useful work that is, however, ecologically destructive. The work creation programs of Communist countries in the twentieth century such as China were often of this kind. But if only ecology is emphasized, the social values and social priorities could be neglected. Clearly, the combination of work that is socially useful and ecologically sustainable is the best alternative. No country is entirely at that level, though it is feasible.

This outline of alternatives shows how we can apply futures alternatives, not only to the topic of work but, also to any other issue or problem, such as war prevention, transportation, education, health, etc. This "futures" approach can involve the public so that they can also explore alternatives and help move the country, or parts of it, in directions not previously considered. The failure to consider alternatives condemns a country and even the world to the old order that is bogged down in obsolescence.

Futures studies is a powerful educational tool that should have a central role in twenty-first century education. "Freedom" has little meaning if people can only choose between obsolete institutions.

ALTERNATIVES TO GROWTH

Meadows and Meadows' book *Limits to Growth* (1976) produced controversy for years. It took the best estimates of resource use and projected them into the future based on the direction of exponential demand. The results showed that consumption of finite resources could not continue without limit, and the projections raised the specter of our uncontrolled growth coming to an end. This way of looking at the future produced shock waves that resulted mainly in denial, for it challenged the conventional belief that change equals progress and that growth capitalism was the right way to conduct life on this planet.

The argument against the belief in limits came mainly from the conventional economists who claimed that as resources disappeared human inventiveness would compensate and that growth would continue. The debate between scientific projections of resource use on a finite planet versus open-ended growth continues. The momentum in the belief in perpetual growth continues because any alternative produces a fundamental threat to capitalism and all other pre-ecological ideologies.

The alternative to continual growth in population and resource use is to make the public domain more important than the "private" domain and to make principles of sustainability more important than principles of private profit. This means a switch of power from the market place to the public political arena, so that human community has more control than private profit.

When controls are proposed that place burdens on industry it is not only western business that objects, but as in the case of the Kyoto Accords, third world nations object to the costs involved in complying. Under a world system based on the dominance of market capitalism, property rights, and competitive market economics it is difficult to move ahead with the development of a sustainable future. As yet no system has been implemented to supercede the world capitalist system and so the many short range "solutions" turn only into dilemmas. If distribution continues to be based on market competition between scarce resources supported by private ownership, high levels of conflict are likely to arise, leading to war and terrorism.

The Romantic Liberal Wing

A common futurist ideology is what can be called the "romantic liberal" approach. It uses polling to see what people "want" in the future. This approach uses personal "desire" to identify what is "desirable." That means that if the people in the United States are polled, many might claim that the current world system is paying off for them as individuals and therefore is a system they "like." This ideology uses personal subjective standards. But since it leads, as it does, to massive poverty, enormous global exploitation of women, and destruction of the environment, an *objective* test of desirability is overlooked by this approach. Though the current world may be personally satisfying to many Americans, it does not meet the standards of being ethically desirable in the sense that it is just for all people.

If the current world system and its supporting institutions lead to such a violation of basic ethics, then the central obligation of any responsible institution is to help transform the world system. But in fact, most institutions are *causing* the poverty and ecocide. *Futures studies should therefore become a way of getting people involved in re-planning and re-creating the future toward closer alignment with the extension of the basic rights of all people.* It soon becomes clear that American corporations and the American government have been, and now are, largely forces involved in the exploitation of people and the destruction of the environment.

The important point is that if a "system" of dominance characterizes the world system, then it follows that people live in a hierarchy of power over which most people have no influence. The top players in the dominance system can be expected to behave in a largely predetermined way, for their roles are guided by their desire to retain their power and use it to their own advantage.

VOLUNTARISM: THE AMERICAN TRAP

A "romantic liberal" approach would try to encourage the people to be personally "responsible." The approach is individualistic and moralistic. It presumes that if people will just learn to be better people—more moral—institutions that are made up of people will change and the world will be better. If changes in personal behavior lead one eventually to political action, a person has gotten beyond the "romantic" level. But if people merely "feel good" about recycling, voluntary simplicity, etc. without political action they may actually be involved in consolation politics that gives them a sense of moral satisfaction but has no effect on the central forces shaping the future.

In a world where the wealthy nations are often glutted and encumbered by possessions there can be considerable personal satisfaction in creating a life of "voluntary simplicity." Ownership of things is a double edged sword, for ownership is reciprocal. Beyond a certain point of meeting basic needs, *things* begin to *own us*. But voluntary simplicity in a developed industrial society is not an effective *strategy for change in the system*. It may provide personal satisfaction, but unless there is sufficient public control over the institutions of production, distribution, and advertising, the growth system will move inexorably toward ecological destruction.

However, environmental education does need to begin with a focus on a person's daily choices in order to sensitize people about the way they affect the environment—how they use wood, metals, non-renewable fuels, and how pollution is connected with everything manufactured. Once people see these connections in their daily lives they then need help to move outward into political and economic areas to focus on needed structural changes.

But if people think that their behavior as consumers is sufficient to produce the necessary change, they will permit the power of the industrial system to continue intact. For instance: in the 1950s and 1960s petroleum fuels had tetraethyl lead to reduce engine knock. People learned that lead was dangerous to human health. Elimination of lead could have used either of the following strategies—personal morality or law. In personal morality, some people could have stopped buying leaded gas because of their concern that it posed a general health risk. Instead it was prohibited by law based on the health risk and phased out according to plan. There would still be leaded gasoline if the elimination required only personal moral choice of consumers, especially if leaded gas was less expensive. Similar approaches could have been used on asbestos, but it too was phased out by law. It would not have been had we relied on personal voluntarism.

MARKET STRATEGY

The other strategy for pre-determined failure is to presume that the market will conserve irreplaceable resources. I have heard capitalist economics professors say that the few remaining giant redwoods will be saved through the market, because they will become too expensive to purchase. The price has in fact gone up but consumption has continued. Without direct conservation and preservation required by law, all trees will be logged until the last one falls. The last one could have a special value as expensive jewelry.

When costs connected with market demand are used as the basis for conservation of resources, the poor are forced into conservation while the rich continue to consume. When environmental choices have serious effects on the entire public, the only workable and fair instrument for sustaining the planet is *enforceable law —necessary coercion not individual voluntary choice.* It is part of the American neurosis to emphasize freedom for individuals and corporations as absence of restrictions and to ignore the very constraints on individuals and corporations that *enhance the freedom of the larger community.* David Saari points out in *Too Much Liberty?* that the American conception of "freedom" led to "most of the valuable property (i.e., manufacturing plants, planes) in the United States being owned by the Fortune 500 corporations (1995, 64)." The freedom of unequals to compete pre-determines such an unequal outcome. Freedom to have a high quality of life should mean clean air, water, good food, jobs, safe communities, and this is all dependent on social organization and enforceable laws.

Personal choice should be increased only until it comes into conflict with the public good. Individualism, consumerism, and personal morality cannot constitute the *main strategy* for creating the future for it ignores the limits of a finite planet and the effects we have on each other. It creates the "tragedy of the commons."

REWARDING THE BAD AND PUNISHING THE GOOD

What needs to be understood from a system standpoint is that **people are now usually rewarded for doing bad things and often punished for doing the right thing.** Such rewards and punishments within obsolete systems leads to anti-social human behavior; and unless the payoff is altered through change in the institutional rules, the outcome will be the same. For example, a CEO of a corporation may threaten the lives of many people by firing them in order to cut down on costs and make the corporation more profitable and more competitive in the global market. If he does, he gets a high salary and his stock value goes up. If instead he becomes mainly concerned with the welfare of his employees and treats the "bottom line" as a secondary consideration, the report on earnings is likely to lead the board of directors to fire him.

Is he a "bad" person? He may be basically a good person in a "bad" institution. But the badness of the institution is really part of the larger context of the particular kind of economic and political system of which the company is a part. However, there are many other ways in which a corporation and an economic system can operate, and those should be the considerations central to futures studies. Such considerations should provide a basis for designing the future by identifying better outcomes and the new rules for the new institutions that will lead to those outcomes.

PEACE STUDIES AS FUTURES STUDIES

Most peace studies have been either Christian-based or Gandhian-based in theory. The first emphasizes "love thy neighbor" and "the Golden Rule," while Gandhian approaches use non-violent resistance and simple living. Techniques of mediation and compromise might be taught. All these have a useful place, but they often ignore the structural basis for violence. (Gandhi saw the need to also address structural causes). Typical programs in international studies focus on ad hoc conflict resolution and ignore the structural basis for war such as the war system. As discussed earlier, the current world system has no overriding law to represent world interests such as universal human rights so war is institutionalized while peace is not.

Since technology, such as nuclear weapons, represent the inevitable direction of the advance in the technology of violence, the world is moving toward genocide if the war system stays intact. But since the United States has the upper hand in leadership through the dominance of military and economic power, it is the least likely to take the necessary steps to make changes in the world system that it now dominates. Though the long-run effect may be global annihilation, the short-run effect is the retention of national power. Typical proposals for survival of people within the current nuclear war system rely on technology. The official United States view has been that it is possible for the *leaders* to survive nuclear war through underground shelters that have already been built in Colorado and near Washington, D.C. The main technological fix is a variation of "star wars"—a faith-based system where missiles are used to shoot down missiles, a carryover from the 1980s Cold War with the Soviet Union. "Ostrich" psychology and technological fanaticism have supported the presumption of survival under the current war system—survival of the military command but not of the general population.

What is clear is that survival of the people and real "defense" will not occur under the leadership of nations, particularly the United States. Two things are needed: 1) good theory, and 2) a world organizational and educational movement to replace national defense with enforceable world law and a world peace keeping system. A number of remarkable non-governmental organizations (NGOs) have been spearheading this needed change; and educational programs should tap into their ideas and strategies, always considering whether they are tinkering with the current world system or trying to produce basic systems change. (Such organizations are listed at the end of the book.)

STRUCTURAL VIOLENCE

In order to go beyond the simple traditional ideas of conflict resolution such as mediation and communication, a study of the *structures that violate people* is a useful starting point for developing peace studies. National sovereignty predetermines that there will be a war system and that big nations will have control in an international system of dominance. Similarly, when competition is used as the way to allocate scarce resources, the rich and powerful will prevail. There will be no "fair" distribution and, therefore, what we have is *structural exploitation*. When people see what is happening, they may try to change the structure democratically—or through violence if democracy is not workable.

Examination of the plight of people such as native Americans, the "untouchables" in India, the homeless in American cities, etc., is a way of moving from specific situations to the analysis of possible structural causes and solutions. When we see the great differences in the health and well being of some groups of people compared with the rest of the population, we can assume that there are structural causes that produce inequality of power. Then plans for structural changes of the primary causes of the violence can provide a basis for a new politics.

POSITIVE PEACE/NEGATIVE PEACE

All the conditions that bring people together to develop cooperative communities might be called "positive" peace. Positive peace involves some conflicts, but they are *minimized* through *democratic processes*, which permit people to work out difficulties without violence. But positive peace between nations will not overcome the problem inherent in a global system in which authority is defined by national military power. Because the twentieth century did not work out a law system at the global level, this "war system" constitutes a major threat to the human future.

"Negative peace" involves a world without war. A world without war may not be peaceful—for various forms of conflict and even violence can continue. But it is a way of moving directly into a world system of control over military power so that national defense is achieved through a world peace keeping system and enforceable law rather than through national military power. The transition requires phased disarmament and system substitution— namely to provide enforceable world law in place of national military power.

The best long-run goal is a world without war and also one with high levels of cooperation, which requires high levels of social justice and human rights. But this may take a long while. Meanwhile the nuclear clock is ticking. North Korea is urgently dangerous—India and Pakistan both have nuclear missiles. And the 6,000 nuclear missiles in Russia and the United States are ready for activation. De-institutionalization of war is the necessary condition for survival of the human race.

The error in many peace movements is to assume that when people are more cooperative, war will disappear. This is not true. There can be high levels of positive peace—cooperation between people—and yet with national military power intact, the world can experience nuclear holocaust. So a world without the war system should be the top priority goal for the twenty-first century: human survival precedes everything else. If democratic processes can also be instituted, positive peace can develop simultaneously. This entails providing for human needs and a common quality of life. But without achieving at least the minimum condition for survival—preventing war—a "negative peace" becomes the necessary but not sufficient condition for survival in the nuclear age.

"I Don't Get No Respect"

This was the line used for decades by comic Rodney Dangerfield after he indicated how he was always mistreated. It always brought a laugh. People could identify with him, for the need for personal respect is universal. The moral premise "worth and dignity of the person" underlies all human interaction—people crave to be treated with respect, but in many social situations and organizations they are not. Even in families respect between parents and children is often absent, and outright brutality is not uncommon. Parents may serve as dictators and the children respond as expected, showing hostility and aggression, or passivity and lack of self-worth.

Some institutions predetermine that there will be little or no respect. The military is the most pronounced of these, and basic training is designed to make a person **lose** self-respect and learn obedience. The recruit is ordered to "respect" his superiors, who often mistreat him so that he hates them; but he must still "show respect" or he receives punishment. Of course, real respect cannot be coerced.

The brutality of Marine training is well known; its psychology is based on getting people to accept total control without questioning. *Humiliation* is important to such training, a device intended to get the self-respect of the person to incrementally disintegrate. Some fraternities use the same humiliation ritual for induction. *Acceptance of subservience to the tormentor* is the key to the required loss of self-respect and the required conformity. The use of autocratic power in some police training is similar, getting people to obey to serve the organization.

The entire world economic system under corporate capitalism serves to institutionalize disrespect, for people are used as means to provide profit for others. Duty and obedience are required of the employee in a corporation, but the employer has the power to fire a person for any arbitrary reason (especially in the United States). Corporations fire thousands when CEOs decide that such a decision will increase efficiency and profits—and in turn permit higher salaries for the CEO.

When structures are hierarchical, the dominance of people over others often leads to exploitation and disrespect. This process is a cause of various forms of psychopathology often leading people to seek psychiatric help. People crave respect, so when they are treated as objects to be manipulated, they often develop not only hostility but also self-hatred or despair.

Even in such autocratic institutions as the military, when squads have experimented with the election of their team leaders by the men in the squad, they have performed better in combat (Boyer 1972, 19). Real respect comes from democratic rather than autocratic organization. People usually show respect for each other in normal social situations. This feeling for others can be seen even following military indoctrination, for many American soldiers in combat refused to shoot at the "enemy" they were supposed to kill.

Democratic institutions increase respect because they involve more equality between people and permit easier communication. But this easily leads to the common belief that in respecting the right of others to hold different views that we should also "agree" with them in order to show "respect." This is where interactive democracy often breaks down and leads instead to conformity.

People's views are often based on incorrect information or prejudice toward other people. In such a case, we should interact and try to correct the views of others, and they should, in turn, do the same with us. This would be real respect for each other as rational human beings and it would increase progress through rational dialogue instead of hypocritical agreement. Lack of respect is the outcome when people are merely the means to other's ends. In contrast, democratic economic units—co-ops as an example—provide a basis for respect and a sense of community rather than being used by others.

The design of future economic systems should put respect for others high on the list of economic goals. Profit making through competition as the dominant means is likely to determine that efficiency will be the primary objective and that people will be exploited as mere instruments to achieve that end. Yet the evidence in studies of corporate efficiency suggests that respect will usually increase output. If respect is to be built into economic systems it will require some form of economic democracy where people have primary control of economic institutions.

Arthur Pearl and Tony Knight, in *The Democratic Classroom*, (1999) show how democracy in schools requires a theory that takes account of respect in a profound way. Teachers need a theory that puts the teacher in the position of respecting the intelligence of students by **actively compensating for the lack of encouragement people have experienced in our hierarchical society**. Unless the power of the student is increased as a participating citizen, an institution such as the school has not shown respect and unless a student is moved from the marginalized edge of the society into acceptance by others the school has not helped develop a democratic culture. *The Democratic Classroom* provides a quantum leap from conventional "how to" teaching methods into the political-social-and ethical basis of an advanced twenty-first century role for the schools, where they are part of the solution instead of part of the problem.

Beyond Tunnel Vision

The inclusion of the study of alternative futures should be a part of the normal education of people, especially Americans, because of the dominant power of the United States in effecting the future of the world. Some approaches recommend changing our basic institutions while others are incremental. These alternative approaches to change need to encourage public debate on how to have a better future. Incremental approaches need to be steps connected with basic systems change.

Human problems will always remain, but the way to resolve them should be through dialogue and discussion. The next century should be a century of dialogue and discussion rather than one of war and bloodshed.

—The Dalai Lama, from his Millennium Message

. . . Streets of Seattle. . . transformed the World Trade Organization into a popular icon for the unregulated globalization that tramples human values on every continent, among rich and poor alike. The guys and gals in the turtle suits, with a little help from overanxious cops, woke up America and maybe the world.

—William Greider, *The Nation*, December 27, 1999

FROM A CORPORATE WORLD TO A DEMOCRATIC WORLD

The primary objective of this book has been to describe ways in which basic institutions of our ostensibly "democratic" society have been increasingly usurped by corporate power and to identify ways in which citizens can work toward asserting more democratic control over their institutions of governance. Though protest is rising world wide to change direction, better theory is needed to guide strategy and movements in the twenty-first century.

First we must understand the character of corporate capitalism. Modern large scale corporate capitalism buys up our government and drives out small scale free enterprise. It mesmerizes us with entertainment opiates and turns us into consumers and producers of trivia. The stress and insecurity of the corporate work place causes rage, hopelessness, and social disintegration. The product is a glutted economy and a public manipulated to buy-buy-buy in order to support the "economy." Production is often used to create profitable materials of war, and nature's resources are depleted at an even more rapid rate to provide concentrated wealth while poverty and homelessness are still rampant. Corporate capitalism, which we mistakenly call "democracy" has no soul and no sensitivity. It is directed only by profit maximization and risk minimization. It runs on inertia and mass indoctrination, with people considered to be discardable objects. The corrupting effect of this concentration of power largely controls our government, and since the United States dominates the world, this corporate power is a basic part of what globalization has

166

become—establishing corporate business world wide using cheaper foreign labor and foreign natural resources (Barnet and Cavanagh, 1994).

As long as our political system is largely controlled by major corporations, no significant progress is likely. So a viable strategy needs first to assert meaningful public control of government and then to dismantle the instruments of corporate rule.

The Marxist view is that capitalism is a phase of historical change which will self destruct by exploiting the working class and thereby lay the basis for revolution. A democratic position, supported in this book, is that corporate capitalism can be de-fanged by eliminating its power to control government. Whether this will occur or not is the test of the potential of people to use effective non-violent democratic power.

STEPS TOWARD STRUCTURAL CHANGE IN OUR CURRENT CORPORATE WORLD

STRATEGY TO ESCAPE THE TRAP

- Use public education at all levels to help people understand the basis for their role in recovering American democracy.
- Avoid a strategy that merely tries to mitigate corporate impacts (pollution, etc.) through regulatory regimes corporations largely control.
- Proceed with incremental steps toward separation of corporations from political control of government.
- Combine legal steps with mass public protest through demonstrations and other means to force changes that reduce the political power of corporations.

UNDERSTANDING THE NEED FOR BREAKING THE CONNECTION:

Bill Bradley, U.S. Senator in 1996, pointed out that "Real reform of democracy, reforms as radical as those of the Progressive era and deep enough to get government moving again, must begin by completely breaking the connection between money and politics (Phillips 2002, 405)."

The conventional view is that investment by the corporations will help produce products for the economy, but there is little incentive to invest in products compared with "investment" in lobbying and providing campaign funds to candidates. For example:

> The Timber Industry spent $8 million in campaign contributions to preserve a logging road subsidy, worth $458 million—the return on investment was 5,725%. Glaxo Wellcome invested $1.2

million in campaign contributions to get a 19 month patent extension on Zantac worth $1 billion—net return 83,333%. Tobacco
spent $30 million for a tax break worth $50 million—return of
167,000%. For a paltry $5 million in campaign contributions, the
Broadcasting Industry was able to secure free digital TV licenses, a
give-away of public property worth $70 billion—that's an incred-
ible 1,400,000% return on investment (Phillips, 326).

The concept of "incentives" for capital investment in free enterprise has
turned out to be very different than the picture sold to the public. If we are
to have democratic government by the people, we will have to find ways to
control the corruption of government through money or the future of the
United States will continue to consist of a corporate-based oligarchy in the
name of democracy.

Corporate capitalism (neo-classical economics) has dominated the United
States and has been promoted world wide by the United States. The public
has been propagandized to accept an ideology of "privatizing" the economic
system and releasing it from public control. This deregulation led to Enron
and other major corporations being exempt from public scrutiny. From 2000
on, one major corporation after another used its "freedom" from public control as a way to cheat the public, increasingly engaging in self serving criminal acts by stealing from its workers, consumers, and the communities where
it operated.

To control corporate power requires that we understand the institution of the
corporation that we have invented. Supreme Court Justice Thurgood
Marshall reminded us that "A corporation is an artificial being, invisible,
intangible, and existing only in contemplation of law. Being the mere creature of law, it possesses only those properties which the charter of creation
confers upon it (*U.S. Supreme Court Reports,* 55 L.Ed 2d p.747)."

However, as Chief Justice William Rehnquist recently pointed out, an 1886
decision made a business corporation into "a 'person' entitled to the protection of the Equal Protection Clause of the Fourteenth Amendment (*U.S.
Supreme Court Reports,* 55 L.Ed 2nd)."

This preposterous decision lingered into the twenty-first century, so that corporate contributions to favored candidates are treated as constitutionally protected "free speech." Under the First Amendment of the U.S. Constitution,
people are guaranteed right of free speech, and by virtue of the 1886 decision, corporations are "persons." This has come to mean that when corporations use their funds to influence elections they are engaged in "speech" and

have the protection of the Constitution. When money is "speech" which can buy candidate elections, corruption of democratic government is guaranteed.

Corporations derive their existence from invented law enacted in each state, which provides a "charter" that gives certain powers, immunities, and tax advantages to those who represent the corporation. Although many corporations are non-profit, the large profit making corporations can use their mass resources to influence, if not control, the political system, and in doing so they become the number one corrupters of American political democracy. The central idea of our political system is that "one person one vote" constitutes the basis for political power. The "We the people" language is crucial and much different from "We the corporations." However, until corporations are prevented from controlling elections with their exorbitant contributions, they will continue to move in the direction Korten has described in his 1995 book *When Corporations Rule the World*. Money that can buy enough television time can usually kill any ballot initiative that has a negative effect on the profits of corporations.

This 1886 decision made it possible for corporations to dip into their vast corporate treasuries and legally put millions of tax deductible dollars into media blitzes, outspending grassroots opponents, often by 100 to one margins—all in the name of "free speech." But a hopeful recent decision involving the state of Missouri could help challenge the 1886 decision and other Supreme Court decisions which have strengthened corporate rule. On January 24, 2000, the U.S. Supreme Court upheld a decision that was appealed from a case in the State of Missouri which placed a very strict limit on campaign contributions (161 F.3d 519). In a reversal of the pattern in place ever since the 1886 corporate personhood decision, a 6 to 3 majority said in effect that the right to free speech does not translate into a right to dominate the election process through large monetary contributions. Justice John Paul Stevens even went so far as to directly challenge the very premise of other rulings since 1886 when he stated in startlingly unambiguous terms: *"Money is property. It is not speech."* If it can be translated into new law, this conceptual reversal from the position that money is speech may help shift the legal basis for corporate power.

Some believe that there was a direct connection between this Supreme Court decision and the protest events in Seattle. It is quite possible that the members of the Court were sensing a shift in the public mood, or the events in Seattle may have been just one more push in a direction in which the Court had already been moving. The activist groups dealing with campaign finance

reform saw a new opporunity as a result of "Missouri." The Missouri decision, which limits contributions to $1000 per candidate, is providing incen-
tive for various groups and states around the country to create new limits on
campaign financing.

In addition, there is other language in the majority opinion which can
embolden groups to push even farther. This Supreme Court decision encouraged Senator John McCain to propose the McCain-Feingold bill in 2001, to
eliminate the loophole referred to as "soft money" (the contribution of
money to political parties, which can then be spent independently on behalf
of particular candidates.) His bill finally passed in March 2002, but it actually raised—doubled in fact—the amount of hard money raised for contributions directly to candidates. So there is finally some momentum for the
idea of campaign financing reform but nothing so far that is effective—only
a weak bill that still permits some soft money to outside groups and is likely
to have little effect on corporate control of elections.

These attempts merely to moderate the influence of big money in elections
keep campaign financing alive as a public issue but deflect the public from *the
real issue which is whether corporations have any right whatsoever to participate
in the electoral process.* Corporations are social inventions and will use their
power to control the political process unless they are entirely separated from
that process. Democracy requires political control by the public and the public must consist of "real" people. This blurring of the legitimate rights of people with fictional corporate institutions is a central error in American politics.

The Missouri decision and rising national and international mass movements
challenging corporate hegemony suggest an opportunity to help reign in corporate political power. Should the political system be "of the people" or "of
the corporations"? People employed by a corporation should have access to
political involvement but the corporation—the fiction created by the public—must then be separated from the political system to make a clearer distinction between the public and private sector. Such pressure helps lead to a
direct re-examination and eventual challenge of the concept of "corporate
personhood" with change in the 1886 law. When this occurs, the movement
will in fact be squarely addressing a central source of corporate power.

Thom Harmann in his book *Unequal Protection* claims that in all these years
that the court has presumed corporations were persons that "the court said
no such thing, and it can't be found in the ruling (2002, 107). He opens up
a question that deserves more attention: Does the decision even have legal
status? Harmann tries to show that the decision was *never a formal ruling of*

the Supreme Court, but only part of the headnotes.* His findings may further erode any presumptions of the legitimacy of corporate personhood.

In the meantime we should consider overcoming corporate personhood as a long term struggle similar to the civil rights struggle. There is a long history of attempts to move ahead in courts and through civil action on this issue and we are still in the middle of the struggle. Buckley v. Valeo in 1976 (387 F. Supp. 135 DDC 1975) involved a majority of the justices declaring corporate money to be a form of "free speech," which led two years later to a landmark case known as First National Bank v. Bellotti, (435 US 765, 1978) where the U.S. Supreme Court overruled a Massachusetts State Statute prohibiting corporations from spending money on ballot initiatives.

Bellotti favored the corporations but there was interesting dissent by Justices White and Marshall stating that "Corporations are artificial entities created by law for the purpose of furthering certain economic ends.... It has long been recognized. . . that the special status of corporations has placed them in a position to control vast amounts of economic power which may. . .dominate not only the economy but also the very heart of our democracy, the election process.... The State need not permit its own creation to consume it (Grossman 2001, 38)."

Even Justice William Rehnquist wrote in another case in 1986 that "to ascribe such artificial entities {corporations} an "intellect" or "mind" for freedom of conscience purposes is to confuse metaphor with reality (38)."

It is clear that "personhood" is still established in law but resides with considerable unease, even by the justices. But the potential power to change this absurd law has barely been tapped, for few people know about "Santa Clara." The public knowledge could result in large scale reaction to a judicial doctrine that has long passed its time.

PUBLIC SHIFT TO DIRECT DEMOCRACY

Conventional politics is called a "republican" form of government. People are elected who are supposed to represent the public. But one critical lack is publicly agreed-upon goals. There are no national goals formulated by the people through democratic process for the future of the United States. Existing "national goals" are mainly those that the office holders create to serve their own purposes and those of corporations that lobby and finance campaigns.

---

* See Vol. 118 of *United States Reports: Cases Adjudged in The Supreme Court* at October Term 1885 and October Term 1886.

Many people would consider our national goals to be the protection of our Bill of Rights—the negative rights which were designed to protect us from government infringement of individual freedoms. But positive rights dealing with basic needs which entitle people to such things as affordable food, housing, a job at decent pay, medical care, and education are also important but largely ignored in the United States. The Universal Declaration of Human Rights which the U.S. supported in its adoption by the United Nations even asserts that everyone has the right to work with fair pay and to have a right to food, clothing, medical care, and education (see Articles 22, 23, 24, 25, 26).

The U.S. has legally recognized an enforceable right only to education. The problem of using states rather than national government to fulfill other basic human rights is that they constitute an attraction which would draw people from other states. For instance since we lack federal medical entitlement, any state that would unilaterally provide free or affordable medical care to all residents would be inviting bankruptcy. So states that start to create new rights need to take account of the economic costs involved. If the prospect of new rights would produce costs to corporations, they currently have the power effectively to resist such change.

In theory, the public can create certain rights in state constitutions through the initiative process. In practice, the existing economic power of corporations to protect their privileges is likely to be used through large propaganda blitzes at election time, influencing the outcome of an election so it favors the corporations. As an example of the effect of this use of corporate money to defeat progressive legislation, very little significant legislation to protect the environment has been passed in Oregon since the 1970s.

So what is needed is to use the initiative process to protect the initiative itself from corporate money. This requires getting enough public support initially to outbalance corporate funds which could be used to defeat the initiative— a test of democracy versus oligarchy. But even if the people prevail at the state level a referendum to restrict corporate spending can still be overturned by the U.S. Supreme Court. We need to not only develop a legal shield to control corporate power but also to have a Supreme Court disconnected from corporate power.

The most rapidly emerging public strategy for gaining control of government by the people is the development of direct democracy, by which people participate directly in formulating political policies instead of relying on representatives. The legal basis for direct democracy in government is the Ninth Amendment of the United States Constitution, which has been used to change statutory and constitutional law within states. The Ninth Amendment reads as follows:

> "The enumeration in the Constitution, of certain rights, shall not be construed to deny or disparage others retained by the people."

One of the implications of this language is that when state legislatures fail to confront needed changes, the people can override their legislatures through direct democracy by using the power of ballot initiatives. The ballot initiative is the name of the process by which citizens can collect a prescribed number of signatures and place their own proposal on the ballot. This expanded use of direct democracy at the close of the twentieth century offered new opportunity, but initiatives can serve not only progressive change but can also be tools for reactionary politics. Both California and Oregon have experienced such use. Money is usually needed to pay for some of the signature gatherers, and big money can be used to support initiatives that serve corporate interests.

Confronting the Source of Corporate Power

Activists working on single-issue campaigns are beginning to adopt more holistic views which allow them to see past the symptoms of problems to their structural sources. From this new perspective, they are starting to formulate strategies aimed at achieving the "systemic" changes which many of us have been advocating for some time.

During the late 1990s, world wide movements have been proceeding rapidly to confront the rising power of the system of transnational corporations. For many years, activists against corporate dominance expended their energies and resources in protracted battles against individual corporations. These same activists are increasingly stepping back and seeing that the entire global political economy has become heavily influenced if not controlled by giant corporations that are now bigger than most nation states. Of the hundred largest economies in the world, 51 are corporations and only 49 are states.

A 1995 article by Ronnie Dugger in *The Nation* urged disparate groups to unite and address the systemic problem of corporate power. It resulted in a founding convention in Texas and led to the formation of the Alliance for Democracy, which now has chapters all around the country and is helping organize grass roots initiatives to control corporate power. One of their most empowering educational tools has been simply to tell the public the history of the corporate rise to power. This history (see Chapter 2) is virtually absent in American political discussion and even American educational systems.

STATE INITIATIVES

Twenty-two states allow statewide public initiatives so citizens can undertake state statutory and constitutional changes. Through signature gathering and a public vote, the initiative overrides the power of city councils, county commissions, and state legislatures which often represent special economic interests. The state constitutional changes resulting *from the people's initiatives* can prescribe the limits and even establish the objectives of state legislative, executive, and judicial action.

Oregon in 1902 was the first to use the state initiative. If there were a similar provision in the federal Constitution for the public to create new constitutional law through a national initiative it would be a useful procedure for taking power away from the corporations and shifting self-governance to the people. But since no such federal provision exists, the power of the states with the initiative is a good starting point to create new rights, at least for citizens of those states. The public can then redirect state agencies and goals of state government and these lead states can serve as examples to others.

DIRECT ELECTION OF BASIC GOALS

In *America's Future: Transition to the twenty-first century* (Boyer 1984) I proposed that the public should vote on goals to direct the future. Through direct democracy, a state initiative could prescribe *goals for the state*. By following these constitutionally determined initiatives, the officials who are elected at the local and state level will then *serve goals mandated by the public*. Currently representatives operate mainly under procedural law and, because money has been so influential in their election, they are likely to give priority to corporate interests. Even in states that have the means of changing state constitutions through the initiative process, this power of the public to engage in direct democracy has been largely overlooked.

NEW HUMAN RIGHTS THROUGH INITIATIVES

During the 1990s, a citizen group which I organized in Oregon has been working on the expansion of rights to include "environmental rights." Two considerations are involved: The right to a clean and healthy environment would confer a prior, inherent, right to the "breather" but no rights to the polluter.

The second right, *the right of future generations to sustained natural systems*, permits standing in court to represent future generations and gives them some claim to the perpetuation of natural systems, streams, forests, watersheds, and genes of species, which are essentially non-renewable. (My local organization, Oregonians for Environmental Rights has copies of the above initiatives.*)

Winona La Duke, who ran as the Vice-presidential candidate of the Green Party with Ralph Nader in 2000, has called for an Amendment to the U.S. Constitution to protect the "common property" of future generations.

Reversing the burden of proof is necessary to enforce a "right to a healthy environment." People need law to protect them from harmful chemicals. For example: for many years the U.S. Forest Service and the timber companies have sprayed defoliants on forests after they were cut. When people claimed that the water they drank from these watersheds was dangerous to their health, they found that the burden of proof was on them to show that they had been injured—that the cancers and fetal deformities were actually caused by the 2-4-D or 2-4-5-T (such as was used in Vietnam). Since they could not prove cause, they had no case. The chemicals continued to be used.

But would it not be appropriate to reverse the rules regarding the release of chemicals into the environment and workplace? This would require that *those who want to use the chemicals demonstrate that they constitute no threat to human health.*

Critics of this proposal say "You can't prove a negative," claiming that one cannot prove that something won't be dangerous. But this is done all the time with pharmaceuticals. Drug companies have to test their drugs to show they are not dangerous before the FDA permits them to be marketed. So in the case of the *voluntary* purchase of drugs sold at the drug store, safety is pretested. In the case of chemicals where people are *involuntarily* subjected to pollution, the burden of proof is now on the people being polluted. This is intolerable.

The illustration provides an example of why the public should be able to vote on such an important idea (which expands human rights) **that the burden of proof in matters of environmental health should fall on the polluter.** If the public does not have a clearly articulated right (achieved for example through a state initiative) public health agencies and the elected members of legislatures will simply chip away at current law to make sure that economics and not public health continues to be the primary concern. When people are elected to office they really have no mandate for what they should do. Party platforms are often ignored or contradicted. We need to change this system by having the public **provide the mandate** by voting for the goals that legis-

---

* Contact this group at P.O. Box 37, Sisters, OR 97759.

lators should work to achieve. Then legislators could legally be held account-able to implement the goals, and if they fail to follow the law created by the public, they could be held in contempt or subject to some form of control for violating the "overriding" constitutional law. This is the way it should be.

ACHIEVEMENTS THROUGH INITIATIVES

Though the public's power to influence national and state elections is severe-ly limited by the overwhelming power of corporate money, states with ini-tiatives have various ways to increase the power of the public. Here are some of the things we have done in Oregon.

Local communities passed initiatives which gave citizens the power to vote on each annexation request of developers involving extensions of city bound-aries. This shifted power from city councils, usually developer-dominated, to the citizens.

- One town (Sisters) passed an initiative requiring the city council to assess maximum systems charges (the costs imposed on communities by develop-ment). Systems development charges are crucial to avoid subsidizing devel-opers for the costs they impose on communities (for water, sewers, parks, schools, police, etc.).

- State initiatives were developed in Oregon to amend the state Constitution which would 1. protect initiatives from changes by the legislature, and 2. protect the initiative from control by large individual and corporate money. These initiatives have not yet been submitted to the voters. An Oregon state ballot measure embodying these propositions achieved the necessary signa-tures in 2002 and will be repeated for 2004. It is called Money is Not Democracy and it prevents corporations from making any contributions to candidates and prohibits soft money. Information is available at www.vot-ers.net/mind.

OTHER STATES

- In 1998, activists in Arcata, California were concerned about the harm caused by corporations and used an initiative to hold two town meetings on the topic of restoring local democratic control over corporations. There is now an ongoing committee charged with the task of developing specific legal means (such as revoking business licenses) by which corporations can be held accountable for violations of law relating to environment, labor, human rights, income tax, occupational safety, and health.

- Wayne Pennsylvania Township passed an ordinance September 9, 2002 that prohibits corporations which have a history of consistently violating regula-tory law from doing business in their town. It is based on the "three strikes and you're out" principle. If the corporation has a history of non-compliance, triggered by a citizen petition, the right to do business in that community can be denied. And new businesses are not permitted to come to the Township if they have a history of violations. An update and copy of this ordinance can be obtained at wwwceldf.org.

■ Arizona recently passed an initiative that provides for public funding of campaigns. It is based on candidates getting a certain level of support through small financial contributions and then receiving funds providing they do not take other contributions. These initiatives, called "clean money campaigns" are in force in Massachusetts, Vermont, and Maine. They do not prohibit candidates from taking major private sources of funds. One result has been to get more candidates involved in the election and another has been to raise the amount of involvement in the election process by citizens. (See www.pbs.org/now/politics/cleanelections.html)

■ In 1998 citizens filed a petition with the California Attorney General asking that he revoke the state charter of Unocal Corporation, which has a long history of massive environmental damage and human rights abuses worldwide. Unfortunately he has refused to take action even though such action is authorized in the State Corporation code. The text of this petition has been published in Benson's *Challenging Corporate Rule* (1999). Benson points out that "citizens of every state, acting through their attorney, have, and always had, the legal authority to go to court to revoke the charters of corporations that violate the law." This book is a guide to citizen action, suggesting a major strategy for helping bring corporations under public control by using existing charters where possible and also upgrading those charters where they are inadequate. Catch 22 in such action is that attorney generals may not even be willing to carry out the law, since they too are so tied to corporate money. But the next step is to try to gain compliance through the courts, though the courts have been subject to similar corruption. Yet the judiciary lifetime appointments have protected courts somewhat from political pressures and corporate money. This last action, combined with strong public movements, is worth trying until money can be removed from corporate politics at a later time.

■ An organization called Tikkun has been developing a Social Responsibility Amendment to the federal Constitution in which "every corporation doing business within the United States with an annual income of more than $20 million must receive a new corporate charter every twenty years and prove a history of social responsibility as measured by an Ethical Impact Report (*The Nation*, May 22, 2000, 24). Micheal Lerner's book *Spirit Matters* details this proposal.

■ Some states—Hawaii and Montana—can already create change through state constitutional conventions. In Hawaii the public votes every ten years to decide on whether a new constitutional convention should be held. Two were held since Hawaii became a state.

■ Wisconsin from 1905 to 1953 had a law that prohibited corporations from engaging in any form of political activity, where breaking the law was a felony and the corporation could be dissolved for disobeying it. This was the language:

> No corporation doing business in this state shall pay or contribute, or offer consent to agree to pay or contribute, directly or indirectly, any money, property, free service of its officers or employees or things of value to any political party, organization, committee or individual for any political purpose whatsoever, or for the purpose of influencing legislation of any kind or to promote or defeat the candidacy of any person for nomination, appointment or election to any political office. (See Jane Anne Morris, p.193.)

The law was on the books until the Federal Election Campaign Act made Political Action Committees legal.

> This Wisconsin achievement indicates that it is feasible to create laws that permit states to control corporations and businesses so that it is unlawful for them to participate in government. This is the kind of action that effectively protects the public sector from infiltration and manipulation by the private sector.

Though political protests may engage large numbers of people they should be part of a strategy that finally creates legal changes which have the power to sustain public control over corporations. Therefore protests need to advocate not only toward structural changes such as revisions in charters but also changes in constitutional and statutory law. Education is needed to help people tie means and ends together, to connect social energy with substantive structural change. Social action without long term institutional direction may be exhilarating and a first step for many in democratic participation but may not create significant change for the future. American education needs to provide people with better theories of alternative futures so that social action leads to real democratic change. See Boyer, *America's Future: Transition to the twenty-first century* (1984).

It is not sufficient merely to control corporations through restrictions on campaign contributions; their basic power must be redefined in law. As Richard Grossman, a leader in the movement on citizen control of corporations has said, "what corporations do, not what they do wrong, is the problem." Corporations have acquired a role in the United States by which they often do massive environmental and social harm simply by carrying on "normal" activities. An objective needs to lead to the transformation of corporations so that they continue to exist but within law that mandates that they provide socially useful and ecologically sustainable contributions to society. *This means removing their power to control government.* They are now the tail that wags the dog.

AFTERWORD

BUSH VERSUS THE WORLD

The bi-polar world of post World War II disappeared when the Soviet Union collapsed. The United States was virtually offered the position of world dominance but it failed to produce any vision of democratic world leadership. Global capitalism continued to drive foreign policy and following the 2002 mid-term "election" of George W. Bush an unprecedented policy emerged. An alarming new strategy for military planning was launched in a document called *Defense Planning Guidance for the 2004-2009 Fiscal Years, Office of Secretary of Defense, 2002.* Vice President Dick Cheney provided the leadership for this initiative with collaboration from Paul Wolfowitz and Donald Rumsfeld. David Armstrong summarized the plan in the October 2002 edition of *Harpers:*

> The Plan is for the United States to rule the world. The overt theme is unilateralism, but it is ultimately a story of domination. It calls for the United States to maintain its overwhelming military superiority and prevent new rivals from rising up to challenge it on the world stage. It calls for dominion over friends and enemies alike. It says not that the United States must be more powerful, or most powerful, but that it must be absolutely powerful.

This imperial plan fit into the other objectives of the Bush administration for it served the wealthy corporate minority, Bush's main reelection constituency. The administration's objective was to shift wealth to the rich and transfer natural resources to the corporations. The main obstacle to their plan was an historically weak election mandate and the struggling economy. The stock market had virtually collapsed and unemployment was high, but the September 11 destruction of the World Trade Center produced an opportunity for the failing Bush administration by making terrorism the central concern. Bombing Afghanistan to kill Al Qaeda terrorists presumably headed by Bin Laden rallied the public around the flag and Bush's approval ratings rose eclipsing his domestic failures. Flags were seen throughout the United States and the way to reelection for Bush became apparent.

Bin Laden personified the threat that gave the Bush foreign policy its new direction. International terrorism provided a Texas model of "High Noon," with Bush vowing to get the outlaws dead or alive. But after the Taliban fell in Afghanistan Bin Laden was still at large, so Bush switched to a similar villain—Saddam Hussein, and military power was directed toward Iraq.

Bush had international cooperation in Afghanistan but vowed he would go it alone in Iraq if the U.N. would not join him. Since the Gulf War, a U.N. mandate had pressured Saddam Hussein to get rid of weapons of mass destruction, so Bush used this as grounds to declare that he would cooperate with a United Nations disarmament process in Iraq only if it led to Iraq's rapid disarmament; otherwise he would wage war whether or not the rest of the world cooperated. The American public was so affected by the searing images of September 11 that the Bush administration was able to connect Saddam with the September 11 tragedy to justify war, even though there was no evidence. *The big lie became the central instrument for public support. The march toward war made truth the first major casualty.*

Bush was unable to get sufficient support from U.N. members in 2003, so with only the help of Britain, Australia, and Spain (but not their citizens) he waged a unilateral and pre-emptive war against Iraq. *This radically belligerent position incited unprecedented protests throughout the world.* He had inadvertently unified much of the world. Never before had so many of the people in the world taken to the streets in the name of peace, making it very difficult for national leaders to side with Bush. A new force for world political change developed.

WEAPONS OF MASS DESTRUCTION

The Bush doctrine centered on the danger of weapons of mass destruction, but this basis for world policy involved a basic oversight. The problem posed by *weapons of mass destruction is not limited to Saddam's presumed weapons: these weapons are a major problem world wide. If the issue is eliminating all weapons of mass destruction, many more nations will be involved including those who have jointed the nuclear club, such as Israel, India, Pakistan, and probably North Korea.*

If the world peace movement is to form around opposition to the Bush administration's global imperialism, it needs to make the general public aware that the *United States is the main producer and repository of weapons of mass destruction.*

MYOPIC IMPERIALISM

By invading Iraq, the Bush administration intended to shift the American electorate's priorities away from public needs toward "rally around the flag" nationalism. But this tactic may be short-lived, for Bush's tunnel vision is blind to the politics of reaction: "for every action there is an equal and opposite reaction."

Throughout Islam, the invasion of Iraq was perceived as a war of civilizations, a Godsend to Bin Laden and other terrorists seeking recruits. If U.S. domination continues, the expanded world reaction could require a level of repressive military power that would turn the United States into a contemporary version of imperial Rome.

AMERICA THE LAWLESS

If we consider the three basic world models anarchy, multilateralism, and dominance, the United States has become a rogue power relying on force to maintain dominance. Abandoning foresight for arrogance and hubris, it now relies on naïve moral certitude and military power. A legitimately moral basis for foreign policy must take the world context into account—culture, economics, ecology, human rights, prior agreements. But the Bush administration ignores context and substitutes self righteous absolutism. Its "defense" plan proclaims that we will spread "democracy" or "freedom" using American military power. But these words are really a cover for corporate capitalism, which threatens to become our new religion. As a religion, it can be imposed on others because "we are right; they are wrong." The world is divided into black and white, good and evil. Instead of building international institutions based on real democracy, human rights and the rule of law, the United States is moving toward global fascism. Undefined, the word "democracy" becomes a useful instrument of imperialism. The terms "democracy" and "freedom" are casualties of this war, along with "truth" and the "rule of law."

Since World War II the United Nations has labored to construct a system of international law, only to see it breached by the American invasion of Iraq. The Bush Administration has taken the United States on the road to international lawlessness, replacing the rule of law with the rule of power. Law is grounded in equality and shared values. By opting out of the United Nations system, Bush replaced the nascent developments of community and international law with the forces of dominance and anarchy. The United States, under Bush, became a rogue nation, a dangerous example of unilateralism to other nations, including the nuclear powers.

PLAYING POKER IN A NUCLEAR WORLD

Though progress in the rule of law has advanced slowly, it has progressed, using treaties and the U.N. to build a more cooperative world. The abrupt setback from the unilateral invasion of Iraq must be seen in relation to a world in which weapons of mass destruction, including nuclear weapons, have not yet been put under any kind of meaningful international control and instead are proliferating. We are still sitting on a volcano—both Russia and the United States have some 6,000 intercontinental nuclear missiles that can be triggered within minutes. A Putin-Bush agreement in 2002 proposed reduction of operational/strategic arsenals to 1,700 to 2,000 but only to store the missiles, not to destroy them. Each country has enough missiles to destroy human life in most of the world and yet the proliferation of nuclear weapons continues, with countries such as North Korea showing the world how these weapons can be useful for new purposes such as attention getting, bargaining, and possibly revenue production.

So what can be done? Is there any basis for moving toward a better future?

The protests against Bush's war suggest that progressive international opinion envisions a world order far different from what Bush is trying to create. Many of those protesting are motivated by a common vision of a post cold-war world free of all weapons of mass destruction, a world in which international law replaces the rule of military power.

CRISIS PROVIDES OPPORTUNITY

If world political movements do not immediately produce specific structural changes, they will at least produce some necessary world education. This crisis, like the depression of the 1930s, can be a time of public awakening and new planning. The following considerations are basic to the future:

International reform

Public pressure and a new administration could redirect the United States to become a cooperative member of United Nations. The international agenda could then include:

- Global disarmament of weapons of mass destruction supported by a UN inspection system such as was used in Iraq.

- An international standing peace-keeping force operating under the United Nations.
- An international legal system for support of human rights.
- A world economic regulatory system that limits economic activity to what is ecologically sustainable.

National Reform

But the U.S. cannot help lead the movement towards a functional world community if it continues to be a corporate oligarchy posing as a democracy. Education and truth are now the crucial tools. Education at all levels needs to focus on the deceptions and myths that we inherited from the twentieth century. Public schools must acknowledge the historical power shift resulting from corporate personhood, for only then will public movements for change become possible. Textbooks must no longer conceal the economic basis for political power in America. Corporate mass media must be exposed as a propaganda instrument serving the power of a dominant minority. Beyond the school system, we need more small newspapers, informed public dialogue, and expanding use of the internet.

Our current historical crossroads represent a major opportunity, and we begin with one great advantage. Not since the 1930s have so many people seen that the economic and military models of the last century are a threat to humanity and nature. It is time to retain and reinvent institutions that are valuable, construct whatever new ones are needed, and revitalize education through the kind of creativity that puts the human race in charge of the future. The breakthrough for Americans will be using democracy to control capitalism and to discover that our up-side down society has been doing exactly the opposite.

SELECT BIBLIOGRAPHY

Alperovitz, Gar. 1996. *The Decision to Use the Atomic Bomb and the Architecture of an American Myth.* New York: Random House.

Anderson, Gerard. 1997. *Annual Report of The Commonwealth Fund.* New York: The Commonwealth Fund.

Armstrong, David. 2002. Dick Cheney's Song of America. *Harpers,* October 76-87.

Arnold, Thurman. 1937. *The Folklore of Capitalism.* New Haven: Yale University Press.

Aronson, Elloit. 1972. *The Social Animal.* New York: W. H. Freeman and Co.

August, Arnold. 1999. *Democracy in Cuba.* Cuba: Instituto Cubano Del Libro.

Bagdikian, Ben H. 1997. *The Media Monopoly.* Boston: Beacon Press.

Barlett, Donald and Steele James. 1998. Corporate Welfare. *Time.* November 9.

Barnaby, Frank, ed. 1988. *The Gaia Peace Atlas.* New York: Doubleday.

Barnet, Richard and Cavanagh, John. 1994. *Global Dreams* New York: Simon and Schuster.

Bartlett and Steele. 1996. *America: Who Stole the Dream?* Kansas City, Missouri: Andrews and McMeel.

Bartlett and Steele. 1998. Corporate Welfare. *Time.* November 9.

Beard, Charles. 1935. *An Economic Interpretation of the Constitution.* New York: Macmillan.

Bell, Wendell. 1997. *Foundations of Futures Studies.* Somerset, New Jersey: Transaction Publishers.

Benson, Robert. 1999. *Challenging Corporate Rule.* New York: The Apex Press.

Black, Charles L. Jr. 1977. *A New Birth of Freedom.* New York: Grosset/Putnam.

Bowles, Samuel and Gintis, Herbert. 1986. *Democracy and Capitalism.* New York: Basic Books.

Boyer, William and Walsh, Paul. 1968. Are Children Born Unequal? *Saturday Review,* October 19.

Boyer, William. 1972. *Education for Annihilation.* Honolulu: Hogarth-Hawaii.

Boyer, William. 2002. *Education for the twenty-first century.* Sacramento: Caddo Gap Press.

Boyer, William. 1975. *Alternative Futures, Designing Social Change.* Dubuque, Iowa: Kendall/Hunt.

Boyer, William. 1984. *America's Future: Transition to the Twenty-first Century.* Westport, Connecticut: Praeger.

Brundtland, Gro. 1990. *Challenge to the South.* World Commission on Environment and Development, Oxford: Oxford University Press.

Brundtland, Gro. 1987. *Our Common Future.* World Commission on Environment and Development, Oxford: Oxford University Press.

Cassidy, John. 2002. *Dot Con. The Greatest Story Ever Sold.* New York: Harper Collins.

Chicken: What You Don't Know Can Hurt You. *Consumer Reports.* March 1998.

Chomsky, Noam and Herman, Edward. 1988. *Manufacturing Consent.* New York: Pantheon.

Chomsky, Noam. 1996. *Class Warfare.* Monroe, Maine: Common Courage.

Chomsky, Noam. 1992. *Deterring Democracy.* New York: Hill and Wong.

Chomsky, Noam. 1999. *Latin America: from Colonization to Globalization,* Australia: Ocean Press.

Clark, Grenville, and Sohn, Louis. 1966. *World Peace Through World Law.* Cambridge: Harvard Press.

Clinton, Richard. 1994. *Finding Our Way Home.* Dubuque, Iowa: Brown and Benchmark.

Cockburn, Alexander. 1997. Unemployment Necessary. *Los Angeles Times,* October 30.

Corning, Peter. 1969. The evolution of medicare . . . From idea to law. www.ssa.gov/history/corning.html.

Cousins, Norman. 1987. *The Pathology of Power.* New York: W. W. Norton.

Cox, Harvey. 1999. The Market as God. *Atlantic Monthly,* March 18-23.

Daly, Herman and Cobb, John. 1989. *For the Common Good: Redirecting the Economy Toward Community, the Environment, and a Sustainable Future.* Boston: Beacon Press.

Dewey, John. 1916. *Democracy and Education.* New York: MacMillan.

Donziger, Steven. 1996. *The Real War on Crime.* New York: Perennial.

Douthwaite, Richard. 1992. *The Growth Illusion.* Canada: New Society.

Dugger, Ronnie. 1995. Real Populists Please Stand Up. *The Nation,* 261 5 (August 21) 159-163.

Eckholm, Erik. 1977. *The Picture of Health.* New York: W. W. Norton.

Eckstein, Susan. 1993. *Back from the Future,* Princeton: Princeton University Press.

Ehrenreich Barbara. 2001. *Nickel and Dimed.* New York: Holt Rinehart Winston.

Epstein, Samuel. 1998. The American Cancer Society: The World's Wealthiest 'Non-profit' Institution. *International Journal of Health Services* (Vol. 29, No. 3).

Epstein, Samuel. 1998. *The Politics of Cancer.* Hawkins, New York: East Ridge.

Falk, Richard. 1971. *This Endangered Planet.* New York: Random House.

Featherstone, Liza. 2002. Walmart Values. *The Nation,* December 16.

Fernandez, Ronald 1994. *U.S. Influence and Intervention in the Twentieth Century.* Monroe, Maine: Common Courage Press.

Frank, Marc. 1993. *Cuba Looks to the Year 2000.* New York: N.Y. International Publishers.

Friedman, Thomas. 1999. From Supercharged Financial Markets to Osama bin Laden: The Merging Global Order Demands an Enforcer. *New York Times Magazine,* March 28.

Garner and Halweil, Brian. 2000. Is Ronald McDonald Really so Different from Joe Camel? *WorldWatch 150 (March):* 52.

Gelbspan, Ross. 1988. *The Heat Is On.* Reading, Massachusetts: Perseus.

Greider, William. 2001. Sovereign Corporations. *The Nation.* 272 17 (April 30) 5-7.

Greider, William. 1997. *One World Ready or Not.* New York: Simon and Schuster.

Grossman, Richard. 2001. Corporations Must Not Supplant "We the People." In ed. Dean Ritz. 2001. 38-40.

Grossman, Richard and Adams, Frank. 2001. Taking Care of Business. In ed. Dean Ritz 2001. 59-72.

Halweil, Brian. 1999. *Farming in the Public Interest.* New York: W. W. Norton.

Hardin, Garrett. 1968. The Tragedy of the Commons. *Science* 162: 1243-8.

Harding, Susan. 2001. *The Book of Jerry Falwell: Fundamentalist Language and Politics.* Princeton: Princeton University Press.

Harmann, Thom. 2002. *Unequal Protection: The Rise of Corporate Dominance.* New York: St. Martin's.

Hawken, Paul. 1993. *The Ecology of Commerce.* New York: HarperCollins.

Heanekens, C. H., et al. 1978. A Case Study of Aspirin Use and Coronary Death. *National Academy of Science's Institute of Medicine* July (1) : 35-8.

Henderson, Hazel. 1995. *Paradigms in Progress.* San Francisco: Berrett-Koehler.

Henry, Jules. 1968. *Culture Against Man.* New York: Random House.

Herman, Edward and Chomsky, Noam. 1988. *Necessary Illusions: Thought Control in Democratic Societies.* New York: Pantheon.

Hersey, John. 1960. *The Child Buyer.* New York: Bantam.

Hersh, Seymour. 1997. *The Dark Side of Camelot.* New York: Little Brown.

Illich, Ivan. 1976. *Limits to Medicine: Medical Nemesis, the Expropriation of Health.* London. Marion Boyars.

Johnson, Bruce. 1997. *Exemplar of Liberty: Native America and the Evolution of Democracy.* West Hartford, CT: Greenwood Press.

Kennedy, Paul. 1993. *Preparing for the Twenty-First Century.* New York: Random House.

Kenworthy, Eldon. 1995. *America/Americas.* University Park, Pennsylvania: Penn State Press.

Korten, David C. 1998. *The Post-Corporate World.* West Hartford, CT: Kumarian.

Korten, David, 1995. *When Corporations Rule the World.* West Hartford, CT: Kumarian Press.

Lapham, Lewis. 2003. When in Rome. *Harpers,* January.

Lappe, Francis Moore. 1982. *Diet for a Small Planet.* New York: Ballentine Books.

Laqueur and Rubin. 1989. *Human Rights Reader.* Devon, UK: Meridian.

Lerner, Michael. 2000. *Spirit Matters.* Charlottesville, Virginia: Hampton Roads Publishing.

Leslie, John. 1996. *The End of the World.* New York: Routledge.

Lifton, Robert and Mitchell, Greg. 1995. *Hiroshima in America: Fifty Years of Denial.* New York: Putnam.

Loewen, James. 1996. *Lies My Teacher Told Me.* New York: Simon and Schuster.

Lutz, Mark, and Lux, Kenneth. 1988. *Humanistic Economics.* New York. Bootstrap Press.

Marien, Michael. 1995. *World Futures and the United Nations.* Bethesda, Maryland: World Future Society.

McDougall, John. 1990. *A Challenging Second Opinion.* NewYork: Penguin.

McDougall, John. 1983. *The McDougall Plan.* Clinton, New Jersey: New Win.

Meadows, Donella and Dennis. 1976. *Limits to Growth.* New York: New American Library.

Meyers, William. 2000. *The Santa Clara Blues: Corporate Personhood versus Democracy.* Gualala CA: III Publishing.

Michael Parenti. 1996. *Dirty Truths.* San Francisco: City Lights.

Moore, Thomas J. 1998. *Prescription for Disaster.* New York: Simon and Schuster.

Morris, Jane Anne. in Dean Ritz. ed. 2001. *Defying Corporations, Defining Democracy.* New York: The Apex Press.

Nader, Ralph. 2002. *Crashing the Party.* New York: St. Martin's Press.

Ornish, Dean, 1993. Eat More, Weigh Less. *Readers Digest 143, (August) 133-5.*

Ornish, Dean. 1998. Intensive Lifestyle Changes for Reversal of Coronary Heart Disease. *Journal of the American Medical Association,* December 16.

Ornish, Dean. 1996. *Reversing Heart Disease.* New York: Ballentine.

Parenti, Michael. 1998. *America Besieged.* San Francisco: City Lights.

Parenti, Michael. 1996. *Dirty Truths.* San Francisco: City Lights.

Pearl, Arthur and Knight, Tony. 1999. *The Democratic Classroom.* Cresskill, NJ: Hampton Press.

Pearl, Arthur. 1982. *Common Sense for the Future*—unpublished text for U. Cal. Santa Cruz classes XIII-2.

Pearl-Cooperstein. 1987. Unpublished text for U. Cal. Santa Cruz class.

Phillips, Kevin. 2002. *Wealth and Democracy,* New York: Broadway Books.

Platt, Anne. 1996. *Infecting Ourselves, How Environmental and Social Disruptions Trigger Disease.* WorldWatch 129. New York: WorldWatch.

Porter, Gareth and Brown, Janet. 1991. *Global Environmental Politics.* Boulder, Colorado: Westview Press.

Reich, Robert. 2002. *The Future of Success.* New York: Vintage.

Rifkin, Jeremy. 1992. *Beyond Beef.* New York: Dutton.

Ritz, Dean, ed. 2001. *Defying Corporations, Defining Democracy.* New York: The Apex Press.

Robbins, John, 1987. *Diet for a New America.* Tiburon, California: Kramer.

Robin, Eugene. 1984. *Matters of Life and Death: Risks vs. Benefits of Medical Care.* Stanford: Portable Stanford.

Roth, Kenneth. 1998. The Court the U.S. Doesn't Want. *N.Y. Review of Books,* November 19.

Saari, David. 1999. *Global Corporations and Sovereign Nation.* Westport, Connecticut: Quorum.

Saari, David. 1995. *Too Much Liberty?* Westport, Connecticut: Praeger.

Scharffenberg, John. 1979. *Problems with Meat.* Santa Barbara: Woodbridge.

Silverstein, Ken. 1999. Millions for Viagra, Pennies for Diseases of the Poor. *The Nation,* July 19.

Sitarz, Daniel, ed. 1998. *Sustainable America.* Carbondale, Illinois: Earth Press.

Slaughter, Richard and Inayatullah, Sohail, edit. 2002. *Knowledge Base of Futures Studies.* CD ROM.

Slaughter, Richard. 1995. *The Foresight Principle.* Westport, Connecticut: Praeger.

Smith, Adam, 1937. *The Wealth of Nations.* N.Y. Modern Library

Spock, Benjamin. 1998. *Baby and Child Care.* New York: EP Dutton.

Starfield, Barbara. 2000. Is US Health Really the Best in the World? *Journal of the American Medical Association* 284 (July) : 4.

The Pentagon's War on Thrift. *New York Times,* May 22, 1997.

Thurow, Lester C. 1989. *The Zero-Sum Society.* Boulder, Colorado: Basic Books.

Toffler, Alvin. 1983. *Previews and Premises.* Montreal: Black Rose Books.

Truman, Harry. 1955. *Memoirs.* New York: Doubleday.

Wasserman Harvey. 1984. *America Born and Reborn.* New York: Macmillan.

Wasserman, Harvey. 1992. *History of the United States Vol. 2, Civil War to the Present.* New York: Houghton Mifflin.

Weil, Andrew. 1995. *Spontaneous Healing.* New York: Alfred Knopf.

Wellstone, Paul. 1997. If Poverty Is the Question. *The Nation,* April 14 15-18.

Wolfe, Sidney 1999. *Worst Pills/ Best Pills: A Consumers Guide.* New York: Pocket Books.

World Commission on Environment and Development. 1987. *Our Common Future.* Oxford: Oxford University Press.

WorldWatch Institute. 1987. *State of the World.* Washington DC.

WorldWatch Institute. 2002. *State of the World.* Washington, DC.

Yost, Jack. 1999. *Planet Champions, Adventures in Saving the World.* Portland, Oregon: BridgeCity Books.

Zepernick, Mary. 2001. Cancer Is a Political Disease. In ed. Dean Ritz 2001. 181-182.

Zinn, Howard. 1997a. *The Nation.* March 10 : 30

Zinn, Howard. 1997b. *A People's History of the United States.* New York: The New Press.

RESOURCES

Alliance for Democracy A national network of local organizations that focuses on controlling corporate power and reforming campaign financing. 681 Main St. Suite 16, Waltham, MA 02451. E-mail: peoplesali@aol.com

The *Community Environmental Legal Defense Fund* (www.celdf.org) provides an activist's guide which helps people get started and opens up a wide range of resources.

The *Council on International and Public Affairs* and their *Apex Press* provides publications that help educate people in protest movements to understand ways to create needed change and yet support the rule of law.

Program on Corporations, Law, and Democracy (POCLAD) is the most useful source of materials on corporate power, the history, and ways to change corporate charters. Contact POCLAD at P.O. Box 246, S. Yarmouth, MA 02664-0246. Tel.: 508-389-1145, Fax: 508-487-1552, E-mail: people@poclad.org.

World Federalist Movement promotes changes in the United Nations to move the world toward the rule of law and federation. Has links to campaign for an international criminal court. 777 U.N. Plaza, 12th Floor, New York, NY 10017. Tel.: 212-599-1321.

World Order Models Project promotes world order values to place conventional and nuclear weapons under international control and fashion new forms of global governance. 475 Riverside Dr. Rm 246, New York, NY 10115. Tel.: 212-870-2391.

WorldWatch Institute is an indispensable source of updated publications on national and world environment. Should be in all school libraries. Publishes an annual "state of the world" report. 1776 Massachusetts Ave. N.W., Washington, DC 20036.

KEY PUBLICATIONS

David Korten's books *When Corporations Rule the World* and *The Post Corporate World* are essential reading. He has also developed a *Positive Futures Network* to facilitate change at: postcorporate@futurenet.org.

Richard L. Grossman and Frank T. Adams' *Taking Care of Business* is an indispensable booklet published by POCLAD.

Thom Harmann's *Unequal Protection: The Rise of Corporate Dominance and the Theft of Human Rights* should also be considered of prime importance.

William Meyers' *The Santa Clara Blues: Corporate Personhood versus Democracy* provides additional legal explanation of corporate power through the 1886 Santa Clara decision. III Publishing, POB 1581, Gualala, CA 95445.

James A. Dator, ed. *Advancing Futures: Futures Studies in Higher Education*. Westport, Ct. Preager. Dator is a pioneer and key figure in the futures studies movement.

Multinational Monitor is one of the best sources for reliable information on world institutions including multinational corporations. 153 P. St. NW WN. DC 20005.

Peace Matters: Newsletter of the Hague Appeal for Peace. Provides linkage with world activities that focus on the reform of peace making institutions. 777 UN Plaza, New York, NY 10017.

AFTERWORD II

BUSH'S SECOND TERM: U.S. DECLINE AND IMPLOSION?

George W. Bush's second term began in January 2005 with the same doubts about the legitimacy of the voting process as occurred in 2000. In many ways the election resembled third world elections with unreliable voting machines and computer systems vulnerable to manipulation. In Ohio, a key state for deciding the electoral vote, people were held up for hours, possibly to discourage them from voting. But the final count allowed Bush to resume office for another four years.

Within the new administration, those who did not always agree with Bush, such as Colin Powell, were shown the exit. Core neo-conservatives, such as Dick Cheney, Donald Rumsfeld and Paul Wolfowitz, the architects of the disastrous Iraq policy, were retained, resulting in a new administration staffed only with "yes men." The ideology of the administration was to be shielded by an even stronger wall against dissent.

There was no indication that the global policy of unilateral dominance would change. The Defense Planning Guidance for 2004-2009, which called for overwhelming military superiority, continued to guide foreign policy. Based on absolutist values of "freedom" and democracy, the policy preserved the central role of corporate capitalism. This administration's self-righteous ideology continued to presume that people would welcome the American conception of freedom, delivered by U.S. military power. The major test was in Iraq.

By January 2005, the Iraq war was a virtual quagmire. Over 1,000 Americans and over 100,000 Iraqis had died (*The Lancet,* vol. 364, no. 9448) with many more wounded. Frustrated by persistent resistance, American military strategy adopted tactics similar to the "destroy it to save it" strategy that was applied in Vietnam. The war for "freedom" had become a recruiting gift for al-Qaeda. The Bush message to the world was that military power, used in the name of "freedom," would substitute for the rule of law. When one is certain one is right, the ends tend to justify the means. But the Bush plan for an American empire failed to anticipate the evolution of a world community of opinion against the United States. World peace, Bush style, was becoming increasingly counterproductive, producing the opposite of intended effects.

American failures helped strengthen the European Union that was beginning to counter balance American world dominance. The EU was moving toward a new integrated regional statehood and its currency, the euro, was becoming stronger than the American dollar.

By 2004 the Bush policy had a pronounced effect on European public opinion. A Pew Research Center survey made in 2004 found only 38 percent of Germans had a positive feeling toward the United States; in France only 37 percent held a positive opinion. Even in the United Kingdom, 55 percent of the public saw the United States as a threat to global peace. This perception was shared in Greece, Spain, Finland and Sweden, where the public viewed the United States as an even greater threat to world peace than Iran or North Korea. (For more on this see T. R. Reid's *The United States of Europe: The New Superpower and the End of American Supremacy*, p. 24.)

In spite of a crumbling Iraq policy and a precipitous decline in worldwide trust of the U.S., George W. Bush was reelected. How could that be explained? Was his administration's domestic policy so effective that it offset the foreign policy? The overriding Bush neo-conservative policy was to shift the public sector to the private sector. Public natural resources were a primary target. National forests and parks were opened to commercial oil and mineral extraction, either through special access or by privatizing and shifting ownership. Forests were opened for logging and protections against air and water pollution were weakened. Policies were given Orwellian names to confuse the public. Plans to cut more old growth trees were called "The Healthy Forests Initiative," lowered air pollution standards came in the form of the "Clear Skies Initiative," faith-based ideology became "Sound Science."

When the energy industries became free to regulate themselves, they did so in pursuit of their own best interests, rather than the public's. Enron became the tip of the iceberg, its bankruptcy costing thousands of people their jobs and retirement savings. Extremes of laissez-faire capitalism overrode the public interest and even corrupted the regulators. Under Bush politics, the pharmaceutical industries infiltrated The Food and Drug Administration, which had been created to safeguard the public, not corporate profits.

Tax policy paralleled resource policy. The rich and the corporations received tax advantages, which redistributed wealth in favor of the top two percent of the population at the expense of the middle and lower classes. Jobs were increasingly outsourced to other countries, and any negative effects were to be handled by the market. Corporations increased profits by shifting production to countries with cheap non-unionized labor and consequently more U.S. jobs were lost than were created. Such policy would seem, on the surface, to spell political disaster in a democracy. It asked the majority to forego their economic future for the benefit of a small corporate minority. But enough of the American public was politically seduced to provide Bush an electoral plurality.

Various factors may explain the Bush reelection, but two stand out—the politics of religion and the politics of fear. Carl Rove, Bush's guiding hand, saw that religious belief could outweigh economic issues and become an election advantage. The evangelical Protestant constituency was especially swayed by the issue of abortion and their belief that United State's government policies should be based on Christian values, not secular rationalism. Once he realized the potential of evangelical support, George Bush shifted to faith-based politics and campaigned in those states where conservative religion dominates. His vague appeal to "values," distracted even the poorest families from such economic issues as employment, wages, unions, and taxes. George Bush's alleged status as a reborn Christian inspired trust among the right wing Protestants and produced votes. Many religious groups, but not all, were enticed by the public money that Bush promised to supply to "faith based" initiatives, which blurred the separation of church and state, but bought votes.

For the rest of the society, whatever their religious beliefs, the Bush campaign's core political strategy became the management of fear. In the 1930s, President Roosevelt campaigned saying. "all we have to fear is fear itself". For Bush it was the other way around. All he had to fear was the public's loss of fear. The 9-11 attacks proved that terrorism poses significant danger. For the Bush neo-cons, terrorism was a ready-made political advantage to be leveraged by controlling and even exaggerating danger to create fear. The government impressed upon the public that the executive branch had secret information about impending dangers and that public safety depended on faith and trust in the President. It became the patriotic obligation of American citizens to empower the executive branch and shield it from scrutiny, even at the expense of civil liberties.

The role of fear, both real and created, may have been decisive in the election. Vice President Cheney, up to the eve of the election, kept repeating throughout the country that Saddam's weapons of mass destruction justified the war in Iraq. The WMD excuse for invading Iraq had long since been refuted, yet it was repeated by all of the administration, like a mantra, until most of the public believed it. Corporate media obediently cooperated until the lie took on the role of self-evident truth. The psychology of the process was well described by Herman Goering in his 1947 World War II Nuremberg Diary:

> *Why, of course, the people don't want war. Why would some poor slob on a farm want to risk his life in a war when the best he can get out of it is to come back to his farm in one piece? Naturally, the common people don't want war; neither in Russia nor in England nor in America, nor for that matter in Germany. That is understood. But, after all, it is the leaders of the country who determine the policy and it is always a simple matter to drag the people along, whether it is a democracy or a fascist dictatorship or a Parliament or a Communist dictatorship, voice or no voice, the people can always be brought to the bidding of the leaders. That is easy. All you have to do is tell them they are being attacked and denounce the pacifists for lack of patriotism and exposing the country to danger. It works the same way in any country.* (Gilbert. G. M. *Nuremberg Diary*. New York: Farrar, Straus, and Company, pp. 278-279)

THE IMPORTANCE OF IGNORING CAUSALITY

After 9/11, the Bush administration always ignored causality, even proposing such nonsense as that the terrorists are after us because they are envious of our success. To accept causality would mean that the terrorists are not monsters, but human beings operating on the basis of human psychology. Acknowledging causality would force the administration to abandon the categorical dictate that terrorists are by nature "evil" and introduce the question of why concerted violence against the United States is increasing. Bin Laden was talking about causality when he declared that removal of American troops from Saudi Arabia would be a requisite for reduction of al-Qaeda attacks. The American bias in favor of Israel and against the Palestinians has long been a cause of anti-Americanism within the Arab world. But the invasion of Iraq generated even greater hostility, prompting hundreds to offer themselves as suicide bombers to carry on a war that, as with all wars, was presumed to be serving a just and necessary cause.

Terrorism, like conventional war (another form of terrorism), is politics by other means and is therefore subject to negotiation. By defining the world in terms of absolute good and evil, however, the Bush policy eliminated the options of negotiation. Absolutism also ruled out historical and cultural analysis when anticipating potential reactions to U.S. policies. In the past, the Bush policy was based on tunnel vision and religious ideology, and there is no indication that his second term will be conducted on any other basis.

FAITH SUPERSEDES SCIENCE

The harm done by faith-based ideology is not limited to American economic and geo-political interests. The Bush administration's ideology has often superseded environmental and medical science, discounting well-founded evidence related to global warming, stem cell research, fisheries, forestry, and pollution's effects on public health. When faith is placed above reason and evidence, there is no public test of truth. Unaccountable power then resides with those who claim to possess revealed truth, undermining the separation of church and state, a foundation of American democracy. Dogmatism, both secular and religious, displaces rational dialogue and intellectual authority. A nation guided by one person's faith can regress into despotism. We are now confronted with such a reality.

THE FINANCIAL HOUSE OF CARDS

Bush maintained the illusion of a sustainable economy by spending and borrowing, thus creating the largest debt in American history out of a large national surplus that existed when he was elected in 2000. Like a person who expands the mortgage on his house and spends the money from the bank as income, this is a "fly now, pay later" approach to finances. "Later" will arrive; though the Bush administration hopes it can be delayed for "four more years," so a future administration will receive the bill. The term "conservative" has been turned upside down and massive debt has been incurred to be passed on to future generations.

The Bush administration, of course, does not rely on banks for funds. They come mainly from other countries—in large part the European Community and China. As Americans buy low priced goods made by cheap overseas labor, they create an imbalance of trade because not enough American goods are sold, so American treasury bonds are offered as collateral to balance the payments. Any future unwillingness of China, Japan, or India to buy the bonds could force the American government to raise interest rates to sell more bonds. The effect of this will be an economic slow down, increased inflation, a likely stock market decline, and possibly another depression.

During its second term, the Bush administration's policies could easily produce an economic implosion with global effects. U.S. neo-con ideology relies excessively upon market forces to bring finances into balance. That is the faith that guided American policy in 1929. It would be a huge price to pay to repeat the failures of the past, when the U.S. left the future to corporations instead of democratic public planning. Striving for world dominance instead of cooperative leadership is heading the United States in the wrong direction. The public urgently needs to cast off the blindfolds provided by the corporate media, see where our society is heading, and change direction to restore American democracy.

Here are some books that can help serve that purpose:

Byrd, Senator Robert C. 2004. *Losing America: Confronting a Reckless and Arrogant Presidency.* New York: W.W. Norton.

Carter, Graydon. 2004. *What We Have Lost: How the Bush Administration Has Curtailed Our Freedoms, Mortgaged Our Economy, Ravaged Our Environment, and Damaged Our Standing in the World.* New York: Farrar, Straus, and Giroux.

Johnson, Chalmers. 2004. *The Sorrows of Empire: Militarism, Secrecy, and the End of the Republic.* New York: Metropolitan Books.

Reid. T. R. 2004. *The United States of Europe: The New Superpower and the End of American Supremacy.* New York: Penguin Press.

Todd, Emmanual. 2003. *After the Empire: The Breakdown of the American Order.* New York: Columbia University Press.

INDEX